Beyond the Black Lady

THE NEW BLACK STUDIES SERIES

Edited by Darlene Clark Hine
and Dwight A. McBride

*A list of books in the series
appears at the end of this book.*

Beyond the Black Lady

Sexuality and the New African American Middle Class

LISA B. THOMPSON

UNIVERSITY OF ILLINOIS PRESS
Urbana, Chicago, and Springfield

First Illinois paperback, 2012
© 2009 by Lisa B. Thompson
All rights reserved
Manufactured in the United States of America
⊗ This book is printed on acid-free paper.

The Library of Congress cataloged the cloth edition as follows:
Thompson, Lisa B., 1965–
Beyond the Black lady : sexuality and the new African American middle class / Lisa B. Thompson.
p. cm. — (The new Black studies series)
Includes bibliographical references and index.
ISBN 978-0-252-03426-8 (cloth : alk. paper)
1. African American women—Psychology.
2. African American women—Sexual behavior.
3. Middle class women—United States—Psychology.
4. Middle class women—United States—Sexual behavior.
5. Mass media and women—United States.
I. Title.
E185.86T447   2009
306.7086'220973—dc22   2008041148
PAPERBACK ISBN 978-0-252-07890-3

For Olufemi Alexander Makinde

Contents

Acknowledgments ix

Introduction
Beyond the Black Lady:
Sexuality and the New African American Middle Class 1

Part 1: Performing Identity

1. Spectacle of the Respectable:
Anita Hill and the Problem of Innocence 21

2. Staging Black Female Desire:
The Drama of Race, Class, and Sexuality 43

3. Black Ladies and Black Magic Women:
Independent Film and Black Sexuality 72

Part 2: Refashioning the Black Female Self

4. Narrating Sexuality in Contemporary African
American Autobiography 97

5. Sex, Travel, and the Single African American Girl:
Andrea Lee's *Sarah Phillips* 118

Epilogue 137

Notes 141

Index 175

Acknowledgments

I could not have completed this book without generous institutional and personal support from a variety of sources. I am indebted to Stanford University's Institute for Research on Women and Gender as well as its Center for the Study of Race and Ethnicity. During my time there I engaged with accomplished faculty from a variety of fields: Al Camarillo, Paulla Ebron, Sharon Holland, Kennell Jackson, Purnima Mankekar, Cherríe Moraga, David Palumbo-Liu, Horace Porter, Mary Louise Pratt, Lora Romero, Roman Saldivar, Renato Rosaldo, and Yvonne Yarbro-Bejarano. I especially want to acknowledge Harry J. Elam Jr., who shared his insights about the theater and the academy.

I am indebted to the Five College Fellowship Program, which allowed me to be in residence as a Mendenhall Fellow at the Smith College English department. During that year I had beneficial conversations with Carol Angus, Anjali Arondekar, Marcy Newman, and Elizabeth Spelman. I also had the great fortune of being a University of California president's postdoctoral fellow at the University of California, Davis, English department and enjoyed the collegiality of Joanne Diehl, Beth Freeman, Patricia Moran, and Riché Richardson. A special debt of gratitude is owed to both Clarence Walker and to the person who served as my faculty mentor, David Van Leer, for their friendship and invaluable feedback on this project.

I had the opportunity to share earlier versions of various chapters with the University of Illinois at Chicago Race and Ethnicity Study Group and in the Circle of Thought Series at the UCLA Center for African American Studies. The staffs of several libraries from coast to coast provided considerable help as I conducted research for, and then wrote, this book. I am particularly grateful to Gerald T. Burke and Deborah LeFond at the University at Albany as well as James Heikkala and Deborah Noyes at the Niskayuna branch of the Schenectady Public Library.

The University at Albany, SUNY has been a nurturing environment for me as a scholar and playwright. A State of New York United University Professions Dr. Nuala McGann Drescher Award and an English department research and writing leave allowed me valuable time to revise the manuscript. I owe the English department's administrative staff, Constance Barrett, Regina Klym, and especially Elizabeth Lauenstein, many thanks for their kindness and patience. My current and former graduate students, Randall Horton, Habiba Ibrahim, Hilary Reed, Stephanie Richardson, and Kelly Secovnie, have been a source of inspiration. I extend special thanks to Iuliu Ratiu, who served as a teaching assistant at a crucial time in the book's development.

I am grateful to my colleagues for their support and camaraderie, especially Judi Barlow, Kevin Bell, Jeff Berman, Ronald Bosco, Maia Boswell, Langdon Brown, Tom Cohen, Patricia Chu, Randy Craig, Glynne Griffith, Jennifer Greiman, Rosemary Hennessey, Janell Hobson, Rachel Jean-Baptiste, Eric Keenaghan, Mark Anthony Neal, Ineke Murakami, Vivien Ng, Marjorie Pryse, Edward Schwarzschild, Paul Stasi, Lynne Tilman, and Laura Wilder. I cannot imagine this book without the assistance of Bret Benjamin, Mike Hill, and Helene Scheck, who not only commented on significant portions of the manuscript but also acted as valuable sounding boards throughout the writing process.

Edward J. Blum and Margaret Mirabelli have my utmost appreciation for reading the entire manuscript and providing thoughtful editorial advice. I also thank my editor at the University of Illinois Press, Joan Catapano, and her assistant, Breanne Ertmer, for their diligence and support.

Becoming a mother during the final phase of this project introduced a stunning array of joys, challenges, and surprises. I realize that this book could not have been completed without the dedicated staff of the Schenectady Jewish Community Center's Early Childhood Education program and my son's other caregivers. I am particularly grateful for the kindness of Cathy Allen, Shawndell Azore, Cheryl Cartier, Amber Hernandez, Nirupama Kapalli, Kelli Potter, Natascha Richmond, Nicole Stabinski, and Stephanie Tovar.

I thank my dear friends who have helped make upstate New York home: Sandra Austin, Angela and Patrick Antinokowski, Alison Belfort, Sharon and James Danoff-Burg, Deidre Hill-Butler, Ifeoma and Emeka Ojukwu, and Durene Wheeler. I cherish the long-standing friendship and unwavering support of Angela Ards, Samuel Biggers, Daphne Brooks, David Campt, Tieal Dickens, Darwin Farrar, Meta DuEwa Jones, Robin D. G. Kelly, David Keiser, Chana Kai Lee, Diana Paulin, Dion Raymond, Sonnet Retman, Rita Rothman, Tracy Scacutto, Darieck Scott, Fatima Washington, and Richard Yarborough.

The friendship and support of three people in particular have made a difference in my life in ways too numerous to list here. I am particularly grateful to Dwight A. McBride for his faith in me as well as his sustained engagement with this project. His suggestions at each step along the way made this a stronger book. I am deeply indebted to Valerie Smith for her generosity and belief in my work. Her esteemed scholarship and dedicated feminist practice inspires me. I am honored to count her as a friend. I owe immeasurable gratitude to my cherished friend Valisa Dougherty, who patiently listened to me ponder the ideas for this project from its inception and always insisted that I keep my eyes on the prize. Our Saturday morning telephone calls have sustained me in ways that are incalculable.

My family's support throughout my life has allowed me to pursue many goals even though it took me far away from them. My brothers, Guy and Robert Thompson, and my sister, Deborah Veley, have each in their own way served as an inspiration. My first teachers were my father, Walter Thompson Jr., who taught me to love the music of language, and my grandmother, Bernadine Holmes, who trained me to value style and substance equally. My most cherished teacher, my lovely mother, Herberdine Thompson, created an environment that fostered my intellectual curiosity, love of books, and desire to explore the world. I owe her more than I could ever repay.

Finally, I want to express my heartfelt gratitude to Adegboyega Makinde as well as to our son Olufemi, to whom this book is dedicated. Their patience, love, and unwavering support made it possible to finish this project. Their presence is a blessing in my life, and they remind me daily of what true success looks like.

Beyond the Black Lady

INTRODUCTION

Beyond the Black Lady

Sexuality and the New African American Middle Class

In October 2003 the love life of Secretary of State Dr. Condoleezza Rice became the object of stinging ridicule in Aaron McGruder's critically acclaimed comic strip *The Boondocks*. For weeks, McGruder's characters Huey P. Freeman and Huey's dreadlocked sidekick Caesar searched diligently to find a boyfriend for the unmarried Rice. The two outspoken suburban black children fashioned a list of possible suitors that included Senator Trent Lott, anti-affirmative action activist Ward Connerly, and libertarian talk-show host Larry Elder. When Huey grumbles, "Condoleezza's just lonely and bitter! She would be a completely better person if she just had the right MAN in her life!" Caesar replies, "All that gal needs is some good ol' fashioned lovin'." In one of the more irreverent strips Caesar surmises that "maybe if there was a man in the world who Condoleezza truly loved she wouldn't be so hellbent to destroy it."

A cultural and political icon, before First Lady Michelle Obama captured the nation's attention, Rice was arguably the most powerful and visible African American woman of our time. When *The Boondocks* suggested finding her a boyfriend as a quick and easy strategy for saving the world, the nationally syndicated strip placed black female sexuality at the center of American and international politics.[1] Not everyone agreed that the topic of Rice's romantic life was appropriate subject matter for a comic strip. Indeed, the members of the *Washington Post*'s editorial board regarded McGruder's scathing satire as so insulting and undignified that they pulled the strip for a week.[2]

Although Rice's political beliefs are fair game, McGruder's decision to link Rice's politics to her lack of a partner is disturbing. By suggesting that the apparent absence of a sexual life makes Rice suspect and dangerous, *The Boondocks* not only ridicules Rice but also blames the destructiveness of U.S. foreign policy on a particular stereotype of black female sexuality. What McGruder considers progressive commentary devolves into a reactionary notion that casts Rice as a repressed *middle-class* black woman whose passion needs to be unleashed. McGruder's strip crossed over to the personal and played upon, and therefore perpetrated, a familiar repertoire of contradictory but damaging stereotypes about black female sexuality.[3]

McGruder is not alone in his preoccupation with Rice as a sexual being. Rice's attractiveness and dating life are central to how the media regards her. In September 2006 Helen Cooper wrote in *The New York Times* that "all Rice needs to do is show up in public with a man, and people start talking. . . . Much imagination has focused on possible romantic links between Ms. Rice and her counterparts."[4] Indeed, biographies of Secretary Rice remark that she has always had a penchant for football players and "bad boys."[5] Despite endless speculation about Rice, however, one is hard-pressed to discover similar interest in the romantic life of other unmarried prominent women such as the former U.S. Attorney General Janet Reno or former Secretary of State Madeleine Albright. Described by a blogger as a "Sally Hemmings for the twenty-first century," Rice has even inspired rumors about a possible romantic relationship with her boss, President George W. Bush.[6] That speculation only intensified when sources alleged that Rice once mistakenly referred in public to Bush as her husband, a Freudian slip that subjected the careful, often pedantic Rice to considerable ridicule.[7] The idea of Rice as Bush's clandestine lover is provocative for many reasons, but what makes the notion particularly striking is the fact that Rice deflects and encourages considerations of herself as a sexual being.

Why would Condoleezza Rice's sexuality be central to the frustrations that many people feel about her political record? How does Rice's background as a middle-class black woman affect discussions of her sexuality? Clearly, Rice's influence and power place her well outside the bounds of the typical middle-class black woman, but *Beyond the Black Lady* is concerned precisely with the convergence of sexuality, representation, and performance of middle-class black womanhood epitomized in Rice's behavior and the responses to her.

The performance of middle-class black womanhood includes a particular set of precepts that determine how black women may construct or present themselves. This performance relies heavily upon aggressive shielding of the body; concealing sexuality; and foregrounding morality, intelligence, and civility as a way to counter negative stereotypes. Conservative sexual behavior is the foundation of the performance of middle-class black womanhood. The notion of performing a class position takes on heightened meaning for African American women because class performance is bound up with the performance of racial and gender identity. Fears of being considered racially inauthentic, as well as anxiety about conforming to derogatory racial stereotypes, place middle-class black women in a delicate position. Through behavior, language, and dress they must publicly signal racial loyalty while simultaneously highlighting class status.[8]

Acting like a black lady became a highly conscious performance developed in part as a response to social codes and ideals of propriety dictated by nineteenth- and twentieth-century reformers who strategized for more humane treatment of African Americans. As Deborah Gray White details in her study of the black women's club movement, "To be kind, gentle, calm, and serene were traits that were critical for women who strove to be examples of perfect black womanhood."[9] Circulating ideologies such as the Cult of True Womanhood and the Cult of Domesticity, which emphasized piety, purity, and submissiveness, held promise for revising notions about black people as immoral. Advocates for Victorian values and impeccable conduct, these black activists established a tradition that positions middle-class women as the arbiters and models of domesticity, chastity, and propriety among African Americans. Therefore, what Evelyn Brooks Higginbotham calls the "politics of respectability" became a foundational ideal of racial uplift and a survival strategy.

Middle-class black women's performance also originated in opposition to various long-standing black female caricatures in American popular culture such as the Mammy, Sapphire, and Jezebel figures. The happy, maternal Mammy, who cares for white families, and the hot-tempered Sapphire, who berates black children and emasculates men, generate misperception of black women as unattractive and asexual; Jezebel, the compulsively sexual temptress, fuels beliefs about black immorality and justifies sexual abuses.[10]

Since the antebellum period black women have suffered sexual violation and the disparagement of their characters. As Daphne Brooks observes, "Black women's bodies continue to bear the gross insult and burden of spectacular (representational) exploitation."[11] Because violence against blacks has consistently been linked with sexual abuse and exploitation, strategies for African American survival have often included reluctance to express sexuality for fear of confirming and conforming to racial stereotypes.[12]

The performance of middle-class black womanhood is tied to impossible standards of respectability. No other group of African Americans find themselves responsible for setting professional, aesthetic, political, moral, ethical, historical, and cultural values. For black women—especially those of the middle class—difficulties arise when they privilege their class performance in order to thwart suspicions about aberrant black female sexuality. To present themselves as ladies, they must either adhere to conservative sexual standards or cloak their sexuality in what Darlene Clark Hine identifies as a culture of dissemblance, a strategy for concealing their private lives while simultaneously performing "openness and disclosure."[13] Both the act of concealment and adherence to conservative rules of sexual conduct hinder middle-class black women's agency. The choice between either betraying their responsibility to the race or embracing their own sexual choices (which may or may not be in line with societal expectations) presents a dilemma. One's individuality and subjectivity is a high price to pay to frustrate demeaning stereotypes.

The desire to present the race at its best inevitably led to literary and cultural depictions of middle-class blacks as overwhelmingly chaste and morally upstanding. Thus real and fictional middle-class women became icons of morality and were put in the service of embodying and preserving African American respectability. Historically, African American writers used middle-class characters to contest racial stereotypes in a variety of ways. Beginning in the antebellum period, African American female writers portrayed middle-class black women who exhibited rectitude because uplift ideology insisted that women embody the highest virtues of the race.[14] Charles Nero notes how race leaders created "tremendous anxiety over the representation of sexuality" in African American literature.[15] Therefore, middle-class characters seldom strayed from established sexual morals in nineteenth- and early-twentieth-century African American writing. In slave narratives, several authors strategically demonstrated the horrors of slavery by describing moments when black women were forced to sacrifice Christian values because of the sexual demands made on them by white men. Early novels and plays followed suit by illustrating the ways racism undermined the stability of African American families by forcing women into immoral circumstances or by making it difficult for them to find appropriate husbands.[16]

Harlem Renaissance authors often constructed chaste and pious middle-class black characters who were self-conscious about their responsibility to "uplift the race." Several, such as Jessie Fauset, Nella Larsen, and Dorothy West, devised heroines who sublimated their sexual and romantic desires to attain higher social and class positions as well as greater financial stability.[17] Moreover, many black female authors cloaked gender issues in racially charged plots that foreground racial concerns over gender.[18] Influenced by

Victorian ideals, novelists, playwrights, and autobiographers often created characters that followed stringent moral guidelines in romantic relationships and even in marriages.

Between the 1950s and 1970s, a major change transpired when novelists from Ann Petry to Gayl Jones began openly addressing the sexual victimization experienced by black women. Many of their characters encounter the harshness of white racism and black male sexism in urban environments.[19] Nevertheless, the figures were primarily working class, rural, or impoverished, so these representations elided middle-class black women. During the struggle for civil rights, especially during the black power and black arts movements, the cultural and political leadership cast the black middle class as problematic because of a presumed tendency toward self-interest, snobbery, and elitism.[20] A concomitant generational shift occurred in the representation of the black middle class in African American literature and drama, reflected in the work of writers such as Amiri Baraka, Alice Childress, and Toni Morrison. Excoriated in the studies of E. Franklin Frazier and Nathan Hare, the black middle class was overwhelmingly depicted as status-obsessed, self-serving cultural imposters more interested in copying whites than fighting for social justice.[21] To further cast them as racially inauthentic, literature also included characterizations of middle-class blacks as sexually dysfunctional and repressed.[22]

Another significant generational shift occurred in the late twentieth century, bringing with it a new representation and assessment of the black middle class. Fewer African American writers created disparaging images of the middle class; instead, several reveal what Trey Ellis calls the "new black aesthetic," which celebrates blackness from the vantage point of the "cultural mulatto" who embraces aspects of American culture usually not considered authentically black, such as rock and roll, prep school, and suburban living.[23] Ellis contends that the new black aesthetic unflinchingly values diversity within African American culture. Writers seem more willing to craft representations of middle-class black sexuality that are neither pathological nor perfect. This refusal to either demonize or valorize the black middle class allows for a much more fluid view of blackness. If middle-class characters no longer have to act as cultural police in order to uphold narrow, essentialist ideals of blackness, then there is room for diverse representations of middle-class black women.[24]

In the spirit of a new black aesthetic, novels, films, autobiographies, and plays also increasingly present the black middle class as a complex and significant component of the African American population. Many contemporary black female writers reject the assumption that racial loyalty prohibits them from writing about sexual desire. Even in autobiographies, black women reject the racial mandate that blacks not "air their dirty laundry." These texts do not attempt to revise beliefs about black hypersexualization by erasing sexual matters; instead, they challenge concepts of acceptable sexual behavior for middle-class black women. Refashioning the black female subject in post–civil rights narratives and performance culture is an attempt by cultural producers to consciously expand the possibilities of middle-class black performance and identity. Under this new rubric, writers extend the representation of the middle-class black woman beyond the image of the black lady.

The term *black lady*, adopted from Wahneema Lubiano's analysis of the 1991 Clarence Thomas Senate Judiciary Hearings, describes the recent incarnation of a figure that comes from a long line of icons of black female respectability.[25] In the early twentieth century the "colored lady," a female member of W. E. B. Du Bois's "talented tenth," regarded her role in representing the race as paramount because "African American female reformers embedded bourgeois respectability in racial uplift ideology."[26] The colored lady was the sort of black woman who subscribed to Anna Julia Cooper's belief that "the intelligent wife, the Christian mother, the earnest, virtuous, helpful woman, [is] at once both the lever and the fulcrum for uplifting the race." Cooper called on black women to battle the "all-leveling prejudice as that supercilious caste spirit in America which cynically assumes 'A Negro woman cannot be a lady.'"[27] The idea of being both black and a lady is a dichotomy that continues to haunt African American women.

Lubiano describes Anita Hill as a figure who embodies the stereotype of the black lady, which, she explains, must be understood in relation to another popular stereotype, the "welfare queen." Society, Lubiano contends, views both categories of black women as aberrant and a drain on public resources because of their perceived dependency on government programs such as welfare and affirmative action. In this way the middle-class black woman devolves into yet another stereotype—a black lady "whose disproportionate overachievement stands for black cultural strangeness and who ensures the underachievement of the 'black male' in the lower classes."[28] Against the backdrop of other more historically charged stereotypes, the image of a highly professional, sexually repressed black lady may seem to be a relief, but she is an equally demeaning figure who merely adds to the litany of misrepresentation. Images ranging from the welfare queen to the black lady trap black women in dehumanizing sexual cliches.

To fully understand the image of the black lady it is necessary to return to Condoleezza Rice, who in part fashions her persona by making her sheltered southern black middle-class childhood a central facet of her personal mythology.[29] Her comportment recalls the image of the black version of the southern belle. As all the biographies about Rice note, she grew up a true black American princess.[30] Her upbringing in civil rights–era Birmingham, Alabama, daughter of a Presbyterian minister and a teacher, provided a childhood firmly ensconced in the southern black middle class.[31] Under her parents' tutelage, Rice learned classical piano, figure-skated, and excelled in Latin. Although she was a classmate of Denise McNair—one of four little girls murdered in the Sixteenth Street Baptist Church bombing in 1963—the secretary of state insists that she never experienced the sting of racial discrimination. Marcus Mabry's biography of Rice explains she was raised to believe "though she couldn't eat a hamburger at a restaurant or a downtown lunch counter, she could become president of the United States."[32] Given her exceptional life history, it is important to assess how Rice resonates within and troubles uniquely "American" constructions of race, gender, class, and sexuality within the United States, particularly among blacks. Rice's background marks her as this era's quintessential black lady. This book is about the black lady—the contemporary African American middle-class woman—and how her sexuality stands in for a host of concerns, anxieties, and fantasies in the minds of others.

Photographs make it easy to understand how Rice's image and appearance strongly engage with the performance of black middle-class womanhood. She often wears a tailored suit, conservative hairstyle, minimal makeup, and a few well-chosen tasteful accessories, such as pearl jewelry.[33] Many white women also wear these items, but it is the presence of a black female body that changes how they signify and resonate. As Mabry explains, "Rice's very posture is a consequence of growing up Negro in Birmingham: the way she holds her head erect, her shoulders square, her chin raised at almost all times. It was meant to project dignity and breeding."[34] Rice and other black ladies present themselves as a challenge to the dominant representation of black womanhood in the public imagination, where one-dimensional images of them as promiscuous, seductive, and sexually irresponsible circulate. It is not only the public comportment but also the sexual conduct of many middle-class black women that defies stereotypical notions about black female lasciviousness and accessibility.

Cathy Cohen and Roderick Ferguson maintain that the black middle class still functions as "the normative antithesis to deviant African American subjects."[35] At first glance, women such as Rice, along with characters drawn from plays, fiction, and film, represent and evoke the ideal upstanding, pious, and respectable African American. Middle-class women, or black ladies, the embodiment of the politics of respectability, play a particular role in policing black behavior, but this book also identifies texts and figures that trouble that notion. Although it is clear that the idea of the black lady continues to govern the way some perceive themselves and are perceived, many authors examined here, by illustrating how expectations about behavior fatigues, warps, stresses, and often destroys black women, seem to suggest they must relinquish that role.

In general, *Beyond the Black Lady* interrogates the central role that black middle-class women play in constituting the African American sexual landscape by examining portrayals of sexuality in post–civil rights era autobiography, fiction, drama, and film and also certain critical moments in U.S. popular culture. The archive of literary, visual, and theatrical texts that I trace emerged in response to, and registers influence from, second-wave feminism and the formation of the largest black middle class in U.S. history. These texts fracture notions of class and racial authenticity and present black women renegotiating social and sexual traditions in which mores, codes, and practices are more relaxed. This study, which intersects cultural studies, feminist studies, and African American literature, draws particularly on the work of African American feminist theorists as they engage with sexuality.

Several African American feminists have addressed the lack of sustained discussion about sexuality in black culture. The often-quoted statement by Hortense Spillers that "black women are the beached whales of the sexual universe, unvoiced, misseen, not doing, awaiting *their* verb" speaks to the dearth of theoretical interventions around black female sexuality.[36] Addressing what they consider to be an absence in African American literature, Hazel Carby and Deborah McDowell have noted the tendency of novelists to "displace sexuality upon another terrain."[37] Frustrated by the tendency in creative and analytical writing to focus primarily on sexual abuses or ignore sexuality altogether, Evelynn Hammonds calls on feminist theorists to foreground black women's "pleasure, exploration, and agency."[38]

The work of other black feminist critics such as Kimberlé Crenshaw, bell hooks, Patricia Hill Collins, and E. Frances White has established a critical framework for understanding African American women's sexuality by exposing how the intersection of sexism and racism continually undermines black female representation.[39] Moreover, Spillers, hooks, Hammonds, and others have called for more developed theories of black female sexuality, emphasizing that these theories must take into account differences in terms of sexual orientation, class, and age.

Spillers identifies sexuality in U.S. culture as the "locus of great drama" and argues in her landmark essay "Interstices: A Small Drama in Words" that "black American women in the public/critical discourse of feminist thought have no acknowledged sexuality because they enter the historical stage from quite another angle of entrance from that of Anglo-American women."[40] Spillers historicizes the erasure of black women's sexuality by linking it to their position as chattel in the antebellum slave marketplace, with the "duty" to reproduce labor without acknowledged sexual agency.[41] As Spillers explains, "[T]he discourse of sexuality seems another way, in its present practices, that the world divides decisively between the have/have-nots, those who may speak and those who may not, those who, by choice or accident of birth, benefit from the dominative mode, and those who do not."[42] Thus she identifies the discursive power denied black women.

In her analysis, bell hooks contends that "representations of black female bodies in contemporary popular culture rarely subvert or critique images of black female sexuality which were part of the cultural apparatus of nineteenth-century racism and which still shape perceptions today."[43] Hooks further describes entertainers such as Tina Turner, Aretha Franklin, and Diana Ross as denigrated sexual objects in sexist American popular culture. Although she provides a useful reading of the ways racism and sexism overlap, her analysis foregrounds how the dominant gaze sexualizes black female bodies.[44] Hooks's argument leaves little room for black female empowerment through sexual representation or for subversive representational strategies presented for a black female spectator. Although Spillers, hooks, and others present important arguments, there is much to be gained by identifying how some black female authors provide what hooks deems "oppositional images of black female sexuality."[45] Texts that rupture the traditional boundaries of proper black middle-class behavior without playing into dominant constructions of black women do just that.

Although most medical and theoretical explorations of female sexuality focus primarily on white women, Gayle Wyatt's and Tricia Rose's scholarship examines how historical events, early messages in childhood, and romantic relationships influence black female identity and sexual health. Their studies, *Stolen Women* and *Longing to Tell,* use interviews, oral histories, and surveys to discern black women's attitudes about sexuality.[46] Rose's subjects, for example, reveal a variety of sexual experiences that defy simplistic categorization; her book encourages readers to consider that a black woman can understand herself as an incest survivor, single mother, and sex worker simultaneously. While Rose questions the inclination to label black women, Wyatt concerns herself with ways those labels affect the overall health of black female subjects and suggests that "every African-American woman can benefit from . . . patiently examining the critical years of her sexual development for evidence of invisible chains that could be binding her to distorting stereotypes, images, messages, and experiences."[47] Her study reveals how past behavior and external messages shape and define the way African American women understand their sexual selves. Further, Wyatt maintains that black women have specific sexual patterns and must learn particular skills to maneuver because American society casts them in such an unfavorable light. After disclosing how she herself was mistaken for a prostitute while waiting for her husband in a hotel lobby, she complains, "The stereotype of the promiscuous black woman persists whether we are standing at a bus stop with our children, on our way to church dressed in our Sunday best, studying at the library for a class, sitting in a business suit testifying before a congressional committee, or standing in a hotel lobby. Age, dress, appearance, and even economic status have much less to do with our image than do race and gender."[48]

Wyatt's thinly veiled allusion to Anita Hill's Senate testimony emphasizes, as in the earlier example of Rice, that even highly esteemed professionals cannot escape the damaging effects wrought in the nexus of sexual and racial stereotypes.[49] Although her study concludes that black women succumb to stereotypes "regardless of age, education, and income," her anecdote also reveals the particular frustrations felt by middle-class black women whose self-presentation and personal accomplishments fail to inoculate them from insults.[50] The work of Rose and Wyatt provided an outlet for their anonymous subjects to discuss their sexuality. Their studies also shed light on how black women cope with the psychic wounds inflicted by disparaging racial and gender classifications. Rarely are black women allowed to reveal such sexual complexity or enjoy a space in which to contemplate and disclose their sexual experiences.

Wyatt and Rose provide significant insight into the ways a broad cross-section of black women view their sexual experiences and identities, and this study augments their work by offering a focused analysis of the literary and cultural representation of a smaller subset of women. This volume deciphers the representation of middle-class women as different from, and also as an integral part of, the African American community. The analysis destabilizes the monolithic conception of black women and considers literary representations to be as important as interviews for revealing how black women understand sexuality.

Beyond the Black Lady is conceptualized around the convergence of two issues: constructions of the black middle class in American culture and moments when contemporary black women writers and filmmakers introduce issues of sexuality into narratives. It broadens the discourse around African American women and complicates the categories of race, gender, and class by offering an alternate reading of the over-determined racial and sexual script that casts middle-class black females as bastions of African American propriety. By drawing on the work of black feminist theorists to contextualize particular cultural products and key episodes in contemporary American popular culture, we can engage in a sustained critique of the strategies contemporary African American women writers deploy when asserting sexual agency in the public sphere.

What are the issues here? As a group, African American women are still characterized as overly sexual in American culture and subjected to harsh criticism in public policy discourse for their sexual and reproductive choices. Single mothers on welfare, for example, are unfairly blamed for the problems of the African American population. As Patricia Hill Collins explains, "Creating the controlling image of the welfare mother and stigmatizing her as the cause of her own poverty and that of African-American communities shifts the angle of vision away from structural sources of poverty and blames the victims themselves."[51]

Defending poor black women has proved tremendously helpful in theorizing black sexuality, but analyzing texts about middle-class women, especially those that challenge stereotypes about black sexuality, reveals how black women from all class backgrounds suffer from sexual misrepresentation. Moreover, this examination reveals the particularly perplexing position that middle-class black women occupy in the national culture and how damaging that role is collectively and individually. Middle-class black women provide a useful lens through which to explore issues of identity, sexuality, race, and class for several reasons. Society's preoccupation with scrutinizing poor and underclass black women often renders the middle class and their experiences invisible despite their economic and professional successes. Consequently, interrogating the unique social location of contemporary middle-class black women as beneficiaries of twentieth-century movements for social change such as second-wave feminism, the sexual revolution, and the civil rights and black power movements illuminates the role of sexuality for all black women.

Twentieth-century white American women writers such as Erica Jong and others have attempted to renegotiate the sexual terrain. Ann Snitow suggests that in the 1970s, under the influence of the second wave and the sexual revolution, white women novelists increasingly began to write about sex.[52] Snitow states that during that period many female authors composed narratives about married women's sexual dissatisfaction. Instead of limiting themselves, as male authors do, to describing protagonists' sexual conquests, women writers explored issues such as sexual repression and gender oppression. This literature complemented the women's movement and allowed women to recognize, extend, and celebrate new sexual opportunities and responsibilities.[53]

In a somewhat belated response, during the late twentieth century African American women's literature, film, and drama also began to depict new images of black female sexuality despite the black community's anxieties about confirming dominant culture's gender and racial stereotypes. The texts examined here go beyond voicing complaints about the effects of sexism and racism on black women's lives. They often express how sexual relationships and experiences raise conflicts for middle-class black women because of the expectations others place on them. In addition, by discussing sexual matters, these compelling narratives lay claim to the humanity of middle-class black women. The work of these writers offers a multiplicity of black identities.

To that end, Evelynn Hammonds asks black lesbians and heterosexual women to begin the project of understanding how each group engages in reclaiming the body and expressing desire.[54] *Beyond the Black Lady* examines how contemporary black middle-class women's narratives and public performances about their sexuality participate in that very same reclamation project. Although Hammonds bemoans the absence of any theory that explores black women's sexuality, it is important to note, at risk of imposing the same line Hammonds draws between creative and theoretical work, that creative expressions by black women provide signposts for theorists to follow and are theoretical texts in and of themselves. As Barbara Christian suggests in "The Race for Theory," "People of color have always theorized—but in forms quite different from the Western form of abstract logic. And I am inclined to say that our theorizing . . . is often in narrative forms, in the stories we create, in the riddles and proverbs, in the play with language, because dynamic rather than fixed ideas seem more to our liking."[55] The black middle-class figures in these texts theorize new and more expansive ways to understand race, class, and sexuality.

In this book I employ the terms *representation of sexuality* and *black middle class* in specific ways. "Sexuality" and "representation of sexuality" signify a discussion of sexual activity, sexual desire, or engagement in a sexual act by a work's characters or author. This includes discussion of the consequences of sexual activity and rejection of sex as well. In particular, this book is concerned with narrative representations of sexual agency. Middle-class black women openly addressing sexuality rewrite their role in African American culture. Lynne Segal maintains that "every time women enjoy sex, confident in the knowledge that *this,* just *this,* is what *we* want, and how *we* want it, I would suggest, we are already confounding the cultural and political meanings given to heterosexuality in dominant sexual discourses."[56] Segal addresses how asserting straight women's sexual desires takes advantage of the social and medical advances that helped give rise to the sexual revolution, but black middle-class women find themselves engaged in a more complicated revolt.[57] When they openly address sexual issues they engage in feminist politics that prioritize women's sexual pleasure and reject a historic role. Because the depiction challenges expectations, it is groundbreaking that writers render middle-class black women as sexual subjects. Their work should be read as a black feminist intervention.

Many theorists and activists acknowledge the importance of sexuality in feminist politics. In "How Being a Good Girl Can Be Bad," Deborah Tolman and Tracy Higgins assert:

> Women's sexuality is frequently suspect in our culture, particularly when it is expressed outside the bounds of monogamous heterosexual marriage. This suspicion is reflected in the dominant cultural accounts of women's sexuality, which posit good, decent, and normal women as passive and threatened sexual objects. When women act as sexual agents, expressing their own sexual desire rather than serving as the objects of men's desire, they are often portrayed as threatening, deviant, and bad. *Missing is any affirmative account of women's sexual desire.*[58]

While Tolman and Higgins describe the general limits society places on female sexuality, for black women suspicions about their sexuality exist regardless of any actions on their part. Not only do they discover that they are "threatening, deviant, and bad" but also that these labels carry historic resonance and continue to circumscribe their experiences. Moreover, because working-class black women are often considered sexually "deviant" whereas middle-class black women are considered "good" but passive victims, narratives that challenge these restrictive binary categories are revelatory.

Beyond the Black Lady charts an affirmative account of middle-class black women's sexual desire and agency because distorted images of African American women are damaging. In *Black Looks,* bell hooks states, "Bombarded with images representing black female bodies as expendable, black women have either passively absorbed this thinking or vehemently resisted it. Popular culture provides countless examples of black female appropriation and exploitation of 'negative stereotypes' to either assert control over the representation or at least reap the benefits of it."[59] Attempts by middle-class black women to assert control over their sexual image are an effective strategy toward reclaiming their sexuality. In the struggle for female sexual empowerment, heterosexual middle-class black women occupy a unique position. If, with their relatively privileged social status, they share the burden of discussing sexuality with lesbian, bisexual, and working-class women—whose bodies are consistently sexualized and suspect—they form a fuller chorus that can more effectively contest stereotypes.

The representation of sexuality cannot be separated from class ideologies and class dynamics. What is the black middle class? For the purposes of this book, "middle class" does not correlate with the financial status of Rice or the fictional characters discussed but rather indicates how images of elite African Americans resonate as arbiters of racial and sexual propriety. Standard definitions of the contemporary black middle class vary, but I am discussing representations of African American women who are generally college-educated professionals and enjoy relative social prestige and economic privilege.[60] Although the socioeconomic status of some of the characters and figures examined in *Beyond the Black Lady* places them outside the economic mainstream of America, they each symbolize gains made during the civil rights era and represent what Stephen Carter dubs "affirmative action babies." I agree with sociologists such as Bart Landry, Alphonso Pinkney, Melvin Oliver, and Thomas Shapiro who characterize middle-class African Americans as constituting both a social and an economic category.[61] This framework takes into account the tenuous political, social, and economic position of most middle-class blacks in the United States and specifically addresses the disparity between the economic position of whites and blacks with similar incomes or education.[62]

In *Black Picket Fences,* Mary Pattillo-McCoy's study of a South Side Chicago neighborhood, she asserts that the black middle class suffers from the "dismissive optimism" of public policies that fail to address their concerns.[63] Her book illustrates how residential segregation challenges the perception of the African American middle class as being out of touch with the broader black community. Although many middle-class blacks relocate outside African American communities, Pattillo-McCoy suggests that they are more likely to live in close proximity to low-income blacks than whites with comparable socioeconomic profiles are to live near low-income whites.[64] Therefore, the black middle class faces many of the same problems as blacks from lower economic groups, including crime, poor schools, and lack of adequate public services.⁶⁵ Although some laud the late twentieth century as a moment of unsurpassed success for some African Americans, Landry and others caution that "it is entirely premature to celebrate the rise of the black middle class."⁶⁶

Other works about the black middle class, such as Ellis Cose's *Rage of a Privilege Class,* Joe R. Feagin and Melvin P. Sikes's *Living with Racism,* and the *Frontline* documentary "Two Nations of Black America" (1998) hosted by Henry Louis Gates Jr., foreground specific slights.⁶⁷ These texts consistently reveal that members of the contemporary black middle class often consider themselves to be a minority plagued by invisibility and discrimination. Other current studies, such as Karyn Lacy's *Blue-Chip Black* and Martin Summers's *Manliness and Its Discontents,* also object to presumptions about the unmitigated privilege of the black middle class.⁶⁸

While recent sociological and historical scholarship analyzes the social, political, and economic experiences of the black middle class, with the exception of Victoria Wolcott's *Remaking Respectability* and Michele Mitchell's *Righteous Propagation* they devote little time to the specific issues women confront, such as sexuality or how such private and personal issues translate into political and social considerations.⁶⁹ Wolcott and Mitchell provide extensive histories of middle-class African American women, but their projects do not significantly analyze fictional representations.⁷⁰

Beyond the Black Lady explores how sexuality helps define the black middle class and how literary and popular representations of middle-class blacks reveal the broader culture's conceptions of African American progress. The innovative plays, films, and books examined in the following chapters question the notion of black middle-class women as racially inauthentic or sexually aberrant and actively fracture embedded discourses about African American identity and culture. This book is organized into two parts. The first, "Performing Identity," includes three chapters that explore images of the black middle-class woman on stage, in film, and in popular culture. The second, "Refashioning the Black Female Self," focuses on examples from fiction and nonfiction. Each work under discussion questions the narrow representational parameters of the middle-class black female subject. Dividing the book in this manner makes apparent how representations of black middle-class womanhood erupt differently in literary texts than in performative genres.

In Part 1, the chapters examine how the performances of black middle-class women in drama and cinema mirror and counter the depiction of black womanhood in the public sphere. The first chapter, "Spectacle of the Respectable: Anita Hill and the Problem of Innocence," analyzes a national scandal with a middle-class black woman at its center. The discussion considers why Hill's Senate testimony created such turmoil and then compares Hill's own account of her experiences, *Speaking Truth to Power* (1997), with her performance in the media and its reception. Hill's assumption of the role of wronged woman disrupts U.S. ideas about sexuality and race, making possible a new role for black women in the cultural imaginary. Hill, as an iconographic "black lady," possessed credibility because she was a demure professional. Yet the vexed response to Hill and her claims indicates that middle-class black women appear unreliable, even when speaking about their own experiences, because professional status, gender, and racial identity somehow render them particularly suspect.

The second chapter, "Staging Black Female Desire: The Drama of Race, Class, and Sexuality," shifts from a publicly identifiable figure to theatrical representations of media-driven events. The experimental play *WOMBmanWARS* (1994) by Judith Alexa Jackson features heroines contending with the ideals of middle-class sexuality and womanhood dictated by the broader African American community. Jackson depicts an African American family confronting Anita Hill's ordeal before the U.S. Senate and Desiree Washington's rape by boxer Mike Tyson. The work emphasizes the ways public attacks on black womanhood distort notions of self and suggests that influences from within the community exact a higher price than that of the dominant culture. Moreover, by incorporating actual footage as well as a fictionalized newscast of these highly charged events, Jackson's provocative drama emphasizes the debilitating effects of the media on black female sexual development and performance. The chapter ends with an examination of P. J. Gibson's more conventional drama *Long Time since Yesterday* (1985). Gibson's play explores the delicate position of middle-class African American women who find themselves attempting to reconcile the pursuit of sexual desire with the need to challenge distorted images of black sexuality and adhere to the black community's conservative expectations.

Chapter 3, "Black Ladies and Black Magic Women: Independent Film and Black Sexuality," considers dominant images of the black lady in contemporary cinema and discusses how Julie Dash's *Daughters of the Dust* (1991) and Kasi Lemmon's *Eve's Bayou* (1997) disrupt that image by using the southern United States as a site where black women reclaim sexual agency. Despite the historical legacy of sexual abuse before and after the Civil War, these narratives feature a middle-class black woman who challenges the community's attempts at restricting her sexuality. Each film is directed by an African American woman and skillfully confronts issues of shame, demonstrates the difficulty of maintaining social status, and exposes the risks women face when operating outside the boundaries of middle-class sexual propriety.

The chapters of Part 2 examine literary narratives that abandon chastity as a marker of black middle-class authenticity. Chapter 4, "Narrating Sexuality in Contemporary African American Autobiography," pairs Jill Nelson's provocative narrative *Volunteer Slavery* (1993) with Lorene Cary's more traditional autobiography *Black Ice* (1991) and analyzes the strategies employed to relay their sexual experiences. Unlike conventional autobiographies by African American women that often conceal sexual issues in order to disprove widely held beliefs about black sexuality, these books illustrate to what degree sexual experiences solidify notions of class identity. Cary and Nelson reveal unflattering, even abusive, sexual relationships between black men and women, signaling a sharp break from traditional African American autobiography and challenging the notion of an "authentic" middle-class black female subject.

Chapter 5, "Sex, Travel and the Single African American Girl: Andrea Lee's *Sarah Phillips*," reads Lee's 1985 novel as a neo-travel narrative that inverts the tradition of sex tourism and casts a middle-class black woman as someone whose social position allows her to pick and choose among white lovers. The sexual exploits of Lee's young heroine signal complete rejection of the role of the black lady and relegate the image of the exotic native woman to an antiquated past. The chapter further addresses how Europe, particularly France—important because of its historic relevance and continued popularity among black expatriates—occupies a unique role in the expression of sexuality among the liberal-minded African American middle class.

The tendency to obfuscate black middle-class sexuality in African American literature and culture leaves very little room for middle-class black women to express sexuality, but this tenuous space deserves some exploration. Narrative and performance texts in which middle-class African American women challenge traditional beliefs rebuke racist and sexist stereotypes. If, as Stephen Ross maintains, one's sexuality represents one's humanity, then privileged black women who rebel against the stagnant representation of black sexuality come closer to full humanity.[71] And the act of affirming their value assures women of a measure of political, social, economic, and spiritual empowerment that benefits all African Americans.

PART 1

Performing Identity

1

Spectacle of the Respectable

Anita Hill and the Problem of Innocence

Anita Hill's role in Clarence Thomas's Supreme Court confirmation saga still fascinates and troubles the United States. The historic turn in the proceedings caused by Hill's testimony about his professional behavior shocked and galvanized the public and placed the issue of sexual harassment at the forefront of the American political agenda. It took more than fifteen years before the Supreme Court justice spoke publicly and at length about the hearings. Thomas's memoir, *My Grandfather's Son* (2007), and his September 2007 *60 Minutes* interview with Steve Kroft reopened old wounds and illuminated enduring national tensions about race, gender, class, and sexuality.[1]

Hill's performance was so powerful and the image of her testimony so lasting that Thomas sought to discredit it. During his *60 Minutes* interview he consistently attacked the basis of Hill's middle-class persona—religiosity, modesty, and cautious manner—and called her public performance disingenuous. Thomas scoffed that Hill "was not the demure, religious, conservative person that they portrayed."[2] And in his autobiography he describes Hill as "rude," "touchy and apt to overreact."[3] Thomas also reports that once Hill's allegations were made public his Equal Employment Opportunity Commission (EEOC) colleagues "called by the score to say . . . that the meek and humble young woman they'd seen on TV was nothing like the abrasive, ambitious person they had known."[4] Thomas's critique of Hill's veracity, coupled with his attack on her performance, calls to mind the tone in some of the media and public reaction to Hill during the hearings. It is as if Thomas and many others found Hill's personality far from what a black woman is supposed to be, offensive and inauthentic.

Hill remains a useful figure, a serviceable black female body, through which debates about racial authenticity and black sexuality can be understood. That hers is a middle-class black body plays quite an important role in depictions of her. Hill's status in American society and culture is confusing and paradoxical. She is a black woman who worked for a conservative administration; she is a beneficiary of affirmative action who under Thomas's leadership helped weaken affirmative action policies; she is a symbol of a feminist cause who until the Thomas confirmation hearings never openly embraced feminism; and she is a middle-class black woman who continues to speak about her sexual life. A conundrum, if not an outright enigma, Hill defies, transgresses, and transcends common stereotypes about African American middle-class women.

Many in the African American community doubted Hill's claims and questioned her intentions. For some, Hill's conservative politics and accusations of sexual harassment against a prominent black man stirred consternation and confusion. Her testimony, however, also signaled the reintroduction of middle-class black female sexuality into the mainstream for public discussion, display, and consumption. Superseding Claire Huxtable—lawyer, wife, and mother on the 1980s' television comedy *The Cosby Show*—Hill became and is now, along with Condoleezza Rice and Michelle Obama, one of the most recognizable and visible icons of middle-class black womanhood. At the time of the hearings, Hill's life and sexual harassment charge against Thomas were discussed in newspapers, magazines, radio programs, and television documentaries, which placed her at the center of U.S. culture and the American imagination.

Even with the passage of time, Hill remains a prominent personality. As a lecturer, writer, and occasional television commentator, Hill, a Brandeis University professor of social policy, law, and women's studies, routinely discusses sexual harassment as well as other issues of social justice.[5] During Bill Clinton's presidency, she commented on the various sexual harassment claims leveled against him by Kathleen Willey and Paula Jones.[6] She also contributed to the national discussion about President Clinton's morality when details of his affair with White House intern Monica Lewinsky came to light.

Hill's continued public prominence, her complex social position, and the delicacy of the harassment charges make her influence on American culture and representations of African American women significant. The hearings prompted the United States to draft sexual harassment legislation and rethink workplace etiquette. And a survey of 137 academics even listed Hill's statement to the Senate Judiciary Committee as one of the top one hundred political speeches of the twentieth century. It ranked ahead of Malcolm X's "Message to the Grassroots," Shirley Chisholm's "For the Equal Rights Amendment," and Lou Gehrig's "Farewell to Baseball Address."[7] Further, the hearings quickly generated several books, documentaries, and critical anthologies that reimagined the interstices of gender, race, class, and justice in U.S. culture. To name but a few, these included Toni Morrison's anthology *Race-ing Justice, En-gendering Power,* Jane Flax's *The American Dream in Black and White,* The Black Scholar's *Court of Appeal,* Geneva Smitherman's *African American Women Speak Out on Anita Hill-Clarence Thomas,* and the *Frontline* documentary "Clarence Thomas and Anita Hill: Public Hearing, Private Pain." Each presented the hearings as a spectacle with a lasting impression on the American psyche.[8]

None of these studies, however, effectively explains what makes Hill such an intriguing figure. Perhaps amid all of the debate about Hill's personality, what was most impressive and most overlooked was her ability, as a middle-class African American woman, to talk about sex and her sexual life with civility and dignity in the face of circumstances meant to distort and humiliate her. As an object of display and as an author, Hill received enough attention to allow more room for middle-class black women's voices in the public sphere beyond their fictional representation.

Media representations of Hill and the hearings provided a script that destabilized and complicated long-standing stereotypes about black women in American popular culture. Throughout American history, men and women of color have been put on display in order to dehumanize and commodify them. During the era of slavery, whites in the South examined and regarded black bodies as objects to be bought and sold, and whites in the North avidly watched minstrel shows that simultaneously mocked and envied black lifestyles. Black women's bodies were especially vulnerable, as enslaved African American women had little, if any, legal recourse against white men who raped them. The end of slavery, moreover, did little to end whites' focus on the black body. During the late nineteenth and early twentieth centuries, lynching marred the American landscape as black men and women were brutally murdered by mobs of whites. These horrific events placed black bodies on display as objects of detestation, scorn, and ridicule. On some occasions even the body parts of victims became highly prized souvenirs for white onlookers.[9] The Thomas confirmation hearings placed middle-class black bodies on display in ways the nation never experienced. Thomas's now infamous high-tech lynching line speaks to the ways that the Senate chamber evoked the ugly voyeuristic excess of lynching scenes in the Jim Crow South. The justice's often noted comparison of the hearings to an act of racial terror particularly aimed at "uppity blacks" foregrounds the class dynamic at play as well as the ways the hearings were a reminder to middle-class African Americans that their presence in the halls of privilege is tenuous at best.[10]

In an effort to protect black womanhood and black women's bodies after emancipation, middle-class African Americans endeavored to shield black women from violence and the gaze of whites. The image of the black lady emerged in opposition to oppression and terror. To combat stereotypes of blacks as hypersexual, middle-class African Americans presented themselves as soft-spoken, chaste, moral, respectable, and dignified.

But when Anita Hill brought sexual harassment charges against Clarence Thomas, the black lady's tools of silence and evasion would not do. Instead, Hill pioneered another path. In an attempt to take back authorial control of her sexual life and personal dignity, Hill departed from the black lady's conventional script. Through her words and actions, she embodied self-respect, self-control, and dignity—hallmarks of the black lady—but broke new ground when she spoke about sexual matters. Even more fully than in her testimony, Hill weaves together in her memoir, *Speaking Truth to Power* (1997), her embodied performance of respectability with a narrative performance that expands notions of black middle-class womanhood. Hill's modest, and creative, self-representation allowed a black female conservative to advance women's sexual and professional rights. Her performance of new middle-class black womanhood has gone a long way toward legitimating black women's voices in public discourse.

"Intensely Private Matters"

Throughout the confirmation hearings, the mainstream print media exhibited a thinly veiled tension between presenting Hill as a trustworthy, respectable witness and regarding her as a promiscuous black woman deserving sexual harassment.[11] Hill received a great deal of sympathy, it appeared, when she presented herself as a conflicted black lady forced to present salacious material to the American public. Her image as a prim professional certainly contrasted with general stereotypes of black women as hypersexual, uneducated, and aggressive. Hill's performance at the hearings and her representation in print have cleared a space for a visible black female subjectivity that is distinctly middle class.

Hill found it difficult, however, to win universal public approval for her testimony because many African Americans considered her accusations against Thomas a racial betrayal, and some conservatives cast her complaint as evidence of a liberal or feminist conspiracy to destroy the nominee. Nell Painter maintains that Thomas and Hill competed for the sympathies of television and print audiences by drawing on the lexicon of American racial and sexual stereotypes. Thomas snatched the role of racial victim, claiming to be a casualty in a scheme to destroy black men, leaving Hill, according to Painter, with "no comparable tradition of a stereotype that had been recognized, analyzed, and subverted."[12] Painter and others have shown that Thomas's use of the lynching metaphor made racism solely a black male burden. Not only did his strategy obscure—if not erase—violence against black females but it also summoned the image of black women aiding in racist plots against black men.[13] Painter concludes, "[C]onsidering that Hill is a beautiful young woman who was leveling a charge of sexual harassment, adapting herself to stereotype and then reworking the stereotype would not have been a simple matter."[14]

Indeed, it was no simple matter, but it would be inaccurate to suggest that there were no recognizable social and historical types by which to identify Hill. When she testified, she confronted a host of cultural claims and notions about middle-class black women. Her class position would not allow her to be easily dismissed with most stereotypes of black women, which tend to focus on the working class, while Hill's conservative association with a Republican administration made it difficult to cast her in the role of the traditional, long-suffering black woman. But her race, profession, attire, and calm persona did contribute to her portrayal as a conventional black lady. Even though the black lady has not figured as prominently in American culture as the Jezebel or Mammy, it was familiar enough to blacks that Hill's proximity to that stereotype shaped how they read and responded to her.[15]

The black lady fills a strategic place in the American imagination, one riddled with complications that reduce middle-class women to social problems. Wahneema Lubiano defines the black lady as being akin to the image of the working-class black woman or single mother, otherwise disparagingly regarded as a welfare queen.[16] In Lubiano's view, Hill represents "the black lady, the one whose disproportionate over-achievement stands for black cultural strangeness and who ensures the underachievement of 'the black male' in the lower classes."[17] The black lady's class status undermines her contributions, given that it is assumed that her success is destructive to the African American community. Many blacks recognize Hill as a problem because she, like other black female professionals, appears to usurp what is considered the appropriate leadership position of the black male. The white majority considers the black lady a problem because it assumes that her successes are gained at the expense of others (whites, males) supposedly more deserving.[18] Most important, the black lady is regarded as cold, ambitious, sexually repressed, and therefore racially inauthentic.

The press repeatedly alluded to Hill's middle-class status in ways that portrayed her as boring, quiet, even sterile, and it steered away from the complexities of her identity as a black conservative. *Time*'s coverage of the hearings depicted, for example, Hill as "this prim law professor" and "a specialist in the dry area of commercial law, a reserved woman who by all accounts is given more to listening than talking."[19] She was acceptable, the magazine suggested, because her professional specialty seemed less glamorous than other areas of law that would draw more suspicion. Because the press did not consistently recognize her as middle class, Hill was forced into a mold from the civil rights era and depicted as "the poised daughter of so many generations of black women who have been burned carrying torches into the battle for principle."[20] Rather than acknowledging or coming to grips with the irony of Hill's conservative politics, the news media absorbed her into an uncomplicated depiction of a monolithic African American culture that has endured many wrongs and fought bravely for its rights.

While a *U.S. News & World Report* article described Hill as "Everywoman, the proxy for all who had ever had a degrading or threatening encounter with a male co-worker," it was her status as an attorney that helped produce that perception.[21] If her profession were less exalted, then as a black woman she would not have been readily considered a stand-in for all women, especially white ones. But her vocation and the circumstances surrounding the hearings allowed her transient universality.

To further support Hill's position as an injured party, *Newsweek* reported that her colleagues insisted "it is unconceivable that the never-married professor would fabricate the allegations against Thomas" and that "little in Hill's life suggested she would one day discuss sexual matters before an audience of millions."[22] Presenting Hill as a hesitant witness supported the notion that only a certain kind of woman would readily complain about sexual topics in public. The press repeatedly emphasized Hill's desire to keep her complaint private and explained her reticence in reporting her experiences as the judge's employee. Emphasizing her reluctance also maintained Hill's image as a proper lady easily considered as a universal "everywoman."

Even the explosive details of Hill's testimony support her representation as a black lady. When detailing the dramatic spectacle surrounding Hill's stoic testimony in its post-hearing coverage, *Time* marveled at her performance and ability to discuss sexual matters with decorum: "Before the days of exhausting and exhaustive testimony would end, Hill would *coolly* and *impassively* detail the nature of Thomas's alleged harassment while she worked for him in government positions from 1981 to 1983. Words like 'penis' and 'breasts' and 'pubic hair' would enter the public record repeatedly in so *somber* and *untitillating* a fashion that no one in hearing room would blanch, let alone smirk or giggle."[23] In direct opposition to the dominant stereotypes of black women, Hill raised sexual matters not as a temptress (after all, *Time* reported, it was nearly impossible to imagine her in the role) but as an insulted lady. Her disdain for the judge's treatment and ability to convey his coarse language with civility supported her image as dignified but prudish. The press mulled in wonderment over her ability to mention sexual terms with such respectability, and her blackness made the task even more remarkable.[24]

Journalistic representations of the middle-class Hill ran dissonantly against the overdetermined stereotype of poor and working-class black women in the public imagination.[25] Her clinical tone frustrated the stereotype of black women as highly sexual, hyperbolic, caustic, unrestrained, promiscuous, loud, and emotional. Her performance contained so little emotion that it completely contradicted expectations of black female vocal expressiveness. Indeed, the belief that audiences regarded Hill as an Everywoman was also derived from the perception of her restrained performance—the hallmark of a typical lady of any race. Able to present distasteful sexual matters before the press, Senate, and television audience, Hill was a marvel.

She was also, however, regarded as an opportunist and traitor to the race. Many African Americans may have believed Hill's version of the events, but there were those who disagreed with her divulging the matter in a public forum. With such a long history of brutality and dehumanization at the hands of and in the eyes of whites, many African Americans still endeavor to conceal black debates and dialogs. Furthermore, the persistent assumption that middle-class blacks enjoy greater privileges, yet fail to advocate for the interests of the broader black community, heightened this disapproval. Hill stood accused of harming the race by discussing sexual harassment, while Thomas attempted to present himself as a race man, with much to lose not only for himself but also for all African Americans. Hill's middle-class demeanor, exacerbated by stereotypes of black women, was the basis for distrust, because she failed to convey the supportive, nurturing, maternal image associated with black females historically, particularly with middle-class black women. As a man, Thomas was expected to behave proudly and sternly. But Hill's stoic disposition reversed gendered notions of racial performance. In some quarters her testimony came to signify a cold, selfish woman interested only in a career that she was willing to advance at the expense of the African American community.

Other participants in the hearings contributed to the public perception of Hill as a self-interested race traitor. Many senators and witnesses responded to her remarkable poise with skepticism. Voicing the same sentiment Thomas would eventually express in his memoir, their former colleague J. C. Alvarez called Hill's performance on October 11, 1991, fake. Alvarez exclaimed, "She played the role of a meek, innocent, shy Baptist girl from the South who was a victim of this big, bad man." Alvarez claimed not to recognize Hill because her performance at the hearings was so inconsistent with her past behavior.[26] He also described what the television audience observed during the hearings—a performance of middle-class black femininity. Whether Hill's testimony was staged is not as important as the fact that others discerned the difference between how she presented herself and what was typically expected from black women and used that difference as evidence of her disingenuousness.

Hill's performance embodied the assumed contradiction between a Yale-educated lawyer and a "meek, innocent, shy Baptist girl from the south." Much like Condoleezza Rice, she flaunted her southern origins to lend herself credence. Yet the strategy failed because throughout the hearings senators usually addressed her as "Professor Hill," thereby foregrounding her profession and by extension her class status. By focusing upon Hill's class and professional standing, the senators successfully alienated many television viewers from Hill. Moreover, when Senator Specter asked that she and he speak not as a senator to a citizen or witness but "one lawyer to another" he was attempting to disassociate Hill from blackness.[27] His aggressive questioning challenged her not as a former employee who was allegedly harassed but as an expert and professional whose experiences distinguished her from most citizens, especially most black women.

Hill's interrogation, occurring as it did before a live television audience, not only positioned her performance directly within the public sphere but also allowed her to influence it. According to Jürgen Habermas, the "liberal model of the bourgeois public sphere" is a place for political discourse among equals to debate issues of the common interest that is separate from the state.[28] African Americanists and feminist theorists have reworked Habermas's concept of the public sphere and extended theories of it to include notions of race and gender. Their contributions help contextualize Hill's contribution to public discourse about sexual harassment and race. Nancy Fraser, for example, warns of the tendency of feminists to misuse the concept of public sphere to "refer to everything that is outside the domestic or familial sphere." Instead, she encourages scholars to focus, as Habermas did, on "the space in which citizens deliberate about their common affairs, and hence an institutionalized arena of discursive interaction; it is a site for the production and circulation of discourses that can in principle be critical of the state."[29] Television was the public sphere's foremost platform in the United States in the late twentieth, and in early twenty-first century, with a twenty-four-hour news cycle and the proliferation of cable networks, it remains a dominant entity. Citizens and government alike use the medium as a forum to engage with political and cultural ideas and influence public thinking.[30]

The intensive exposure of the hearings altered the coverage of political events by the U.S. media. In this instance the televised hearings informed citizens about sexual harassment as well as various dimensions of middle-class black life. After the story broke and the cameras ran, various women's groups organized to pressure the government to respond to their concerns about Hill's mistreatment by the senators. These citizens were able to exercise power because they had the opportunity to "mediate between society and the state by holding the state accountable to society via publicity . . . so that state activities would be subject to critical scrutiny and the force of public opinion."[31] During the hearings many women demonstrated their power by influencing the process; they contacted their congressional representatives and spoke out on talk-radio programs.[32]

Another function of public discourse is to categorize and recategorize the subjects of interest to the society, and this was particularly evident with Hill's entry into the public sphere. There are moments when those who are less powerful, such as Hill, intervene in the public discourse in ways that redefine the marginalized.[33] Hill helped to redefine black women by providing an alternate narrative to the popular rendering of black female bodies. As feminists have suggested, the public sphere also includes "alternative" or "subaltern publics" that "parallel discursive arenas where members of subordinated social groups invent and circulate counterdiscourses to formulate oppositional interpretations of their identities, interests, and needs."[34] These subaltern publics contribute to broader discourse and influence their own representation. Yet during the Hill-Thomas hearing, Fraser contends, the diverse voices of alternative publics were missing:

Absent from the mainstream public sphere was the sort of black feminist analysis that could have corroborated and contextualized Hill's experience. As a result, African-American women were in effect "asked to choose . . . whether to stand against the indignities done to them as women, sometimes by men of their own race, or to remember that black men take enough of a beating from the white world to hold their peace." In other words, there was no widely disseminated perspective that persuasively integrated a critique of sexual harassment with a critique of racism.[35]

Fraser identifies the conundrum black feminists confronted at the time and continue to face when issues of racial and gender rights seem to collide.

Fraser, however, neglects the moments when black women addressed the problems that emerged in the Hill-Thomas confrontation.[36] And when black women spoke publicly about Hill's testimony, they followed many predecessors on the long path of African American participation in the public sphere. Throughout the nineteenth and twentieth centuries, as Michael Dawson and others have shown, African American activists, including Frederick Douglass, Booker T. Washington, W. E. B. Du Bois, and Ida B. Wells, not only contributed to the mainstream public sphere but also used their own counterpublic sphere to challenge the dominant culture.[37] Until the 1970s, the black counterpublic, mostly composed of men, included representation from various economic classes. Since that time the black public sphere has deteriorated because of the "combination of structural shifts in the international and American political economy, the consolidation of the political right's domination of public discourse and policy under President's Reagan and Bush, and conflict and diverging interests within the Black community."[38] Dawson identifies the black feminist agenda, which insists on acknowledging gender oppression along with race, as one of the most salient diverging interests to have disrupted the black counterpublic.

Dawson discounts how African American women have created and constituted a long-standing counterpublic of their own, one that has intersected and complicated the counterpublics developed by African American men and white women. Chronicling the history of several prominent black women's national organizations in *Too Heavy a Load*, Deborah Gray White concludes that "black women persistently spoke on their own behalf on issues of race leadership, negative stereotypes, woman's suffrage and woman's rights, and civil rights and civil liberties."[39] It is clear that by the time Hill testified, a black female subaltern counterpublic sphere had long existed and been a vibrant site for debate and dialog. It is equally important to acknowledge, however, the diversity among black females. White explains how differences influence the ways in which activists define priorities and agendas: "Seldom did African-American women organize across class lines. Poor, working-class, middle-class women all organized nationally but mostly within their own groups. Although it cannot be said that black women always chose race over other aspects of their identity, it can be said that race, *along with* gender and class were variables *always* factored into whatever national organizations did."[40] Organizations reflected their constituency's concerns, and it is important to distinguish among the various contributions each segment makes in reshaping the image of African American womanhood.

This black female subaltern counterpublic provided Hill with quick and steady support. It championed Hill for her intervention, for allowing black women to play a pivotal role in altering workplace policies, and for forging alternate representations of black women. When the hearing first began, a host of black feminists mobilized under the name African American Women in Defense of Ourselves. This organization provided a framework for a dynamic cross-section of women across the nation. Nellie McKay suggests that Hill's decision to "bear witness" encouraged others to "protest loudly the racial-sexual politics that wantonly dismisses African-American women's experiences, or slanders their collective character."[41] McKay's defenders of black women's collective character imagine themselves as inclusive; the architects of the campaign, however, were primarily professional and middle class.

Although Fraser does not specifically identify black feminists as a subaltern public, their role as one became more visible during the hearing. Indeed, because of the Senate hearing, the subaltern public of black women reentered the national discourse as advocates for their own issues.[42] The most poignant example of the influence of middle-class black women in the public sphere was the Sunday, November 17, 1991, full-page advertisement placed in *The New York Times* by African American Women in Defense of Ourselves. The campaign, initiated by black feminist academics Elsa Barkley Brown, Deborah King, and Barbara Ransby, was intended to "carve out a public forum," specifically for the views of black women.[43] The ad, signed by more than 1,600 women, responded to the media's failure to identify and consult with black feminist intellectuals and detailed specific objections to Thomas's nomination as well to the tone of hearings. The campaign repositioned black women as arbiters of American values instead of objects within the debate.[44] It also drew attention to the racial and sexual stereotypes that had plagued the hearings and denounced them for continuing to do harm to black women.

While *The New York Times* ad supported the media-driven idea of Hill's Everywoman universality it also reclaimed her specificity as an African American woman: "We are particularly outraged by the racist and sexist treatment of Professor Anita Hill, an African American woman who was maligned and castigated for daring to speak publicly of her own experience of sexual abuse. The malicious defamation of Professor Hill insulted all women of African descent and sent a dangerous message to any woman who might contemplate a sexual harassment complaint. . . . We will not be silenced."[45] Instead of being ashamed about sexual abuse and quietly trying to dissolve sexual stereotypes, the ad makes these issues public matters—just as Hill did with her testimony and public performance.

The rapidly executed and far-reaching crusade of African American Women in Defense of Ourselves "revealed an invisible but potentially national network of Black women that already existed."[46] The organization demonstrated just how many black women disapproved of the new Supreme Court justice and were outraged by the way in which Hill was treated during the process of his confirmation. The events surrounding the hearings impelled black women to speak in the black public sphere and make a formal response. In order to exert the most influence, the ad addresses the sexual mistreatment of all black women, not just Hill: "We wanted to specifically speak out in opposition to the sexual abuse and degradation of black women, including that of Hill, to condemn what we felt certain were misogynist and reactionary policies and practices by Thomas, and to dispel any erroneous notions that he enjoyed ubiquitous support among Black women."[47]

Despite the desire for inclusiveness their protest could not provide a univocal display of African American women's opinions. Drafting the advertisement was difficult, and although the voices of black women who supported Thomas were heard during this process the ad articulates only the views of those who opposed the nominee. As Deborah White has explained, black women of different classes have traditionally lobbied, mobilized, and advocated separately, and they continue to do so. The ad campaign, which found support on college campuses and among professional women, was predominantly a black middle-class and feminist crusade.

Scholars have tended to minimize the importance of class in the response of black feminists. Just as Hill's treatment by the African American community at large was due in part to her class status, class considerations also influenced the style and mode of intervention by African American Women in Defense of Ourselves. As a group of professionals they were able to secure the substantial financing needed to place the ad. In addition, *The New York Times,* the newspaper of record, targets an affluent, educated readership. Although the ad eventually ran in African American newspapers in seven large cities, it nonetheless reached only a narrow, very specific metropolitan and predominantly middle-class audience.[48]

The strategies of African American Women in Defense of Ourselves could not preclude the specific concerns of members' professional identities and experiences. The defense of Hill was couched in universal terms and underemphasized class in favor of the ideal notion of a black female subaltern counterpublic, but the collective was forced to choose in the end between racial solidarity and class affinities. The tensions revealed showcased the difficulties with holding a position that equally takes into account race, gender, and class.[49]

Revealing Testimony

Six years after Thomas's confirmation Hill finally made a play to define herself before the broader public that had cast her as a poster child for sexual harassment, used her to advance women's rights, and vilified her character. In a lighter moment during the hearings, Senator Howell Heflin asked Hill whether she was motivated by a desire to write a book. At the time, she answered no.[50] She apparently changed her mind and published an autobiography because she felt "no longer content to leave the assessment to others, for they cannot know what I experienced—what I felt, saw, heard, and thought."[51]

The book goes a long way in remaking, controlling, redefining, and complicating her image in the American popular imagination. Autobiographies and memoirs, according to James Olney, serve as "metaphors of self" in which an author purposefully constructs his or her "self" for an audience.[52] In addition, autobiographies within the African American tradition have a place of prominence. From Frederick Douglass's numerous works to those of Sojourner Truth, Booker T. Washington, Ida B. Wells, W. E. B. Du Bois, and Malcolm X, black autobiographies have been central documents by means of which black men and women have endeavored to wrestle authorial control over their selves away from socially and culturally dominating whites.[53] Hill's autobiography also includes her analysis of sexual harassment and reveals her more progressive, post-hearing views on gender, race, and politics.

All in all, Hill's memoir accomplished an amazing feat. Much as she did at the hearing, she was able, in *Speaking Truth,* to uphold the morals and mores of the black lady while at the same time be open about her sexual life. By engaging these contradictory elements—her status as a middle-class black woman and willingness to talk about sex—Hill supplies a primer to her performance during the hearings. Despite being a Yale-educated law professor, Hill adopts the image of wronged Everywoman. She accomplishes that performance by depicting her actions as those of a pious black lady. She foregrounds her differences from the hypersexual stereotype of the black woman to further invoke outrage at being humiliated by Thomas and the senators. At the annoyance of Thomas and his supporters, Hill emphasizes her class ascension and religious and moral upbringing to support her image as intelligent, professional, respectable, and innocent.

As a response to Senator Heflin's suggestion that she had frivolously placed herself at the center of Thomas's confirmation, Hill portrays herself as a contemplative, private person. Explaining her rationale for writing the memoir, she assures readers, "I do not undertake this endeavor lightly. I have never had much interest in writing anything beyond legal articles and essays. The very idea of a book of personal reflection is counter to my nature. I do not eagerly share with strangers the personal aspects of my life. . . . But it is as important today as it was in 1991 that I feel free to speak" (7).

Reentering the public forum provides Hill an opportunity to reclaim her name and repair her reputation.[54] In *Speaking Truth* she contextualizes her experience during the hearings and presents strategic details about her personal life. She attempts to rehabilitate her image through the narrative while asserting her sense of proper boundaries. In the memoir, the line between public and private, as well as what Hill considers her natural and unnatural self, is constantly explored and manipulated. She reiterates her right to speak, to define her self, and in doing so carves out a space for middle-class African American women to discuss sexual matters. Paradoxically, though, writing a memoir seems to be at odds with her avowed inclination toward privacy; therefore, the book represents another performance of Hill's public self—a narrative performance that reveals as well as shields.

Throughout the nineteenth century, African American autobiographers tended to begin with statements of being: "I was born." Hill, however, starts her autobiography with her "birth" in the public eye on October 11, 1991, the moment she first entered the Senate chamber to testify in the Thomas hearings. Almost immediately, just as she and Thomas began their statements, the memoir turns to her childhood years in a small Oklahoma town. She explains how segregation introduced her to racism and how attending integrated schools taught her about assimilation. Her knowledge of violence came from the assassinations of Martin Luther King Jr. and President John F. Kennedy as well as from stories about her grandfather and his run-ins with the Ku Klux Klan. Despite the gravity of those events, she emphasizes (much as Condoleezza Rice does) her insulated southern childhood and stresses that her large family never discussed the social and political changes erupting around them. When Hill admits, "The civil rights movement was a remote and abstract experience" (45), she dispels lingering perceptions of herself as a black activist determined to destroy the conservative Supreme Court nominee.

More important than clarifying her politics, Hill also provides subtle details about her sexual history and identity. She downplays her physical attributes and emphasizes her academic accomplishments in order to nullify perceptions of being a sexual temptress. Instead of relishing her triumph over adversity she consistently describes herself humbly: "I was not athletic, nor did I think of myself beautiful in the homecoming queen way. I had a pleasant round face that from age seven was adorned with glasses thick enough to correct my nearsightedness, and that did not seem to change much with age. I looked and indeed was very bookish. I remained that way during high school and college" (45). This description embraces the image of the innocent studious girl "with a pleasant round face." Hill's "bookish" appearance as a teenager translates into her future self-presentation as an adult. By downplaying physical attractiveness, she foregrounds academic and professional success and promotes her image as a desexualized political innocent.

The packaging of *Speaking Truth* is consistent with its content; Hill transcends derogatory racial and sexual stereotypes with her upstanding middle-class demeanor. The black and white, Annie Leibovitz photograph selected for the dust jacket makes this point graphically. In silhouette, the contemplative Hill wears a loosely fitted white shirt that portrays her as stylish but modest. Hill seems conscious of her professional packaging as well. In the FBI interview described in the memoir she recalls, "[The FBI interviewer] asked if there was anything in the way I dressed or carried myself that might have led Thomas to believe it was appropriate to talk to me about pornography or make otherwise suggestive remarks. . . . I answered that I had dressed then, as I did at the present time, rather conservatively, and certainly in a way appropriate to an office setting" (118–19). Aware of how she is read by her interrogators—a black woman who probably acted in a seductive or sexual manner—Hill answers carefully and reinforces how her private presentation during the FBI interview at her home replicates her public appearance.

After establishing herself as a black lady, the memoir covers more intimate ground as Hill discusses the details of relationships with former boyfriends as motivations for rejecting Thomas. With guarded language, she makes revelations about her relationships but never undercuts her image as a private, chaste black lady. Hill maintains that while working for Thomas she kept careful boundaries between her professional and personal attachments. As she did during the hearing, she explains, "I had friends from school with whom I socialized and had begun to meet others as well. I was dating two or three men casually, but even if I had not been, I would not have considered dating Thomas" (69).[55] Although she admits to being unclear about the exact number of men she dated, she emphasizes that her relationships were only "casual"; by presenting them as informal dates she implies minimal sexual involvement. Clearly, Hill wants readers to understand that she was not at a loss for possible suitors. This passage challenges the perception of her as asexual or undesirable but shields her from accusations of promiscuity.

Hill makes an even stronger case about her romantic life while working for Thomas when she explains the circumstances around her decision to leave the Equal Employment Opportunity Commission: "I had not planned to return to Oklahoma; I had not planned to go into teaching. I would leave behind me in Washington a budding relationship with a young surgical resident for whom I cared very deeply. But the opportunity to leave the employ of Clarence Thomas and to be nearer my family was most compelling" (80). Hill not only contemplates how the career change will affect her professionally but also notes the potential harm to her personal life. Mentioning past relationships also underscores her marital status, and Hill seems to imply that Thomas's harassment forced her to sacrifice a potentially serious relationship.

Hill's former boyfriend remains nameless and faceless, but the vague narrative construction of him solidifies several of Hill's objectives. The strategy not only maintains their privacy but also shrouds the relationship so the former suitor evokes the image of the ideal man. She provides few details about him or their relationship but does mention his profession. His status as a physician is crucial because it counters suspicions that she hoped for a relationship with Thomas as a way of advancing her class status. Her boyfriend's career also upholds her identity as a proper middle-class woman. Once married, he, the doctor, and Hill, the lawyer, would become a real-life *Cosby* family, but Thomas's behavior disrupts that black middle-class fairy tale.

Enlisting former boyfriends as proof is a delicate strategy, but Hill had already used it successfully during the hearings to reinforce her standing as a proper black lady. It works in the memoir, too. Quoting the testimony of another former boyfriend, John W. Carr, Hill defends her character and substantiates her charges against Thomas. Carr stated that while enrolled in Harvard University's JD-MBA program he "developed a social relationship with Anita Hill."[56] Although he indicates that they were involved with each other, she describes him as "a friend whom I met when I worked for Clarence Thomas" (159). Despite these inconsistencies, Carr's testimony on October 13, 1991, characterized Hill in a manner consistent with her own self-presentation. Carr, another professionally appropriate suitor, proved that Hill had a "normal" social life while still allowing for her to maintain the image of a "proper" young woman.

Carr's testimony was also important because it confirmed that Hill confided in him during their relationship about Thomas's behavior. "She was very uncomfortable talking about these events," Carr recalls, "and said that she did not want to go into any detail about the actions that so upset her."[57] Hill's discomfort and reluctance to discuss the offensive incidents (even with her boyfriend) buttresses her characterization as modest. Under Senator Joseph Biden's questioning Carr gingerly explained the nature of their relationship:

> THE CHAIRMAN: Mr. Carr, you were dating Anita Hill. I assume that's what you meant by having—we use a lot of euphemisms in this town and an old-fashioned word—you were dating Professor Hill at some point in the past, is that correct?
>
> MR. CARR: I think that's close.
>
> THE CHAIRMAN: Okay, well, maybe—
>
> MR. CARR: Let me explain, if I may? When you say "dating" I think of a relationship that was going on.
>
> THE CHAIRMAN: I admit that I find it difficult—I mean these phrases . . . did you go out alone with her from time to time? [Laughter]
>
> MR. CARR: Yes, I would characterize it that we met, we dated, and the bulk of our relationship was on the telephone getting to know one another.
>
> THE CHAIRMAN: I see. Now—
>
> MR. CARR: I guess I would say we didn't get but so far.
>
> THE CHAIRMAN: I understand that. [Laughter][58]

The precise and delicate manner in which Carr describes their relationship—what he says and what he refuses to say—attempts to place Hill beyond suspicion in the eyes of the panel. Senator Biden's clumsy response elicits repeated laughter because he is endeavoring to force Carr to define in a word or two a relationship that is too slippery, too complex, to articulate.[59]

Senator Alan Simpson alluded to Hill's sexual orientation in his questioning and various press interviews, so she also found it necessary to establish her heterosexuality.[60] She addresses the issue directly in her memoir. The violation of her privacy and the threat of being labeled a lesbian (whether true or false) in the national media angers Hill. Before stating her sexual preferences, she questions the appropriateness of the entire line of thought:

> In one statement, no part of which was made in my presence or objected to by the chairman of the committee, Senator Simpson questioned my background, character, and "proclivities." Journalist William Safire gave definition to the term "proclivities," lest there be any doubt that Simpson was questioning my sexual orientation and following up on earlier efforts to get Oral Roberts law students to state that I was a lesbian. . . . Even if the claims about my sexual orientation had been true, in pursuing the information the newspaper seemed only interested in satisfying the public about intensely private matters, unrelated to my claim. (216–17)

Throughout the autobiography Hill accomplishes what the senators and the press failed to do: she reveals her "proclivities" with much fervor but without actually mentioning sex. She confirms her heterosexuality by using such terms as *seeing, steady,* and *dating* in reference to men instead of more suggestive language that might bring to mind stereotypical images of aberrant black female sexuality. She asserts that her sexual orientation is an issue unrelated to her claim against Thomas, but lesbianism would undermine her position as the Everywoman and jeopardize her black lady status.

Hill's friendship with a colleague, Shirley Wiegand, raised the most suspicion about her sexual orientation. Hill tries to clarify the nature of their relationship by emphasizing that although Wiegand is an attorney, she did not attend to Hill's legal needs but "was stuck with the uninteresting job of hand-holding" (207). Hill praises Wiegand for providing a "lifeline to reality" during the ordeal but complains, "Some in the press would even misrepresent that true friendship, to exploit the salacious and unfounded suggestion that our relationship was sexual in nature" (207). She reprimands the Republican senators for "looking for statements from anyone who would attest to anything negative about my professional competence, my personality, or my sexuality" (208). The concept of a "negative" sexuality is problematic, however. Although disavowal of lesbianism allows remaining within acceptable boundaries for the ideal of middle-class black womanhood, it nonetheless seems to further the notion that lesbianism is abnormal, troubling, and wrong.

After explaining her sexual orientation and relationship history, Hill's memoir shifts to disclose a more intimate health matter, one where her private life, physical life, sexual life, and public life intersect in painful ways. She reveals that during the months leading to the Thomas confirmation she endured both physical and emotional pain. "I was suffering from a medical condition that seems to run in my family," she confides. "My uterus was covered with tumors that caused me considerable pain and discomfort. Each day I would rise to moderate pain that increased as the day wore on" (91). Although the dramatic revelation shatters her privacy, the disclosure softens Hill's image, making her appear more vulnerable and feminine. The condition explains her aloof, distant manner during the hearings and her grave manner in public. Although at the time, she says, embarrassment kept her from disclosing the diagnosis to her family, divulging her medical history in the memoir gives Hill corporeality without sexualizing her middle-class black body.

By sharing this delicate health matter Hill once again garners sympathy. She goes into great detail about her frustrations with her gynecologist, who "speculated that a hysterectomy was inevitable but said he would treat my condition with painkillers until the discomfort became unbearable" (93). She concludes the narrative theme by describing how just a few months after the hearings a surgeon performed a myomectomy to remove the growths, which were benign. The surgery left her uterus intact, but she nonetheless felt depressed and "hollow inside" (261). The possibility of a hysterectomy and her feeling of emotional hollowness draws attention to the possibility of perpetual emptiness, of no partner and no children.

Speaking Truth to Power reveals Hill's awareness of the performative aspects of her committee testimony, and with the memoir she weaves a narrative performance of middle-class values with her embodied performance during the hearings. She recounts Senator Biden's difficult questioning on October 11 and admits feeling trapped by the cameras. Yet she explains her performance almost as if evaluating an actor onstage, "I resolved to become as motionless as possible. I had to be impervious to the lights and to the heat as well as the natural reactions of my body. Though I felt each one of the senator's attempts to humiliate me, I vowed not to so much as twitch. I ignored the numbness in my legs and even the pain from the tumors in my abdomen" (187).

Choosing a stoic stance, the nearly immobilized Hill responded to the obtrusive questioning with poise. Despite physical distress unknown to the public at the time of the hearing but providing a new layer of meaning for the reader, she brought dignity and attention to the issue of sexual harassment. In the memoir, stoicism reads as an act of strength instead of detachment for she not only endured the glaring lights and senators' scowls but also actual physical distress. Revealed as a multiply injured woman—by Thomas's sexual harassment, by the personal effects of his harmful behavior, and by physical pain—Hill, in her memoir, joins a long tradition of strong black women.[61]

By the end of her memoir Hill is transformed. Surviving all ordeals helped her accept her new public role. Part of her recovery has meant working on "reconstituting my relationship with various communities of which I had been a part because of my race, gender, and profession" (343). Using the metaphor of quilting, she discusses her attempt to put together the strained, torn, and disparate fabrics of her life. In the stitching, a new self is made. The quilting image signifies a return to a lasting tradition in southern and black rural cultures, one that underscores her connection to African American womanhood and her origins. As Roland Freeman suggests, quilting is central to African American culture for reasons that include "more than just the aesthetics. . . . it keeps us warm, it soothes our pain and relieves our burdens, it commemorates important occasions, it preserves family history, it demonstrates skill, it encourages social interaction, and it supports intimate communication."[62] Hill's status as a single professional black woman contributed to the spectacle of the hearings, but it is a domestic image that concludes her autobiography.[63] Although invoking domesticity could be considered a gesture toward traditional notions of womanhood, in this case it symbolizes new commitment to more radical racial and gender politics.[64]

After the hearings, Hill observes that the momentum generated there mobilized many segments of the American public. She differentiates between the flurry of activism surrounding sexual harassment, such as the efforts of the African American Women in Defense of Ourselves, and her specific role in moving the discourse forward:

> The energy created by the furor over the hearing continued at a high pitch for months. . . . It did not occur to me that all of the activity was about me, because it was not. The activity was about every woman who hurt because of the hearing. The hearing exposed a vacuum of understanding so massive and powerful that it would have sucked all of me into it had I not tried so hard to hang on to what was left of my life. Thus while others were organizing, rallying, and protesting against the hearing, I was trying to keep the experience at bay and to regain my health. (260)

Hill casts herself as an individual who was simply a catalyst for change, not the focal point. She seems to recognize that African American feminists and others found ways to organize on the subject of sexual harassment without allowing her limitations as a political conservative to direct the discourse in the public sphere.

Hill's decision to testify placed black middle-class womanhood at the forefront of the movement to end sexual harassment. Hill and her supporters heed Audre Lorde's decree: "Your silence will not protect you."[65] Indeed, by speaking and performing, Hill may have protected other women from suffering from similar abuse in silence. As Fraser notes,

> Publicity, then, is not only a weapon against state tyranny, as its bourgeois originators and current Eastern European exponents assume. It is also potentially a weapon against the extra-state power of capital, employers, supervisors, husbands, and fathers, among others. There was no more dramatic proof of the emancipatory side of publicity in relation to private power than the way in which these events momentarily empowered many women to speak openly for the first time of heretofore privately suffered humiliations of sexual harassment.[66]

Fraser recalls the "consciousness-raising" this episode created among different segments of women in the United States. Hill's participation in the hearings succeeded in teaching the public about the issue of sexual harassment, and it also made middle-class black women more visible architects of black political strategy. Hill's intervention in the black female subaltern counterpublic also allows black women to envision themselves as sexual subjects who can voice sexual matters, desires, or complaints. Her intervention in the public sphere helped humanize African American women, if not to the rest of U.S. society then at least to each other.

The spectacle of the hearings and Hill's mistreatment by the process was cause for alarm. Her experience proves that simply obeying the dicta of middle-class behavior will not save black women from misinterpretation or mistreatment. Unlike moments throughout American history when black bodies have been on display to be beaten, tortured, and dehumanized, Hill, through perseverance, wisdom, and savvy, found ways to define herself time and again, even to a hostile audience. She demonstrated numerous ways to grasp control over public image through her embodied performance and narrative self-constructions. Sexual harassment, like other forms of abuse, is about power, not the victim's sexual signals. Acknowledging that power dynamic grants black women agency to either discuss sex openly or refuse to discuss it at all without worrying about how their sexuality shapes perceptions of race.

Hill frames her testimony and her autobiography as pedagogical. *Speaking Truth to Power* ends with an open letter to the 1991 Senate Judiciary Committee in which she chides them for their callousness. She hopes that they did "indeed learn from the experience of 1991" (354). The tone of coverage of the Hill-Thomas episode sparked by Thomas's memoir suggests that at least the media has learned. Her appearance on ABC's *Good Morning America* and her *New York Times* op-ed both granted Hill a national forum to address Thomas's comments. Most mainstream media organizations granted her a measure of respect that was lacking when her statement was first leaked.[67] Hill's national reemergence as a public intellectual who advocates for women's issues has further extended her influence.[68]

At the end of the memoir Hill acknowledges how the hearings shaped and reshaped her. "I wanted to weep as well," she mourns, "for I knew that I had lost something that nothing could ever replace. Just what it was I could not be sure, but inside I knew that I would never be the same" (197). What changed for Hill also changed for many middle-class black women who were no longer invisible in popular culture or workplaces, churches, and communities. This increased visibility was something to be celebrated.

Hill's legacy allows Americans, especially blacks, to think about the middle class differently. In particular it invites them to rethink the role of middle-class black women. Contemporary middle-class black women are no longer relegated to a fictional representation on a popular television show that can be dismissed as unreal. Nor can they be written off as subordinate to black men—middle class or otherwise. Further, literary and other cultural texts have also expanded the notion of black womanhood. African American women were working in autobiography, fiction, film, and drama at the end of the twentieth century. In their work, they broadened the representation of middle-class black women with heroines who revealed how issues of sexuality determine black female identity and circumscribe black women's power.

2

Staging Black Female Desire
The Drama of Race, Class, and Sexuality

> DANNY: If there's one thing I know, that's women. That woman is lying. She prob'ly bought the tape herself. Can you see a man like Clarence Thomas in a porno shop? (*Gets another beer from fridge*) She's probably mad about him marrying a white woman. You know how you sistas are.
>
> SAPPHIRE: Calm down honey... you're getting those beads of wet rage on your forehead.
>
> DANNY (*Gets another beer*): Damn straight I'm mad. Can't let the oppressor... how'd my man put it... "high-tech lynch" us. Black folks got to learn to stick together.
>
> SAPPHIRE (*Attending to lamb chops baking in oven*): Correct me if I'm wrong, but ain't Anita Hill black?
>
> —Judith Alexa Jackson, *WOMBmanWARS* (1994)

Judith Alexa Jackson's character Danny in *WOMBmanWARS* (1994) raises a crucial question about Anita Hill's status within the African American community. Danny regards Hill as "that woman" with suspect motives. Sapphire, Danny's wife and the play's protagonist, challenges him and in so doing provides a counter-image of Hill which Hill holds an equal claim to being part of the black race regardless of her allegations to the contrary. As Sapphire and her family witness Hill's ordeal before the U.S. Senate, Sapphire defends the aggrieved lawyer in order to show allegiance to black womanhood and challenge assumptions about black authenticity. In this chapter I examine Jackson's performance piece and P. J. Gibson's drama *Long Time since Yesterday* (1985) as theatrical representations of black middle-class women defending their sexuality and asserting sexual agency.[1]

In *WOMBmanWARS* and *Long Time since Yesterday*, black middle-class women defend their sexuality in light of cultural stereotypes about black female sexuality and discuss sexual identities with respect to racial, gendered, and economic positions. Jackson draws on sexual scandals from American popular culture to highlight women who have survived sexual violation by embracing their own integrity. *WOMBmanWARS* redeems Anita Hill as a resilient heroine; in this performance she is a strong woman who perseveres despite being center stage in a national spectacle. Gibson, however, extends the depiction of the tragic middle-class woman in *Long Time since Yesterday*. Her characters explore their sexuality only to discover that the sexual revolution of the 1970s, purportedly enjoyed by middle-class white women, holds fewer pleasures and greater pain for black women. Both Gibson and Jackson endeavor to problematize cultural understandings of race, class, gender, and sexuality by addressing racial stereotypes and considering the varied ways in which a middle-class black woman's public performance places her in a precarious position.

Gibson's and Jackson's representations not only suggest different ways for others to imagine black women but also reveal strategies that black women use to resist the distortions propagated throughout American culture. As Glenda Dickerson maintains, "The depiction and perception of African-American woman in this country through stereotypes has garbled her voice and distorted her image. The real tragedy is that the African American woman herself has too frequently bought this distortion."[2] The dramatic creations of Jackson and Gibson intervene in this tragedy. Their plays stage black women seeking to assail cultural distortions, clarify black women's voices, and construct new means of sexual presentation and integrity.

Gibson's and Jackson's cultural interventions follow a long history of African Americans' creative use of the theater. Just as autobiography has expressed the African American sense of self from Frederick Douglass to Anita Hill, theater has operated as a dramatic literary format that publicly represents a group to itself and to others. Throughout the nineteenth and twentieth centuries, as Daphne Brooks suggests, drama has been a unique and vital genre in African American presentations of identity and community. African American drama comments on race and the ways in which society contends with the tensions and traumas caused by racism. Because the genre allows for communal watching of characters that embody ideas, abolitionists before the Civil War used drama to persuade audiences to challenge slavery. Henry "Box" Brown, for example, a slave who had freed himself by using the postal system to mail his body north in a box, regularly reenacted this great feat to astounded audiences.[3] In the years following the Civil War a host of antilynching dramas juxtaposed the morality of African Americans with the brutal lawlessness of southern whites.[4] A major advocate for the centrality of drama, W. E. B. Du Bois pushed for African American theater to be staged in institutions located within the black community. Du Bois felt that, unlike other genres, African American drama could "reveal real Negro life as it is."[5] Theater's immediacy and role within American culture placed it in an incomparable position.

Nevertheless, drama has often been subordinate among blacks to other literary and performative genres. In "Writing the Absent Potential," Sandra Richards laments the continued absence of most theatrical texts and criticism from African American literary anthologies. Most African American literary criticism, she explains, analyzes poetry, fiction, and some autobiography, but most critics regard "drama as a disreputable member of the family of literature."[6] Richards seeks a reassessment, for she believes the underrepresentation of plays in the African American literary canon ignores the centrality of performance in African American culture.[7] William Branch insists that at the outset of the twenty-first century the central question for black theater remains, "What themes should Black dramatists consider, what forces of history must they re-examine, and how will they reconcile the great need to *counter*-propagandize with the essential focus of theater as a means of entertainment rather than sermonizing?"[8] His comments and rhetorical question speak to how playwrights use black middle-class characters and themes to counterpropagandize and sermonize about African American culture, gender, and society.

During the twentieth century, African American theater consistently rendered the black middle class, particularly the middle-class heroine, as a tragic figure.[9] In dramas from Angelina Grimke's *Rachel* (1916) to Adrienne Kennedy's *Funnyhouse of a Negro* (1964) black middle-class women find themselves inconsolable or suicidal because they cannot confront circumstances caused by racism. In these texts black middle-class characters often sacrifice personal needs and desires for the greater good of the race or because of the burdens of blackness. Many of these representations also suggest that being middle class creates deep ambivalence about identity and that integration leads only to tragic ends. Characters find themselves facing madness, murder, suicide, or at the very least unhappiness. Plays focusing on the black middle class often feature characters confronting death, depression, and suicide. They include such works as Amiri Baraka's *The Dutchman* (1964), Talvin Wilks's *Tod, the Boy, Tod* (1990), Kathleen Collins's *The Brothers* (1982), Alexis

Deveaux's *Tapestry* (1976), and Kennedy's *Ohio State Murders* (1992). Black middle-class figures are rarely depicted as heroes in contemporary drama but are more likely presented as racially confused and political sellouts.

The representation of middle-class African American women in African American theater often mirrors that of the late nineteenth- and early twentieth-century literature. Early African American drama emphasized racial uplift and featured chaste and pious black middle-class characters.[10] In addition, plays by black female writers such as Pauline Hopkins, Eulalie Spence, and Georgia Douglas Johnson showcase black suffering while highlighting respectability, morality, and honor.

This tendency in African American drama to present middle-class women suffering in the name of racial uplift changed dramatically during the black arts and revolutionary black theater movements. In the 1960s, artists were called on to create black art for black people that voiced anger with the racial status quo.[11] Unfortunately, that meant presenting the black middle class not only as tragic but also as an anathema to the well-being of the broader African American community. Plays such as Alice Childress's *Wine in the Wilderness* (1969), Baraka's *Great Goodness of Life: A Coon Show* (1967), and Kennedy's *Funnyhouse of a Negro* (1962) feature middle-class characters confused about their role in forging black equality. With the exception of Kennedy's work, the plays either relegate black middle-class women to supporting roles or make them nonexistent.[12] In the 1970s, black female playwrights such as Ntozake Shange, Aishah Rahman, and Pearl Cleage acted as architects of a new theatrical sensibility and began to develop work that showcased the complexity of black women's lives. Playwrights after the civil rights era, such as Suzan-Lori Parks, Lynn Nottage, and Anna Deavere Smith as well as Gibson and Jackson, moved the African American theater tradition forward beyond the "racial uplift" paradigm.[13] Although African American women have approached drama in innovative and diverse ways, unfortunately, many of their plays have often focused narrowly on the experiences of rural or working-class black women.[14]

In the same vein as Branch, Parks theorizes about the necessity of broadening theatrical notions of blackness and argues that "there are many ways of defining Blackness and there are many ways of presenting Blackness onstage." She ponders the effect of changing the standard conflict in African American drama: "And what happens when we choose a concern other than the race problem to focus on? What kind of drama do we get? Let's look at the math:
. . . BLACK PEOPLE + X = NEW DRAMATIC CONFLICT (NEW TERRITORY)."[15]

New territory for black theater includes centering African American female characters in plots that venture beyond the standard realist rendition of black and white racial conflict. Focusing openly on sexuality, for instance, forces audiences not only to confront gender issues, as Anita Hill did during her Senate testimony, but also to reckon with the intersection of race, class, and gender. Presenting middle-class characters makes class a central issue; exploring race, sexuality, and class simultaneously responds to Parks's insistence on using a dramatic formula that moves beyond standard racial conflict—to witness and contemplate the complex intersections of race, class, gender, and sexuality for middle-class black women.

It is rare to discover African American dramas that feature black women characters negotiating the conflict between their own sexual desires and middle-class social mores. Both *Long Time since Yesterday* and *WOMBmanWARS* challenge the theme of the isolated, tragic middle-class figure and bring to center stage women who struggle with sexual choices and the expectations of others.[16]

Both plays intervene in what Evelynn Hammonds designates as the "black (w)holes," or missing parts, of the African American cultural, literary, and sexual landscape. Hammonds explains that black women, historically denied sexual agency and subjectivity, need to make their sexuality visible in a way that empowers and emancipates instead of imprisons and distorts. She concedes, however, "To this date, through the work of black feminist literary critics, we know more about the elision of sexuality by black women than we do about the possible varieties of expression of sexual desire. Thus what we have is a very narrow view of black women's sexuality."[17] Reading Gibson's and Jackson's plays as feminist projects reveals the difficulties middle-class black women experience when they endeavor to explore, protect, or re-imagine their sexual lives, given the distorted images of black women that dominate the American imagination.[18]

Because black female playwrights engage directly and subtly with demeaning stereotypes and tropes that circulate in the public sphere they must consider how their plays reflect upon, undermine, reinscribe, or reinforce racial, gender, and class clichés. Gibson and Jackson provide two different renditions of middle-class black women subverting sexual stereotypes. In *Long Time since Yesterday*, all but one of the women contemplates or attempts suicide when faced with difficult sexual and romantic choices. But the play departs slightly from the trope of the tragic middle-class lady by exhibiting a full array of black middle-class women as sexual subjects. Similarly, *WOMBmanWARS* challenges the notion of middle-class black female sexuality as a commodity only in the service of the African American community. Instead, Jackson's play illustrates the hazards for those who ignore or sublimate their sexuality. *WOMBmanWars* combats strategies of concealment that prioritize worries about reinforcing "negative" racial stereotypes about both black men and women.

In order to confront contemporary issues of black female sexuality, Gibson and Jackson adopt what Tania Modleski defines as the "principle of reverse," a term she derives from Maya Angelou's autobiography *I Know Why the Caged Bird Sings* (1969). This principle "describes the mimicry of 'oppressed groups, who often appear to acquiesce in the oppressor's ideas about it, thus producing a double meaning: the same language or act simultaneously confirms the oppressor's stereotypes of the oppressed and offers a dissenting and empowering view for those in the know."[19]

To apply Modleski's use of this concept to Gibson's and Jackson's work it is useful to return to the notion of the subaltern counterpublic created and sustained by black women. Gibson and Jackson put in play the principle of reverse by first raising the specter of the oversexed black women, thereby engaging or activating the social stereotype. Next, they set out to reveal the stereotype to be chimera by complicating the monolithic notion of black female sexuality. Gibson presents a variety of middle-class women, whereas Jackson connects black women's experiences across class to show their interdependence.[20]

Staging stereotypes in order to counter them is an unstable tactic. As Coco Fusco observes, theater practitioners must be wary of adopting "the strategy of reworking cultural stereotypes." It is often unclear whether "the artists' ironic reinterpretation of an established paradigm can be discerned by different audiences," which makes it possible for these plays to "inadvertently recapitulate[e] the scenarios they seek to subvert."[21] The only alternative to avoid an audience misreading, however, is to maintain the culture of dissemblance and never directly address black women's sexuality. Besides, Gibson's and Jackson's engagement with African American sexual stereotypes complicates and expands the categories black and female by centering middle-class women.

These plays also illustrate the costs of sexual stereotypes for black women's psyches. *WOMBmanWARS* portrays what occurs when others deem black middle-class women out of control, and *Long Time since Yesterday* explores the dangers of African American women accepting distorted images of black sexuality. In both plays black middle-class women suffer. In Gibson's tale several of the central characters consider self-destruction (and one succeeds); Jackson's women—some drawn from life—undergo extreme punishment for asserting themselves. Both plays suggest, however, that the presumption of tragedy for middle-class women is an outdated trope. Most characters endure. Just as Anita Hill announced herself with her autobiography, the experiences of the characters in these two plays declare the importance of issues of sexuality in forming the individual and collective identities of black middle-class women.

Fighting the Race, Sex, and Class War

With her complex title *WOMBmanWARS,* Jackson, although unwittingly, alludes to Anita Hill's gynecological problems during the Senate confirmation hearings. The title announces that a black woman's body is a battlefield upon which gender issues are staged. Jackson's choice of the "womb" as metaphor is ironic considering Hill's health concerns, for it once again signifies the importance of procreation, and black women's bodies, as the vital center of their identities. But the play also shows the assault on the black woman at the physical level, her womb emblematic of the most personal and sexual parts of her body. If the quilt is the image that Hill chooses to express community and individual redemption, it is the womb that Jackson seeks to reclaim in order for black women to be whole.[22] Her message is not completely literal. As a *San Francisco Chronicle* reviewer remarked, "[D]espite its limitations and redundancies *WOMBmanWars* is often effervescent and not at all as didactic as the title suggests." The review then applauds how Jackson "attempts to balance feminist polemics with poetry, public flash points with private friction."[23] The performance piece, which premiered at the Institute of Contemporary Art in Boston in 1992, has also been performed at San Francisco's Lorraine Hansberry Theater, La MaMa E.T.C., P.S. 122, the New York Shakespeare Festival, Ujima Theater Company and Hallwalls in Buffalo, the North Carolina Arts Festival, and Just Us Theater Company in Atlanta.

WOMBmanWARS emphasizes the ways public attacks on black womanhood undermine notions of self, and it suggests that influences within the black community exact a price as high or higher than the dictates of the dominant culture. Moreover, by incorporating footage of actual and fictionalized newscasts of highly charged events, Jackson's provocative play emphasizes the debilitating effects of media on black female sexual development and performance. The national media tends to characterize African American men as overwhelmingly criminal and violent, but the news tends to depict black women as welfare-dependent and hypersexual. In television programs as well they are constructed as whores, whether in hip-hop videos or made-for-television movies. This fictional black woman—the one the national media considers authentic—is sexually available and comfortable flaunting her body. By placing a television monitor onstage, Jackson is able to use as a backdrop conventional media representations of black women. *WOMBmanWARS* invites the audience to conjure up stereotypical images by showing familiar television clips featuring characters who mimic many of the voices that shape and define authentic blackness.

Jackson, a writer and performance artist, has explained that she created *WOMBmanWARS* as a response to "twenty-one or so odd hours of prime-time woman-bashing" that she witnessed during the Anita Hill–Clarence Thomas Senate Judiciary Hearings in October 1991.[24] The piece also considers Mike Tyson's rape of beauty pageant contestant and college student Desiree Washington that same year. *WOMBmanWARS* not only highlights the problems black women encounter when they defend black womanhood in private spaces but also dramatizes the public spectacles (or wars) that transpire within the African American community. Jackson reenacts these moments in American culture as a "spectacle of voyeuristic excess" and attempts to frame the transgressions against individual black women as linked to the media spectacles that assaulted them.[25] *WOMBmanWARS* casts these very public episodes as symptomatic of the struggles of all black women. Moreover, instead of focusing solely on middle-class women, Jackson's play reveals the connections between the middle class and working class to demonstrate how the sexual spectacles involving Hill and Washington affected the extended community.

Jackson suggests that the broader African American community compromises black women because it often judges racial loyalty and authenticity on unquestioning support for problematic black men such as Thomas and Tyson. The play features black women who reject the belief that race loyalty trumps personal, political, sexual, and gendered identities and shows how they become ostracized for failing to embrace their role as defenders of the race. Jackson condemns the expectation that black women will remain silent regarding sexual matters. She exposes how black leaders and the broader community insist that black women relegate any discussion of sexual mistreatment to the private sphere. Policed by the threat of condemnation or accused of pandering to a feminist agenda often regarded as white and middle class, black women are forced into public silence when prominent black men victimize them.

Jackson restages two highly public struggles between black men and women in a fashion similar to Anna Deavere Smith's one-woman shows

Fires in the Mirror: Crown Heights, Brooklyn, and other Identities (1993) and *Twilight: Los Angeles, 1992* (1994), both of which examine the intersection of racial and class conflicts in order to illuminate notions of American identity. Both playwrights work in an era when increasingly "real-life drama seemed to be a definite point of fascination for the public."[26] Like Smith, Jackson documents and illuminates volatile social moments in contemporary American culture. Although Smith shows many sides of a conflict, Jackson makes no gestures toward impartiality. Instead she reinterprets events from the position of the marginalized. Both Smith and Jackson raise the specter of race because they are women of color playing characters who represent a variety of racial and gender subjectivities, all confronting difficult matters. Jackson suggests that "a solo performance affords the actor the opportunity to explore her own anima/animus and to present evidence of that dichotomy by portraying both the male and female characters in the play."[27] The solo black female performer using a documentary format, however, also forces the audience to rethink the role of black women in national "historical" events.

Instead of discovering the "truth" about public traumas, Jackson uses the documentary format to examine and trouble the "record" of experience. The form of "documentary drama is now—as it has been at previous times in American history—part of the culture's attempt to explain itself to itself."[28] This theatrical style also allows Jackson to reinterpret two disturbing moments in African American popular culture, where, in contrast to Smith's emphasis on ethnicity and race, Jackson highlights gender and sexuality. Her methods also diverge from Smith's in that Jackson weaves a fabricated story, using as threads the narratives of public, visible women. Bridging the fictional and nonfictional illustrates the connections between private and personal battles for gender equality and public and publicized ones. It also helps underscore the links between the middle class and other black women.

Set during October 1991, *WOMBmanWARS* juxtaposes a family watching the televised Thomas-Hill Senate hearings with a reenactment of Washington's encounter with Tyson. The scene shifts from Desiree Washington's hotel room, to the home of Sapphire and Danny, to the Senate chamber (often represented by still photographs and video footage), and to a black church. As Sapphire and Danny struggle to make meaning of the Thomas-Hill hearings with respect to their individual racial and gender views, they also endeavor to raise their little girl, Danisha. Jackson uses a variety of famous faces, voices, and images to signify the all-consuming, constant, invasive influence of popular culture. The repeated shift between Hill's and Washington's stories foregrounds the connections between these two public events, and the fictional family's response shows multigenerational disparity in experiences of sex and gender.

As the title *WOMBmanWARS* suggests, each member of Sapphire's family is at war in some fashion, and the wars reveal the complex and interconnected structures of race, gender, class, age, and sexuality in black America. Sapphire's name recalls the stereotypical black woman as the "emasculating black bitch" whose boorish strength and volcanic anger undermines black masculinity and dominates the black family. A working wife and mother, Sapphire is not only at odds with her husband, Danny, over how to guide their child but also with her own notions of womanhood. Danisha is at war on two fronts: a neighborhood boy's sexual harassment (he wants to look up her dress) and her parents' ambivalence (they wanted a boy instead of a girl). Danny is at war with himself and American society because of the narrow notions of fatherhood and masculinity offered to blacks.

Among Jackson's plethora of characters is the symbolic, unsettling, figure of Gorilla, who represents an attenuated stereotype of the black lady, a woman alienated from the African American community and invisible to the broader society. As Gorilla delivers a monolog during a dream sequence, the actor's back is toward the audience, a gorilla mask attached to the back of her head. Gorilla's extensive diatribe reveals a woman obsessed with her impressive accomplishments, possessions, and appearance—perhaps reflecting how many in the American public viewed Anita Hill. Gorilla boasts, "Was summa cum laude at Harvard. On the Dean's List at Yale. Taught law three years at Oxford. And was a Fulbright Fellow twice. My clothes are all designer. . . . My scent is politically correct."[29] Culturally smug, Gorilla brags that "while simultaneously cultivating a taste for arias by Mozart, I have successfully suppressed any urge to explore Hip Hop, Be Bop, or rap" (154). Distancing herself from black musical forms, bragging about educational achievements and professional credentials, and gloating about her expensive garments, Gorilla seems a black middle-class nightmare reminiscent of those scathingly criticized in E. Franklin Frazier's *Black Bourgeoisie*. Confused and frustrated, however, that her assimilation does not translate into acceptance, she asks, "No Gorilla could have achieved all of this. So why do I get the impression that your perception of me has still not changed?" (155).

Morphing into an ape, Gorilla begins to use African American vernacular. She grows more aggressive and livid and then threatens, "Don't let me have to go dere. Don't let me have to act like no nigger! I ain't tryin' to play dat see" (155). As her anger mounts, Gorilla becomes inarticulate, and her performance of class and gender identity disintegrates. Eventually reduced to a variety of easily distinguishable stereotypes, the middle-class black woman becomes a terrorizing, masculine black brute. When the stage directions state that Gorilla "gets up and begins to move downstage menacingly," they direct the actor to evoke primitivism and savagery. Jackson exposes how the middle-class black woman is perceived in daily life despite wearing the right clothes or holding the proper academic degrees. In the eyes of American culture, Jackson suggests, a brute lies beneath the polished veneer. Instead of smugly enjoying her success, the black middle-class woman must confront forms of dehumanizing racism, just like blacks from all other socioeconomic backgrounds.

Jackson employs the gorilla because it is the animal most often used—both in the past and the present—to describe blacks. Here she follows the theoretical work of Hortense Spillers, who considers the labels under which black women labor and offers a rationale for reclaiming and revising their meanings: "In this regard, the names by which I am called in the public space render an example of signifying property *plus*. In order for me to speak a truer word concerning myself, I must strip down through layers of attenuated meanings, made an excess in time, over time, assigned by a particular historical order, and there await whatever marvels of my own inventiveness. The personal pronouns are offered in the service of a collective function."[30]

The stereotype of the African American as a gorilla was evoked in another public spectacle of the 1990s: the attack on Rodney King. After King, an African American motorist, was crushed like "a can," as he related during the trial, investigators noted that Laurence Powell, a Los Angeles Police Department officer, had commented in a computer message that an earlier domestic violence police call to an African American family "was almost as exciting as [the movie] *Gorillas in the Mist*." The gorilla in this context, and in Jackson's play, represents the primitive, the barbaric, the exotic, and the animalistic. The gorilla is also coded masculine, so it mocks black women's femininity. Playwright Jackson uses Gorilla to humanize the dehumanized, explode the stereotype of the animalistic black, and link middle-class blacks to racist iconography.

Gorilla destabilizes the newly emerging stereotype of the middle-class black lady by offering a caricature to compare with Hill's actual performance.[31] In her introduction to *Race-ing Justice, Engendering Power* Toni Morrison explains that Hill "as a black woman" was a "contradiction itself, irrationality in the flesh . . . . She was a mixture heretofore not recognized in the glossary of racial tropes: an *intellectual* daughter of black *farmers*; a *black female* taking *offense*; a black *lady* repeating *dirty words*."[32] Gorilla enacts onstage the absurdity Morrison identifies, and that makes Hill and others like her unintelligible to the broader public.

Even those in the black middle class disdain the black lady for her dispassionate and proud disposition.[33] The character Gorilla, however, allows Jackson to perform a stereotypical black middle-class identity and undercut it at the very same moment. Jackson also uses the principle of reverse to critique how other African Americans stereotype the black middle class. The play suggests that blacks who traffic in simplistic, misguided characterizations are participating in the very same dehumanizing ethos as those who perpetuate other racial stereotypes.

Stereotyping the middle class is not a new phenomenon in African American literature or drama. Stereotypes that regard the black middle class as sellouts help police black identity around narrowly defined ideals of authentic blackness.[34] Middle-class figures, especially those such as Hill whose politics are deemed antiblack, are considered lost and alienated from their true selves. Thus, Gorilla represents a tragic imitation of African American identity. As the newly emerging stereotypical middle-class black lady, Gorilla represents Anita Hill and Washington as well. Instead of siding with Hill or Washington, or, conversely, seeing them as self-interested black women, however, Jackson questions the flat characterizations of the middle class. In placing Hill's and Washington's stories side by side, *WOMBmanWARS* makes it possible for the audience to question how class and sexuality operate in public debates.

Jackson then introduces the voice of Clarence Thomas's mother in order to demonstrate the similarities between black women of different classes. Speaking from Pin Point, Georgia, Mama Thomas represents the "folk" left behind by successful African Americans such as her son. Speaking of her son, she explains, "I neva thought I was no smart woman. Leastwise, nobody ever said I was. But, I kinda like to think my genes is in 'im somewhere" (175). The inclusion of Mama Thomas creates a dialog between the black lady and the matriarch (or Mammy). It also reminds us of the link between women like Hill and African Americans from less privileged socioeconomic backgrounds. Hill (like Thomas) comes from an impoverished rural background, and in her Senate testimony she emphasized how those who raised and nurtured her also influenced her notions of justice and morality. By including Mama Thomas, Jackson casts Clarence as the traitor to the race, rather than Hill, because in violating an African American woman he violates the bedrock of the race. Mama Thomas is the missing traditional black matriarch of the Horatio Alger story that Thomas invoked during the hearings. And if Mama Thomas's sympathies lie with Hill, that closes the gap between working-class and middle-class black women.

Although middle-class and working-class women do not interact onstage, Jackson brings together their seemingly disparate voices to illustrate that the victims of patriarchy and sexism come from all strata of African American society. Because Gorilla and Mama Thomas both use African American vernacular in their monologs, Jackson is able to fuse the identities of the black middle-class lady and the long-suffering black matriarch. No matter what a black women does professionally, she is subject to being stereotyped. By rendering her female characters as complicated, complete figures, Jackson critiques those stereotypes. Further, the voice of Thomas's mother allows the inclusion of poor black women in the struggle against gender subjugation, thereby short-circuiting claims that gender struggles involve only the middle class.

Jackson also explores many tensions between African American women and men that are continually debated in popular culture. She depicts the black church, another site of black performance, as an institution that plays a role in the oppression of black women. The church's reactionary sexual politics support black male claims for their proper place in the patriarchal order. Jackson's character The Reverend invokes the names of Adam Clayton Powell and Marion Barry to remind his congregation (and the broader black community) of other incidents when a black woman brought down a successful black man. Through complaints voiced by political, academic, and religious leaders as well as criticisms from anonymous African American men, Jackson dramatizes the overwhelming disapproval of black feminist politics that Hill and Washington experienced. She restages, for instance, the public celebrations of Tyson's release in Harlem and elsewhere and evokes rejection of black feminist politics when she has The Reverend plead, "Black women have got to stop stomping on the black man's dreams. . . . We are not saying, the black man is perfect. You got problems? Don't run to the enemy. Don't call 911. Come to the church . . . that's what you do. That's where we can begin to sort things out. Pray for him black woman but don't bring the black man down. Raise him up. Raise him up" (174).

The minister, a historically significant figure in African American culture, reminds his congregation that the support of black women depends on their silence and loyalty. The Reverend also symbolizes the power of black patriarchy and traditional black political culture. Jackson includes the black church, especially its ministry, in order to illustrate the overwhelming chorus of voices that circumscribe black women's lives. As the voice of the black establishment, its institutions, and its patriarchy, The Reverend implores black women to support the men of the race but then threatens that otherwise they will carry the blame for black America's problems.[35]

To further depict the "war" between genders, Jackson reminds her audience that successful middle-class black women are blamed in particular for the disintegration of the black family. Sapphire's husband, Danny, complains that she is eclipsing his role within the family: "Oh . . . you got a job, so you the boss now huh? You in charge" (179). If the family and church critique black women for undermining black men, African American intellectuals blame them as well. To illustrate this, Jackson creates a televised interview:

> REPORTER: Our last interviewee wanted to remain anonymous. (*Speaks into camera and holds blue dot in front of face*) "There's a high level of anger among black men, be they low-income or professional, that black women will betray them; that black women are given preference over them to use them. Black men feel that white men are using this black woman to get another black man." (*Reporter removes blue dot; speaks into camera*) Dr. Alvin Poussaint, psychiatrist and consultant for *The Cosby Show*. CUT! (178)

The Reporter exposes Poussaint and reveals how widespread such opinions are in black America—even among elite scholars. Again moving quickly between fictional and nonfictional characters, Jackson uses an actual prominent academic, Poussaint, because of his authority as a Harvard professor and his connection to *Cosby* (one of the most notable markers of black middle-class life in U.S. popular culture), which gives his opinion a certain credence and irony as well.[36] Just like The Reverend, Poussaint represents established patriarchal notions about black women's roles. Contrasting Hill's painful testimony with the domineering chorus of African American critics helps explain why she remained silent for so many years.

Although *WOMBmanWARS* articulates some of the problems black women face, Jackson casts the conflict as a matter damaging to both genders. She attempts to address the rift between African American women and men through the play's spiritual center, Anima/Animus, who signifies good and evil as well as "the male/female that exists in us" (145). The unisex spirit of Sapphire's unborn child (a baby miscarried before Danisha's birth), Anima/Animus speaks from the womb to bemoan the degradation of the female in African American culture. Anima/Animus seeks to politicize and educate the audience by claiming:

> Anima you don't hear much about these days. Can't even find it in the dictionary. It means female soul, from the roots an, "heavenly," and ma, "mother," recalling a time when all souls emanated from the Heavenly Mother. When all souls were male and female. When all souls were Anima/Animus.

> Well, that's how it was long ago. But somewhere in the middle of Herstory, history intervened. Where once both sides were considered equal—the woman side became the sequel. Don't soundbites simplify things? I'm using soundbites because attentions spans are so short in the twentieth century. (158)

In hope of unifying black people, Jackson suggests that the denial of the female degrades and diminishes both women and men. When female sexual agency is sacrificed for the good of the race, she asserts, it dehumanizes all African American people.

WOMBmanWARS also demonstrates the complicity of middle-class African American women in their own subjugation. Jackson suggests that women play a central role in maintaining the belief that African Americans must always present a "positive" image to ensure the community's survival. In a scene replicating a person-on-the-street interview, a black professional woman shares her opinion of Hill: "'I hadn't been a Thomas supporter until now. She's making it up. She wants to do a movie or something.' Rhonda Jenkins, secretary. Northeast" (177). Jackson presents a hostile atmosphere in which no one trusts the word of black women, not even other black women, and middle-class women are particularly suspect because they are considered overly ambitious.

This atmosphere of distrust extends to the family. The subplot of Danisha's initiation into womanhood points to the way black mothers enforce a double standard. Danisha's scuffle with a neighborhood boy damages her dress and prompts her to complain "I'm ruint." The dress, symbolizing Danisha's character and virtue, is beyond repair, much like the lives and reputations of Hill and Washington. When Danny discovers that his daughter fought a boy, he punishes her. Danny asserts that if Sapphire fails to teach Danisha proper behavior, then it becomes his responsibility to make sure his daughter learns how to "be a lady." Disciplined by her father for fighting and undefended by her mother, Danisha learns that behaving like a "lady" is more important than protecting her body. Although Danny and Sapphire are not middle class they are concerned with teaching Danisha codes of middle-class respectability because being considered a lady will ensure her class mobility. Their daughter discovers that if she silences herself she avoids further pain and scrutiny and finds acceptance. The process of silence and dissemblance seems to recreate itself with every generation.

The confrontation between Danisha and her parents signals a major shift in the narrative. Jackson no longer uses high-tech gimmicks or satirical language. Instead, the play takes on a somber tone. When Sapphire fails to support her daughter, she teaches Danisha that she alone must bear the consequences of revealing the harassment. Sapphire's and Danny's response to Danisha also explains Hill's prolonged silence. When a woman (especially a black woman) talks about sexual abuse, no one will believe her. Sapphire understands that Danisha's testimony (like Hill's) will be met with punishment. "My heart knew it would be my job to break you," she admits. "To break your spirit before you were grown and some stranger came along and did it. I had to do to you what my mother did to me and her mother did to her. To protect you from your dreams" (182). Watching Hill testify, however, Sapphire sees that black women have options other than acceptance and silence. Hill's plight helps Sapphire recognize that it is she, in fact, who undermines her daughter's sense of identity with conflicting messages about sexuality and the importance of being a lady. When Sapphire finally recognizes her part in diminishing her daughter's spirit she disrupts the pattern of complicity, vowing that this is "the last day I stand back and watch your spirit cry" (182).

To further illustrate how the public influences black women's private choices and lives, Jackson dramatizes events in Desiree Washington's hotel room to explain what led to her encounter with Tyson. She receives a telephone call from the boxer and argues with her roommate, another pageant contestant, about whether to go on a date with him. Armed with a camera and giddy about the prospect of riding in a limousine, Washington appears innocent and Tyson seems deranged as he lifts weights and fantasizes about his prey. Yet Jackson's representation of Tyson is inconsistent with the way in which she renders other black men and women as equal victims of dehumanizing racial, gender, and sexual stereotypes. Tyson is depicted as nothing other than a brute; when Washington speaks to him on the telephone, he is truly a gorilla, "lifting weights lasciviously" and imploring her "to come over" (162). Jackson fails to provide background to explain how Tyson became a sexual predator, thereby leaving stereotypes of aberrant and explosive black male sexuality intact. Although she positions her play as addressing both genders, Jackson neglects to problematize ways in which black men are cast in public spectacles. Because of this oversight, she misses an opportunity to illustrate the connections between black men and women—how tropes of black male violence and female promiscuity are damaging. Her failure to address the stock image of Tyson undermines the subversive strategy she employs in the representation of diverse black women.[37]

Similarly, Jackson's representation of Hill and Washington as "innocent" robs them of personal and sexual agency. In "'You're Turning Me On,'" Michael Awkward suggests that the real Washington unwittingly participates in her own victimization. Awkward comments, "A key to successful objectification of the female body is persuading women of the benefits for them in masculinist formulations of women's erotic utility. The cultural imposition of notions of the appropriateness and inevitability of the female body's figurations as the site of recreational phallic desire, in other words, depends on the success of phallocentricism's institutionalizing of its perspectives to the extent that they are unquestioned by large numbers of receptive female accomplices."[38]

Jackson demonstrates Awkward's point by focusing on Washington's role as a beauty contestant. Much like Danisha enticed by promises of cake, or Hill lulled by her professional ambitions, the star-struck Washington finds herself lured by proximity to celebrity. Desiree explains to her fellow beauty contestant, Miss Indy Anna, "Girl, he has a LIMOUSINE! And he wants to take me. Show me the sights I have never seen before" (161). Washington's innocence, and image as a good girl, is constructed as naïve and eager. Although the mainstream press and popular opinion question her judgment during the trial, it becomes clear that "Tyson's attractiveness to Washington as an escort, then, was tied specifically to his celebrity status, and that status is conferred upon him literally as a consequence of his masculine power."[39] Jackson effectively ties the victimization of Hill and Washington to the very same male privilege that makes Tyson and Thomas powerful.

The black community disapproves of Washington's or Hill's decisions to accuse black men of sexual violations publicly. Jackson returns to the church, where she introduces another character, The Good Christian Woman. This character—a symbol of the early-twentieth-century's respectable "colored lady" and reminiscent of those who populated such organizations as the National Association of Colored Women—speaks for black women who found fault with Washington's charges against Tyson: "Some kind of Beauty Queen. Had no bizness being there that time of night. She knew what was what. Paper says there weren't nary a sign of struggle. Teach preacher. No bruises of any kind. She knew what she was doing. . . . Never did put up a fight. And now she cry raped. Beauty Queen my good Christian foot. (*Stomps good foot for emphasis*)" (181).

The Good Christian Woman with the good Christian feet advances the argument of those African Americans who did not believe Washington or felt she should have concealed the incident for Tyson's sake. Just as Sapphire teaches Danisha how to behave to her own detriment, the broader community of black women, often with the church's blessing, routinely regulates and maintains boundaries of proper sexuality. Jackson reveals the church's double standard because The Good Christian Woman never criticizes Tyson for inviting a young woman to his hotel room at "that time of night." A severe case of blaming the victim, this approach subtly exonerates the guilty while heaping shame upon the wronged.

Although some blacks castigated Washington, many members of the national media regarded her differently than Hill because of her youth. The coed's class status also bolstered her position and gained her support by the mainstream media.[40] Compared with Tyson, Washington is believable. A *Newsweek* article explained that "Tyson's accuser came across as the perfect victim. Now a scholarship student at a Roman Catholic college, she was barely eighteen when she arrived at the beauty pageant. Growing up in Rhode Island, she was apparently the all-American girl: She played softball, ushered at her church, and volunteered as a Big Sister. The court heard about her high school days as a varsity cheerleader, class president, and most outstanding sophomore."[41]

If Washington is cast as the perfect victim, what is the profile for the imperfect victim? Black women from poor backgrounds who are not college students become scapegoats. Washington's honesty and sexual innocence are assumed because she is middle class. Although Jackson does not fully develop her in the plot, both Washington and Hill represent chaste, pure, and vulnerable middle-class black femininity.[42] That stock depiction reinforces the figure of the black lady and helps demonstrate it to be as dehumanizing as more familiar stereotypes such as Jezebel or Mammy.

Jackson criticizes contemporary news journalism for their sensationalist coverage of the Thomas-Hill and Tyson-Washington stories. The spectacle of black sexuality dominated the reporting while other national events such as the Iran-Contra affair received less notice. Jackson juxtaposes slides of print-media headlines about Hill and Thomas with the character Reporter reading coverage about prevailing political corruption and racist violence:

> REPORTER (*Speaks into mike*): October 12, 1991: THOMAS'S ACCUSER TELLS OF OBSCENE TALK AND LASCIVIOUS ADVANCES!
> Other news: former assistant secretary of state admits (*she yawns*) guilt in Iran/contra scam.
> JUDGE PREFERS DEATH BY ASSASSIN'S BULLET OVER LYNCHING!!
> Other news: all charges dropped against Oliver North. (*Looks bored*).
> (176)

The mainstream coverage reproduces images and stereotypes that overdetermine the construction of black sexual representation and identity. Multiple exclamation points, capital letters, and alarming language draw attention to the salacious Thomas-Hill hearings that dominated the nation's attention while the bored Reporter delivers what some would argue was the far more important news about the Iran-Contra affair with little emphasis.

To counter media representation and African American disapproval, *WOMBmanWARS* ends with a litany of voices. First, there is chanting by the "natives," which sounds much like reports about public sentiment during Thomas's confirmation hearing: "Black. Witch. Must. Die" (184). Next, each icon or stereotype of black womanhood is called upon to speak her name, starting with Jezebel. The performance ends with a proclamation: "My name is Anita F. Hill. I believe my Self. I believe me. (*lights fade as she chants in Danisha's voice*) Go Anita. Go Anita. Go Anita. (*fade to black*)" (185). Hill's voice rises, she is transformed by her stalwart presentation of her version of events. Her testimony, and by extension Danisha's and Washington's, defends all black women. The performance ends with Hill asserting belief in herself and her ability to maintain integrity in the face of damning cultures and subcultures.

More than fifteen years later the nation continues to debate whether to accept or believe women like Hill (or decide whether the truth actually matters). Jackson's final scene emphasizes the importance of African American women keeping faith in themselves and encourages them to see themselves as part of a community. Danisha's voice, which is heard last, assures that the cycle of black women's complicity has been disturbed if not completely destroyed. The litany of names calls up the perceived and the real connection among black women from all strata of black life and undermines the power of racial, sexual, and gender stereotypes. Moreover, Danisha's chant—"Go Anita"—encourages black women to find ways to combat what Kimberelé Crenshaw calls their "intersectional disempowerment."[43]

WOMBmanWARS places turbulent moments in late-twentieth-century American culture onstage in order to show how black women's lives continue to fascinate and shape the country's notions of sexuality and power. Jackson's insistence on situating an African American family's struggles at the center of the plot shows the power of public narratives in the private sphere. In restaging such ugly moments as Hill's testimony and Washington's rape, the play forces audiences to consider the role middle-class black women continue to play in defining appropriate notions of African American sexuality in public discourse.

Rethinking Tragedy: P. J. Gibson's Black Middle-Class Heroines

Not all contemporary black theater follows the lead of Anna Deavere Smith or Judith Alexa Jackson by focusing on contemporary national events. And unlike most African American dramas, many plays by P. J. Gibson, a professor of English at John Jay College of Criminal Justice and former arts administrator, feature middle-class heroines in urban environments.[44] In her introduction to *Destiny's Daughters,* Gibson explains that her "mission [is to] create plays and roles . . . which were not limited to maids, whores, prostitutes, and addicts." Instead, she writes "strong, fully developed, complicated, interesting, financially sound characters."[45] Gibson has also published poetry and short stories, including erotica. *Long Time since Yesterday,* her most-produced play, enjoyed its world premiere at the Henry Street Playhouse in the 1985 New Federal Theater production. Subsequently it has been produced more than sixty times at venues such as the Donovan Rhysburger Theater at the University of Missouri and the Kuntu Repertory and the New Horizon Theater, both in Pittsburgh. Critics regard the piece highly for its willingness to "investigate racial realities" such as racist beauty standards, "identity and racial politics, sexuality . . . and love."[46] In 1985 the play won an Audelco Award for best drama, and Gibson won the playwriting award.

Other plays by Gibson, such as *Shameful in Your Eyes* (1971), *Konvergence* (1973), *Void Passage* (1973), *Ain't Love Grand* (1980), *Unveilings* (1981), *Clean Sheets Can't Soil* (1983), and *Brown Silk and Magenta Sunsets* (1985), also feature women struggling with intimate relationships. Gibson's dramatic interests broaden representations of black women by exploring middle-class narratives. She humanizes middle-class black women by presenting them neither as ideal ladies nor inauthentic victims. Instead, she shows that middle-class African American women are "ordinary" people who have problems different from those of working-class women but not more important or complex. She also emphasizes the diversity among middle-class females and deliberately "set out to bring to the stage the great variety of black women that she had observed during the years when she lived in Pennsylvania, New Jersey, and Washington D.C." Gibson notes that "she found these women fascinating, especially those who had lived a dual life-style: they had grown up poor, then through education, marriage or some trick of fate or fortune had slipped into the middle class."[47] Her decision to write can be linked to her politics. In a 1999 interview with the *Pittsburgh Post-Gazette,* Gibson explained that "too many times black people are portrayed as impoverished or criminals . . . when the curtain rises on a suburban home, well-decorated and with women who are highly skilled professionals, it makes the audience feel good about seeing themselves as other than the stereotypical images."[48] In *Long Time since Yesterday* she makes the diversity of the black middle class clear through characters of different class origins and a wide range of sexual behavior, from promiscuous to chaste.

Some dramatists are troubled by Gibson's focus on the middle class. Alice Childress, a celebrated playwright, bemoans artists who focus on the middle class: "It is a serious self-deception to think that culturally ignoring those who are poor, lost, and/or rebellious will somehow better our image. . . . Black writers cannot afford to abuse or neglect the so-called ordinary characters who represent a part of ourselves, the self twice denied, first by racism and then by class difference."[49] Representing the black middle class, however, does not necessarily mean neglecting other classes, and middle-class characters do not make African Americans appear more agreeable. Nor does their portrayal erase the ugly issues of racism. Instead, Gibson's depictions show that difficulties of the middle class originate outside the black community as well as within it.

In *Long Time since Yesterday* Gibson complicates a variety of sexual stereotypes, such as the asexual black lady, predatory and masculine lesbian, and hypersexual black woman in order to uncover the real, genuine women behind these myths. She takes her characters beyond stereotype to show the complexity of their experiences, emotions, and lives. Gibson suggests that middle-class black women's public performance is designed to please their race and class constituency, and when they breach that expectation they face dire consequences. *Long Time since Yesterday* reveals through tragedy how the burden of performance takes a toll on those whose behavior must uphold African American respectability.

Gibson considers it tragic that social ideas and myths invade black women's sexual lives and prohibit many from experiencing sexuality without the oppressive social standards that regulate women's actions or the derogatory labels that damage black women's psyches. *Long Time since Yesterday* blatantly juxtaposes life and death, being and nonbeing, fulfillment and emptiness, suicide and procreation, and sexual satisfaction and sexual frustration in an effort to show the significance of the private struggles of middle-class black women against their role as public models. Although many dismiss the problems middle-class black women face because they enjoy relative privilege compared with working-class or poor black women, Gibson's play suggests that their problems are also grave. She casts middle-class black women's sexuality as a matter of life and death, with death the answer for those who face a lack of emotional satisfaction.

In nineteenth-century African American theater, life was represented by freedom from bondage; death was slavery. Abolitionist dramas such as William Henry Brown's *The Drama of King Shotaway* (1823) and William Wells Brown's *Escape; or, A Leap to Freedom* (1857) depict desire for freedom from bondage at any cost and emphasize that there is no life without individual liberty. During the early twentieth century, decades after emancipation, lynching plays by Georgia Douglas Johnson, Alice Dunbar Nelson, and W. E. B. Du Bois suggested that living under the threat of death robs blacks of true freedom.[50] Later dramas such as Lorraine Hansberry's *A Raisin in the Sun* (1959) consider life to be gaining one's civil rights and figurative death to be the lack of self-realization or actualization brought about by a racist society. During the black arts era, playwrights wrote dramas that consider death a price to be paid for liberation from the suffocating perils of racism.

Contemporary dramas such as *Long Time since Yesterday* move away from broader African American struggles and couch freedom in terms of personal fulfillment. Even while plays such as Robert O'Hara's *Insurrection* (1998) satirize America's history of racial oppression in an effort to open new ground, they place issues of sexual identity in relation to race. Like O'Hara, Gibson uses death to underscore what is at stake for black survival if personal fulfillment is thwarted. In an era with the largest black middle class in American history, what is "life"? Conversely, in the post–civil rights era, what is "death"?

Long Time since Yesterday foregrounds private, personal conflicts around sexual matters and reveals the stifling consequences of middle-class black performance for women. Gibson explores how issues of sexuality destabilize the bonds between black women and undermine their sense of self. The play also illuminates problems that emerge when black females try to regulate each other's sexual identities, experiences, and explorations and highlights limitations of the sexual revolution of the 1960s and 1970s for middle-class black women. Gibson reminds the audience that most black women who breach the boundaries of sanctioned behavior face horrific consequences. Nearly all the characters consider suicide when romantic conquests fail to bring happiness, and one does kill herself because of the shame she feels for a lesbian affair. The unhappy heroines reveal sexual repression as a particularly demoralizing pitfall of middle-class life. In these ways Gibson's work fits with that of other contemporary black playwrights, including Adrienne Kennedy (*Funnyhouse of a Negro*, 1964), Talvin Wilks (*Tod, the Boy, Tod*, 1991), and Alexis DeVeaux (*Tapestry*, 1976), who often use tragedy to depict the horrors of middle-class African American life. Theirs is a narrow representation of the middle-class figure, so weak, so misunderstood, and so frustrated that death, often by suicide, is the only option for addressing life's difficulties.

Not unlike the popular television series *Desperate Housewives*, *Long Time since Yesterday* focuses on privileged women who find themselves reconsidering their lives (especially their romantic and sexual lives) after the suicide of an old friend. The play takes place in the present at Janeen's suburban New Jersey home after her funeral. Her death reunites Janeen's five college friends, Laveer, Alisa, Panzi, Thelma, and Babbs. Through a series of flashbacks the play exposes the tensions among the women and unveils the reasons for Janeen's suicide. Unlike the tragic heroines in earlier African American dramas, often destroyed by the perceived contradiction of being black and middle class, it is primarily the burden of sexuality and class that haunts Gibson's characters. All the characters regard their sexuality as foundational to their emotional lives, and the play's central character, Janeen, ends her life because of an empty marriage and a longing for more passion, acceptance, and control.

The most explosive conflict transpires between Laveer, a promiscuous heterosexual artist, and Panzi, a physical therapist and closeted lesbian. Since their college years both women have competed for Janeen's affections and loyalty. Gibson depicts Janeen as a sexual innocent, unclear about her desires, beholden to black bourgeois values, and easily manipulated by stronger-willed and more experienced friends. Janeen, a stereotypical frigid, chaste, middle-class woman, finds herself torn between Laveer, who is generally regarded as a wanton and undiscriminating "nonconformist," and Panzi, a "predatory" lesbian.[51] The play suggests that black women are vulnerable and victimized by opinions about their sexuality. In addition, Gibson shows that no archetype explains the complexity of women's sexual choices or identities.

Throughout *Long Time since Yesterday* Gibson presents Laveer, with her wild sexuality and strong influence over the group, as both disruptive and glamorous. When they are children, Laveer explains sexual matters to Janeen, whom she considers a "spineless twerp," and Janeen receives the information bashfully.[52] Laveer's and Janeen's friendship is particularly troubled by their roles as teacher and student because of Laveer's self-assurance and adventurousness. Gibson upends the tragic middle-class, black-lady theme when the promiscuous Laveer faces no tragic consequences. Instead she boasts, "I'm going to do everything, travel all over the world, have great lovers . . . see all kinds of things and be famous, but . . . I'm going to have to experience tragedy. Artists have to do that, you know. So I'm going to die at twenty-one" (219–20). It is Janeen, however, who follows the proper middle-class black path and succumbs to depression and finally suicide.

Not only does *Long Time since Yesterday* depict a woman who ignores the pressures of black middle-class sexual decorum but the play's progressive rewriting of middle-class black female sexuality also comes from Gibson's ability to represent six very different women who experience varying degrees of sexual contentment.[53] Thelma, an unmarried doctor, struggles with an underdeveloped appreciation of her own beauty. The divorced Babbs, a conceited television anchorperson, finds herself reluctantly celibate as well as suicidal. Babbs and Thelma each confide during their reunion that they are depressed about their narrow prospects for romantic and sexual contentment.

Not all of the characters, however, face bleak futures. Other than Laveer, Alisa, a married preschool director and mother of five, boasts of being the most fulfilled. Alisa confides that her marriage still includes sexual adventure:

> ALISA: Besides, it wasn't all as bad as it seems. During that dreadful cast-wearing stage ... (*To Thelma and Panzi*) You know, the itching part right smack in the middle where the pencil and ruler don't reach ... Lloyd and I discovered some nice kinky positions.
> THELMA: Do tell.
> BABBS: A noted reason why the Reynolds clan continues to grow.
> ALISA: Well, someone among the group has to perpetuate the growth of mankind. (223)

Gibson shows that despite the emphasis on repression, the sexual lives of some middle-class black women shape the core of their emotional well-being. Laveer and Alisa, the most self-assured, are the only sexually satisfied members of the group. Given that one is single and the other married, Gibson refuses to offer a traditional middle-class lifestyle as a formula for contentment. Laveer's ability to forge a life outside the bounds of proper middle-class behavior allows her to emerge self-confident and dynamic. Although Alisa has a husband, she stresses the expressiveness and experimentation within their sexual relationship. Unlike Janeen, marriage never distorts Alisa's sense of herself, nor does she accept that sex is only for producing offspring. Gibson suggests that whether middle-class black women are married or single, denying sexual agency will threaten their self-worth, undermine their humanity, and estrange them from the broader community. Alisa's and Laveer's college friends remain proper black ladies and so find themselves unhappy and frustrated because they lack sexual and emotional fulfillment.

Even as a young girl, Laveer criticizes the limits placed on proper black ladies:

> LAVEER: Well, hell ...
> JANEEN: Laveer ... your mouth?
> LAVEER: What about my mouth?
> JANEEN: It's filthy.

LAVEER: So.
JANEEN: It's not ladylike.
LAVEER: But it's fun. Besides, I'm not sure I want to be a lady.
JANEEN: Everybody should want to be a lady.
LAVEER: Not if we have to end up like our moms. Yelk! Too many "I can'ts" or "I shouldn'ts" for me.
JANEEN: They're respected.
LAVEER: So who cares about being respected? I want to be daring, risky. ... And what's so great about being a virgin and never kissed? I want to kiss somebody. I want to stick my tongue in ... (*Thinks*) Darrel River's mouth and let him put his hands right here (*Indicates her small breasts*). (218)

Laveer rejects any notion of ladyhood that shackles body and mind. It is clear from their exchange that both young girls understand that propriety is about more than sex; it is about language and action and grammar—linguistic as well as physical. Laveer rejects the entire repressive performance of middle-class womanhood.

The conversation with Janeen highlights the conflicts inherent in the discourse of respectability and reveals how middle-class performance is a totality of gestures as well as a style of living. All of these components make a woman a lady. Membership within the black middle class limits actions, speech, and, finally, sexuality. Laveer's provocative comments and bold ideas are contrary to maternal dictates about proper behavior. Virtuousness and respectability strike her as drab alternatives to an adventurous life, sexual and otherwise. Yet by initially presenting Laveer as a girl rebelling against her community, Gibson expands the possibilities for middle-class black female identity and upsets the notion of the tragic middle-class black heroine. Laveer not only survives youthful sexual experimentation but also enjoys several lovers as a single adult. Unconventional, she finds professional success and enjoys an exciting personal life, retaining her friends' respect as well.

Gibson suggests that for middle-class black women social pressures to act like a true "lady" often mars sexual experiences. Most of the women in *Long Time since Yesterday* conform to the expectations of middle-class black community, and this strategy leads to tragedy. Parental and peer pressure to pursue the American dream overwhelm Janeen, and instead of reveling in her happiness she finds herself miserable. She cannot articulate, much less pursue, her needs and desires. She cannot satisfy her self. After entering a marriage arranged by her parents, Janeen complains about feeling scrutinized: "Half the world didn't know I was going to make love before I got married. You should see how those people look at you. Even now . . . Sometimes, when I'm shopping at the supermarket. One of the Trees will come up to me, look down at my stomach, and give me that look which says, 'When are you going to put that screwing you and Walter are doing to some use? When are you going to make a baby?' I tell you it's embarrassing" (252–53).

Although married, Janeen feels ashamed for enjoying nonprocreative sexual intercourse, even with her husband. She considers marriage an institution that primarily serves the broader middle-class black community rather than herself. During sex Janeen cannot help but imagine her parents and their social circle judging her.[54] Much like Anita Hill's testimony before the Senate and the nation, the middle-class black woman's sexuality finds itself on display once again. The performance of middle-class black womanhood, even within the confines of marriage, takes precedence. Janeen is trapped by the conventional role of the black middle-class woman held up as proof of black humanity and dignity in the midst of a white supremacist culture that denigrates, but desires and exploits, the black female body. The display and performance of middle-class black respectability as displayed by Anita Hill— hiding her body, wearing prim blouses and long skirts, and refusing to speak or think about sexual matters—becomes a trap that prevents Janeen from enjoying her sexuality.

Janeen confesses feeling even more on display when she and Panzi make love. This act of sexual experimentation could have allowed her to reclaim her sexuality and redirect her life, but the affair only increases her paranoia about being the object of the community's gaze. Trying to accommodate the expectations of her parents and their friends provokes an extreme case of middle-class angst and shame. Imagining their devastating judgment keeps Janeen from relishing either her sexual relationship with her husband or her lesbian fling with Panzi. She is completely paralyzed. The pressure to conform stifles her desire for sexual adventure and experimentation and eventually leaves her suicidal.

The possibility that Janeen is also a lesbian is never considered. Instead, her surviving friends focus on the horror Janeen's husband's felt when he discovered his wife in bed with Panzi. Surprisingly, it is the unconventional Laveer who leads the charge in blaming Panzi for the death, although she knows that Janeen's husband raped Janeen in retaliation. In this way *Long Time since Yesterday* traffics in homophobic stereotypes—Panzi is not just another middle-class black woman looking for a satisfying relationship but rather a lesbian predator. The portrayal of a healthy black middle-class lesbian, or even further a black middle-class lesbian couple, would truly be an innovative rendering of the new dramatic territory for which Suzan-Lori

Parks asks. Instead, Gibson reiterates the stereotype of the lesbian predator and the suicidal middle-class woman. She fails to thoroughly broaden the notion of black womanhood.

Gibson's plot repeatedly uses suicide and death to exemplify the differences among the friends. The thriving women who determine their own fate never regard death as an answer, but the long-suffering ones who allow the demands of middle-class traditions to suffocate them do consider ending it all. The play's consideration of suicide not only toys with the title of Shange's extremely successful choreopoem "For Colored Girls Who Have Considered Suicide When the Rainbow Is Enuf" but also with the concerns featured in it. At first glance, the preoccupation of Gibson's elite sisterhood with their sexual lives seems self-indulgent compared with Shange's mostly working-class heroines. But the use of death in *Long Time since Yesterday* follows Shange's lead by insisting that audiences consider the sociocultural and political value of black women during a time when so much attention and hysteria is focused on black males. And through this tragic figure Gibson depicts how traditional middle-class black values stifle women's sexuality, retard their sexual development, and distort their sense of self.

Laveer, while a college student, insists that Janeen orchestrate a mock funeral so Laveer can thwart or control death and tragedy, so it is ironic that the play opens as the women gather after Janeen's funeral. The funeral ceremony represents a vehicle for reinvention and transformation for Laveer, but fantasies of death help the other women mitigate their horrible disappointment with life. Laveer's friends follow the prescribed path to contentment, but it brings only misery.

Much like Janeen, Babbs contemplates suicide because she is disappointed with her middle-class life. The links between death and sensuality are clear in Babbs's description of a recent suicide attempt: "I took myself a sensual bath, in a tub of perfumed bubbles. Put on my sexiest gown. Fluffed up my face. Turned on the oven. Blew out the pilot. Reclined my body on my bed in a manner befitting Cleo herself and waited.... Unfortunately, my neighbor's car alarm went off for the sixth time that week. The ringing gave me a headache, so.... The rest is history. I opened the windows, got dressed, went out for some fresh air, and much to my chagrin am very much alive" (233). Babbs prepares for suicide as if for a rendezvous with a lover. She beautifies herself in anticipation of her next life, where she will be the desired and appreciated. Shaken from stupor by the car alarm, Babbs returns to life, defeated. Much like her simplistic expectation that physical beauty guarantees happiness, Babbs anticipates that suicide will provide relief. But she fails to reclaim her life. Gibson suggests that women who fail to define and control their sexuality ultimately lose the ability to control their lives.

In contrast, Laveer's funeral performance during college allows her to triumph, figuratively, over death. Anticipating an early death as the cost for fame or as a punishment for her unconventional lifestyle, young Laveer robs death of its power by planning her demise. Performing a symbolic suicide provides momentum to maintain her rebellious journey into adulthood. She is the only one who chooses an unconventional path. A painter, she travels internationally and brags about having so many lovers that there are "too many to count."[55] Laveer allows Gibson to trouble the tragic black middle-class theme and reverse the image of the black woman as a Jezebel. Although promiscuous, Laveer is admired by her friends and adored by her lovers. Her successful career and education place her outside the world of traditional expectations, and she fulfills her childhood dreams.

The play ends with Janeen's surviving friends feeling disillusioned by their failures. Thelma asks, "Look at us. Listen to us. All those years of dreaming: the places we thought we'd be, things we thought we'd be doing. . . . And what have we become? Drunks, dykes, nonconformists, crusaders, hiders."[56] Bleak reality falls short of promise, dreams, and expectations. Uncritically accepting middle-class values leads to unhappiness and, ultimately, death. After Janeen's suicide, however, it is clear that death frees only the victim. Whether married, divorced, or single, middle-class black women must renegotiate the expectations of their community as well as their own hopes for the American dream.

Although *Long Time since Yesterday* centers on sexual relationships and sexual liaisons, Gibson, like Jackson, shies away from staging actual sexual encounters. Instead, she elects to have the characters describe intimate moments, relying on the imagination to animate Laveer's past as well as Janeen's and Panzi's caresses.[57] Sandra Richards's argument in "Writing the Absent Potential" is useful here. After complaining about the absence of black theater within the African American literary canon, Richards theorizes about the power of absence. She asserts that when a playwright leaves text open, it allows a director to imagine how "the unwritten, or absence from the script, is a potential presence implicit in performance."[58] Despite her omissions, Gibson's script gives directors the opportunity to stage the women's affairs. Actually presenting black women performing sexual and sensual acts on stage might offer a more potent challenge to the image of black middle-class women as sexless, and by permitting her characters to perform as sexual beings before the audience Gibson might create a more commanding reversal of demeaning stereotypes.

Gibson's and Jackson's plays illustrate how stereotypes of black hypersexuality and standard notions of middle-class chastity confound black women. In the early twentieth century Alain Locke observed that "the Negro playwright has to abandon his puppets of protest and propaganda and take to flesh and blood characters and situations."[59] The complexity of Gibson's flawed vulnerable characters allows black women to exist as more than middle-class icons. Although, Jackson, by presenting figures from public life creates the "propaganda" Locke wants writers to eschew, her placement of Hill and Washington in relation to a fictional black family's story shows the importance of addressing long-standing images. Jackson rescues Hill and Washington from their respective media spectacles and turns them back into flesh-and-blood women navigating spectacular situations.

Disregarding black women's sexual desires, autonomy, and rights keeps people from recognizing African Americans in all their complexity and humanity. Jackson suggests that black female invisibility harms the African American community as a whole, and both *Long Time since Yesterday* and *WOMBmanWARS* reveal the consequences for individual black women unable to live completely and express themselves. Ignoring the demand to stay silent about their sexual experiences allows black women an opportunity to not only explore their sexuality but also determine the limits and parameters of so-called racial loyalty.

Except for the examples that Jackson and Gibson provide, few works in African American theater explore the joys of the erotic from the perspective of a black female; plays rarely celebrate middle-class black female sexuality or desire without apology. Perhaps contemporary African American theater will include more representations of the black middle class that go beyond tragic heroines who embody morality for the race. Representing the experiences of African Americans from the perspective of the diverse middle class provides new images and permits black theater to more fully explore the influence of sexuality on identity. The work of Gibson and Jackson suggests a framework for future plays. Perhaps performance art, with lesser dependence on theatrical structure, provides a space for celebrating the black female body and sexual pleasure.[60] Jackson ends her play with a ceremonial chant, a mantra or litany to encourage black women to adopt self-love. It is reminiscent of the close of Shange's "For Colored Girls Who Have Considered Suicide." These prayers, these meditations, speak to the hope that black women will become full participants in the universe of signs instead of remaining what Hortense Spillers calls "the beached whales of the sexual universe."[61]

3

Black Ladies and Black Magic Women
Independent Film and Black Sexuality

The southern middle-class black woman plays a distinctive role in the African American imagination—she is the ultimate black lady. Like Anita Hill, many of today's most visible iconic black ladies such as Oprah Winfrey or Condoleezza Rice, and prominent women of other generations like Dorothy Height, Coretta Scott King, and Rosa Parks, hail from the South. Each made unique contributions to American life, but what makes them similar is that each woman's public conduct evoked honor, dignity, propriety, and modesty. Coretta Scott King was the quintessential black lady. At her funeral, many spoke of her bravery as a movement leader, but their comments also emphasized her poise, grace, dignity and "regal bearing." Even those who may not have shared King's political leanings were complimentary about her character.[1]

What comments would there have been, however, if a second husband or better yet a "companion" had survived Coretta Scott King? Unlike her iconic counterpart Jacqueline Kennedy Onassis, she never remarried, nor did she have a publicly visible romantic partner in the years after Martin Luther King Jr.'s assassination. Onassis's fruitful publishing career allowed the former first lady to distinguish herself professionally, but for many unaware of King's continued work advocating for human rights the extended widowhood made her another type of martyr. In this she was unlike Myrlie Evers, widow of civil rights activist Medgar Evers, who remarried in 1975 and charted a more visible and public contribution to African American politics as the only woman to chair the NAACP. Coretta Scott King was primarily identified as a grieving widow who spent her years safeguarding her husband's legacy.

As her funeral proved, King functioned in the African American imaginary as royalty. Holding to the black middle-class code of propriety, she never acknowledged rumors of her husband's alleged infidelity; instead, her silence bolstered the image of their relationship and family as impeccable, solid, and proper. She is but another example of the middle-class black woman sacrificing her own integrity for the imagined needs of the African American community. The South, and the southern woman, epitomized by women like Coretta Scott King, remains at the root of middle-class black identity.

As Houston Baker makes clear in *Turning South Again*, "Where the south and black southern being are concerned, I believe such rehashing forms the crux of a psychodrama of framing, performance, signification, and, ultimately *being* for the black American."[2] Despite the horrid past of chattel slavery, the South remains the most identifiable homeland for many African Americans. In their hearings before the U.S. Sentate, both Anita Hill and Clarence Thomas sought in part to prove their blackness by evoking their southern heritage. Baker's observation anticipates black cultural producers' repeated turn to the South to renegotiate notions of black identity. For black women artists, however, revisiting the South raises historically charged issues of sexual agency. The South is the primary site of black female sexual exploitation and debasement, the place where slaveholders in the antebellum period and white employers in the postbellum period sexually abused black women. The black female body not only suffered sexual exploitation from white slave owners but also reproduced the slaves who helped maintain the Peculiar Institution.[3]

This history and conflicted experience makes it ironic that the most acclaimed black woman filmmakers have chosen the South as the location for their first feature films. Kasi Lemmons's *Eve's Bayou* (1997) and Julie Dash's *Daughters of the Dust* (1991) use it as a site to explore black female sexual agency and place black middle-class women at the core of their narratives. Lemmons sets *Eve's Bayou* in a fictional parish in Louisiana in the early 1960s, and Dash locates hers on the Sea Islands off the Georgia coast at the turn of the twentieth century.

Lemmons and Dash reclaim the South for black women and dispel myths about their bodies being "ruined" or "damned." Their films weave intricate narratives that foreground black women's negotiations with the suffocating notions of black middle-class propriety, respectability, and responsibility. Both directors use the southern landscape as a metaphor for black female exoticism and excess and contrast it with repressive black middle-class mores; the fertile soil, willow trees, murky swamps, white sand beaches, and sugarcane fields are stark contrasts to stifled passions. Lemmons and Dash skillfully exploit the romanticization of southern culture in ways that justify the region's continued hold on the black imagination.

They also evoke nontraditional black spirituality rooted in the southern United States. Hoodoo, a term commonly used in the African diaspora to refer to West African–based systems of spiritual and medicinal healing, and other forms of African spirituality propel significant portions of both narratives. The female characters who operate outside the boundaries of proper behavior use indigenous religious practices to assert new forms of personal identity. Like black ladies, these conjurers, juju, or root women occupy respected places in the community although their power and beliefs are sometimes feared and ridiculed. The filmmakers' use of spiritual practices are not precise or necessarily accurate, but their narratives incorporate indigenous spirituality to demonstrate the ways that being black and female reside outside normative boundaries. The middle-class figures grow to respect these modes of religious or spiritual expression because it is often through accepting hoodoo or encountering other folk forms of worship that these women find the freedom to express their sexuality. Instead of nonconforming spirituality being identified with savagery and hedonism, these traditions allow them to embrace the sensual.

Screening Race, Gender, and Class

Daughters of the Dust and *Eve's Bayou* challenge the overdetermined narrative of middle-class black romance presented in numerous movies released since the 1990s. The long list of popular films includes *Boomerang* (1992), *Hav Plenty* (1997), *Love Jones* (1997), *Soul Food* (1997), *The Best Man* (1999), *Two Can Play That Game* (2001), *The Brothers* (2001), *Deliver Us from Eva* (2003), *Breaking All the Rules* (2004,) *Something New* (2006), *Daddy's Girls* (2006), and *Why Did I Get Married?* (2007). Considered "feel-good films targeted at the black community, . . . [that] assume a middle class audience" they often feature handsomely dressed, attractive professionals in luxurious settings, navigating the pitfalls of urban romance.[4] Many of these movies recycle the same actors and possess similar storylines. Almost like offshoots of *The Cosby Show*, their plots distance African American characters from the racism, poverty, and violence that is so prevalent in urban dramas. Instead of being central, race is an incidental feature of these films. Even African American culture appears peripheral, its presence evident mostly through a film's R&B- and hip-hop–inflected soundtrack or the occasional use of the latest slang. Besides presenting an insular black middle-class universe, these comedies consistently feature the black lady as professionally exceptional but personally doomed. Often regarded as frigid and asexual, she is continually frustrated by the inability to find satisfying intimate relationships. The striver's career and possessions substitute for unfulfilled sexual desires.

Although they are from a different genre than the films of Lemmons and Dash, *The Best Man* and *Soul Food* vividly illustrate the conventional representation of middle-class African American women and establish how the figure of the black lady operates in contemporary film. Romantic comedies provide some of the most visible and enduring images of middle-class blacks. Depictions of middle-class women are so dominant that Lemmons and Dash, as well as the movie-going public, cannot help but be influenced by the images.

The Best Man's Jordan (Nia Long), a highly driven television executive at BET, is considered a "control freak" whose investment in her career sabotages any possibility for companionship. Jordan's friends present her professional success as the barrier to a relationship, especially one with Harper (Taye Diggs), whom she's loved since they were in college. The movie takes place over the course of a weekend, when a group of old college friends reunite in New York to celebrate the marriage of Mia (Monica Calhoun) and Lance (Morris Chestnut). The plot turns on the revelation that the best man, Harper, once had a night of passion with the bride-to-be. Their indiscretion carries more significance because it calls into question Mia's sexual purity.

Compared to Jordan, Mia is sweet, passive, and devoted. It is Mia's virginity and "goodness" that initially capture Lance's attention. Lance, a star athlete and womanizer, describes the single, ambitious Jordan as "too damn sassy and independent" and warns his best friend, "She might make more cheese than you someday bro. . . . Hey man, I love Jordan, you know that right? But let's face it dog—a woman like that don't need no man, she's one step from being lesbian." After Lance's tirade, the men all snicker in agreement. What makes their laughter particularly stinging is that they are all handsome, intelligent, successful, and ambitious—male versions of Jordan herself. Instead of valuing her, however, they mercilessly ridicule Jordan. The middle-class woman (or black lady) represents a problem to be avoided; she is too independent, too intelligent, and too self-sufficient. The men declare her a threat and a romantic outcast who resonates to them in the same register as "the lesbian."

Jordan never denies her ambition. She insists on covering the wedding to advance her career and only ceases after her persistence is met by reproach and annoyance. Jordan also understands her personal failures. During a tension-filled romantic afternoon with Harper she confesses that she has not had sex in six months. And she has to think back further than that to recall when she last experienced "good" sex. Jordan's attempt to consummate her relationship with Harper fails miserably, and she suffers the typical fate of a middle-class black woman: being left on her own when Harper decides to remain with his less ambitious and far less successful girlfriend. The more traditional bride fares much better. The film constructs Mia's one-night stand with Harper as a good girl's fleeting moment of justifiable revenge against her wayward man. Even after her indiscretion is revealed, Mia triumphantly joins her college sweetheart in matrimony.

Like Condoleezza Rice and Anita Hill, *Soul Food*'s Teri (Vanessa Williams) also has her personal life and sexuality scrutinized by others. She, too, is punished socially for focusing too much attention on her career. She is depicted as a workaholic corporate lawyer who is destroying her marriage. Her husband has a sexual tryst with Teri's flirtatious cousin because Teri refuses to support his desire to leave his law practice and pursue his music career. Teri's plight contrasts significantly with the experiences of her younger sister, Maxine (Vivica A. Fox), a contented homemaker whose devoted husband, the audience discovers, dated Teri in high school. The sisters' different marital experiences only reinforce Teri's characterization as a middle-class professional shrew. She suffers heartache because she's too centered on material gain and professional advancement, preoccupations that prevent her from realizing the value of family and love.

The family values Teri's financial achievements only when they need her to pay for a wedding, funeral, or other major expense. When the family matriarch dies, Maxine is considered the one who truly maintains family tradition even though Teri's financial stability grounds them in equally important ways. At the end, the newly divorced Teri is depicted as damaged goods.

Popular African American romantic comedies like *The Best Man* and *Soul Food* consistently reward women who pursue traditional female roles. They present the desperate social circumstances of professional black women as the result of misplaced priorities and aggressive personalities. In essence, these films uphold and further the cultural stereotype of the black lady as cold, prim, and passionless. They also, in light of bleak marriage rates for black professional women, send an alarmingly conservative message and signal a backlash against the recent academic and professional successes the women have enjoyed.

In their period dramas, Dash and Lemmons subvert the stereotypes perpetuated by contemporary romantic comedies. *Daughters in the Dust* and *Eve's Bayou* escape the clichéd depictions of sexually frustrated, but highly professional, black middle-class women. The directors endeavor to redefine contemporary notions of black womanhood from a historical perspective but without becoming mired in the horrors of the past. Critics have rightly pointed out that Dash's groundbreaking feature film "created a new way of seeing, and reading" African American life.[5] Indeed, *Daughters of the Dust* is a black feminist film that places black women at center of African American history. But it and *Eve's Bayou* are also landmark depictions of black women's beauty and sexuality. Both Dash and Lemmons force viewers to think about middle-class women and the sexual values attached to them in more dynamic ways.

Instead of merely evoking southern culture, Dash advocates for a "New World African aesthetic" that honors a nonlinear African storytelling style. She considers her work "based upon the way an African griot would recount a story's history, would recount a tale based upon West African deities, like Ogun, Osun, Yemoja" and asserts that "contemporary filmmaking by African American artists is very much a part of the continuum of the past and the writers from the '60s."[6] Although use of this New World African aesthetic collapses and simplifies various West African spiritual, regional, and tribal traditions, the strategy does allow *Daughters of the Dust* and *Eve's Bayou* to celebrate an alternate belief system that honors black people, black women in particular.[7] In an interview with Houston Baker, Dash defends her narrative style: "I think we need to do more than try to document history. I think we need to probe. We need to have the freedom to romanticize history, to say 'what if,' to use history in a speculative way and creative speculative fiction."[8]

The tendency toward speculative fiction is evident in Lemmons's film as well. The work of the two extends beyond reimagining black history; the films specifically reimagine black womanhood within a spiritual tradition that harks back to indigenous modes of expression, power, worship, and respect. Their reliance on the religions of the African diaspora allows the films to move beyond retelling sorrowful stories of black female suffering and sexual abuse. Instead, they offer some black women as sexual agents whose choices complicate conventional notions of middle-class sexuality; they also provide filmic renderings of middle-class women who are unfulfilled and romantically frustrated.

EVE'S BAYOU

Eve's Bayou, one of "the most financially successful independent film[s] of 1997," caused critic Mia Mask to ask a despicable but telling question: *"Eve's Bayou:* Too Good to Be a Black Film?"[9] The film did enjoy critical acclaim: Lemmons was awarded the Independent Spirit Award for Best First Time Feature, and the film was nominated for seven NAACP Image Awards. The distancing of the motion picture from the genre of African American cinema partially derives from Lemmons's break from typical renderings of black life, which led some critics to wonder if it was genuinely a "black film." *Eve's Bayou* revises the overbearing iconography of African American females through a subtle and diverse representation of southern black middle-class women.[10] Within the strict confines and historical conventions of the upper-middle-class black family, Lemmons renders four very distinct female characters, each of whom have different temperaments and motivations.

Eve's Bayou relates the tale of a popular black physician, Louis Batiste (Samuel L. Jackson), and reveals how his philandering unsettles his wife, Roz (Lynn Whitfield), who holds to a notion of a middle-class family. Roz's reactions to Louis's misdeeds shape how their two daughters, fourteen-year-old Cisely (Meagan Good) and the titular Eve (Jurnee Smolett), a precocious ten-year-old, imagine their futures as middle-class women. The film's spiritual center, Louis's sister, Mozelle (Debbi Morgan), is critical to Lemmons's unconventional rendering of black sexuality.

Although the patriarch is at the center of the film, *Eve's Bayou* offers an unusually layered portrayal of black middle-class womanhood. While literature, film, and drama repeatedly depict middle-class African Americans either as repressed, shallow, and self-loathing or as unblemished moral leaders, the Batiste women encompass a more complex range. None are asexual Mammies, hypersexual vamps, outcast lesbians, or emasculating tyrants. Lemmons also disregards the impulse to treat middle-class blacks as perfect citizens who rigidly adhere to normative codes of conduct or apolitical, self-interested, unenlightened sycophants. Instead she endows her characters with both admirable and disagreeable qualities that foreground their humanity and complexity.

This visually stunning film uses vivid colors, a haunting soundtrack, and delicate lighting to evoke the danger, mystery, and romance of the southern United States. The "stylish, southern Gothic tale" makes use of a gumbo of spirituality, biblical allusion, and mysticism. Louis Baptiste undermines his position as a popular and respected physician with a rampant promiscuity that embarrasses and finally devastates his wife and children. Exposure of his infidelities erodes the family's polished veneer. Scandal and tragedy result, particularly victimizing the young daughters. By watching their parents interact, the girls learn how to become conventional colored ladies. Yet their Aunt Mozelle's alternate model of womanhood at least allows Eve to redefine what it means to be a black middle-class woman. Through Mozelle, *Eve's Bayou* reveals how middle-class black women develop creative strategies to undercut conservative notions of female propriety and responsibility.

The first scene establishes the class and social position of the Batiste family in the southern community of Eve's Bayou. The camera pans from the dark, mysterious bayou to a wooded yard filled with expensive automobiles. Slowly the audience enters a large, beautifully adorned residence filled with laughter and zydeco music. The house teems with jovial, well-dressed black guests of various hues, dancing, gossiping, and laughing. The dining-room table and sideboard boast a lavish spread of Creole cuisine and champagne. The Batiste children laugh, play, and flippantly recite lines from Shakespeare.[11] As the host, Louis, surrounded by an adoring family, friends, and community, takes pleasure in being the focus of gossip in the small parish.

The opening scene also introduces the primary challenges facing the Batiste clan: sibling rivalry, marital betrayal, misplaced intimacy, and emotional estrangement. In a moment of competition Eve and Cisely vie for their father's attention. When Louis dances with Cisely in front of the crowd, Eve retreats to the carriage house. Pouting, she falls asleep. Later in the evening, however, she is awakened by her father's sexual encounter with party guest Matty Mereaux (Lisa Nicole Carson).[12] This act of infidelity, and the fact that Eve witnesses it, signals the family's eventual destabilization and departure from proper middle-class decorum. Ironically, Louis immediately calms Eve, who stoically apologizes for frightening Mrs. Mereaux with her startled scream and later allows Cisely to provide an alternate and sanitizing version of the episode. Despite Cisely's attempts, however, Eve remains traumatized by observing the incident. The moment is a catalyst for her maturation, and like the adolescent Laveer in *Long Time since Yesterday* she is now encouraged to question the advantages of becoming a colored lady if doing so requires her to privilege decorum and poise over acknowledging unpleasant reality.

Matty Mereaux completes the landscape of black womanhood in *Eve's Bayou* and serves an important purpose. From the onset, the film contrasts the flirtatious, voluptuous Matty with the glamorous yet respectable Batiste women. When Matty dances a slow grind with her husband at the party, another guest whispers that Matty's husband "ain't the only one getting it." Clad in a tight, shiny black dress covered with hot-pink flowers, Matty embodies the stereotype of the Jezebel. The spectacle of her full body and the close-up of her buttocks invite derision from another guest; even Eve's grandmother, Gran Mére (Ethel Ayler), conveys her irritation in sarcastic Creole. Matty's physical excess signifies sexual excess.

It seems simple to read Matty as a tainted woman, but her status is much more complex. Her marriage to a college professor, Lenny (Roger Guinevere Smith), secures her middle-class position, and because she and Louis were childhood friends it seems possible that Matty may also come from a relatively privileged background. Nevertheless, her improper, "loose" behavior jeopardizes (and in some ways negates) her social standing. The example she sets warns the girls that middle-class status depends not only on where one comes from but also how one conducts oneself.

The prominent Batiste women contrast with Matty, and their role in the community suggests the subtle ways in which the performance of black middle-class identity passes from generation to generation. But Roz and Mozelle offer divergent role models for the young Batiste sisters. Eve's burgeoning adolescence and her older sister's nascent womanhood force the family to confront Louis's infidelity. His betrayals compel both girls to locate themselves within the universe of black womanhood. Both Eve and Cisely define themselves in relation to, and often in opposition to, the older women they most admire or to whom they are closest. Cisely competes with her mother, Roz, while Eve patterns herself after Aunt Mozelle.

The Batiste family history is crucial to understanding the sisters' choices and roles. The legend of Eve's Bayou frames Batiste womanhood in terms of African American history. Their ancestor, an African slave—the first Eve—worked as a conjurer and healer. According to legend, her "powerful medicine" saved the life of her owner, General Jean Paul Batiste, who was stricken with cholera. In gratitude he freed her and gave her land (acres of bayou); afterward, "perhaps in gratitude," she bore him sixteen children. The family's origin harkens back to slavery yet attempts to position the matriarch Eve as powerful.

In addition to historic symbolism, *Eve's Bayou* employs biblical references. Eve symbolizes the first human woman, often denounced in Christian cultures for original sin because she disobeyed God and ate from the tree of the knowledge of good and evil. The matriarch Eve used her knowledge to save her master's life, thus earning freedom and ensuring a privileged life for her descendants. But the first Batiste Eve's freedom is conflicted by concubinage with her former master, underscoring the ways sexuality complicates the lives of her female descendants.

Eve gained freedom because of her knowledge as a healer, but that freedom is questionable given her role as concubine and mother of her former master's children. Her special status within the slave community is disconcerting; the relationship with the father of her children calls to mind the relationship between Sally Hemmings and Thomas Jefferson as well as arrangements between other white men of means and countless enslaved black women of the antebellum South that Lorraine O'Grady regards as a "still under-theorized, historic relationship."[13] It is more complicated than the obvious features of exploitation and abuse. Eve's descendents gain valuable land in the bayou because of a powerful white man. Instead of the usual arrangement—a female slave as property that produces property (more slave babies)—the Batiste family inherits land and social prominence through the matriarch's body.

The land represents bondage as well as liberation for the Batiste clan. The original Eve's sacrifice of her body (if it was a sacrifice) makes it possible for Louis to become a respected, even envied physician. But sexuality proves to be a thorny issue in the lives of her female descendants. Ironically, her female progeny find *their* choices limited and their lives complicated by gender, sexuality, and class status. Nonetheless, Eve and Mozelle, who inherit the gift of "sight," try to control their destiny while Cisely and Roz fall victim to the dictates of middle-class decorum.

The spiritual gifts that give young Eve and Mozelle agency also derive from their family origins. It is not only their ancestor's role as a concubine that changes the family's destiny but also her skills as a healer and conjurer. Black female sexuality and black magic, both considered mysterious, powerful, wicked, and uncontrollable, are the foundation of the Batiste family's financial and social standing. The same space their ancestors occupied as slaves is now the location of their grand home.

For Lemmons, family history is but one tool to disrupt stereotypical depictions of black womanhood. The bayou symbolizes African American dynamism, boundlessness, hope, and power, a deep, dark space offering both beauty and danger. An area of slow-moving water coming from a river or lake, often overgrown with reeds, the bayou is as languid as the colored ladies of the story. The film treats the landscape as an additional character that is female, even maternal. Given the Batiste family history, the gendering of the land as female is particularly intriguing. Spirituality, land, and sexuality all resonate as elements controlled by women, and in Eve's Bayou those elements destabilize middle-class propriety.

Another icon of black womanhood competes for the young Eve's loyalty, the witch doctor Elzora (Diahann Carroll). Lemmons's casting choice is worthy of note, being that Carroll has become the epitome of the middle-class black lady because of roles in films such as *Paris Blues* (1961), *Sister, Sister* (1982), and especially the groundbreaking 1968–71 television series *Julia*. Until *Cosby*'s Clair Huxtable (Phylicia Rashad), Carroll's Julia was the most significant black middle-class character in television history. Carroll starred in this acclaimed situation comedy as a young mother and nurse, widow of a Vietnam War soldier, who raises her young son within a multiracial community. After a long tradition of comedies with black women as domestic servants, *Julia* presented the first professional black woman character on network television, and the part solidified Carroll's role as the quintessential colored lady. Although she played a nurse in a northern city, Carroll's Julia carried herself with the dignity and poise of a southern lady.[14]

As Mozelle's rival, Elzora paints her face white and wears a head wrap. With Carroll in the role, Elzora is desexualized but still attractive. She lives in the swamp and performs readings in the market for a dollar; she also, like Matty, resides outside parameters of the black middle-class community. As D. Soyini Madison observes, however, "the margin Elzora occupies is reminiscent of the brazen and fearless outcast—the mad woman who has no 'place,' only the one of her own choosing. She is fearless but she is also feared, taunted, and ironically believed. She is the embodiment of an ancient, dark spiritual root, another archetype from the black diaspora, mocked yet avenged."[15] Mozelle, also gifted with second sight, remains within the black middle class, but Elzora's brazen use of hoodoo places her well outside the community of respectable women.

Roz best fits the cultural stereotype of the middle-class black woman. Lemmons portrays her as untouchable, asexual, and respectable. Although she is not a high-powered professional like Jordan in *The Best Man,* a similar fate befalls Roz. Carla Peterson points out that in order to become respectable the black female body is normalized and made "culturally white" by performing in ways that are "regulated and disciplined." That is what Roz does. In order to maintain her status as a colored lady she uses strategies of decorporealization and normalization.[16] In order to uphold her middle-class identity Roz presents her black female body as attractive but desexualized. Matty and other women in the film flaunt their sexuality (in order to attract Louis), but Roz is portrayed as shrill, unhappy, desperate, frustrated, and vulnerable. She refuses to compete with others for her husband's affections through sex, and the demands she makes on him are based on family, duty, responsibility, and morality. She performs what she perceives as the role of the proper middle-class black woman who uplifts the community by adhering to the highest codes of conduct.

Roz's performance of the normalized black female identity only allows her to demonstrate passion through motherhood, and it is her son, Poe, who receives a disproportionate share of her attention. His affections substitute for Louis's neglect. She embodies the role of the ideal middle-class housewife (a doctor's wife no less) and mother, with her power confined to the domestic sphere. Unlike the barren Mozelle, Roz's role as mother defines and normalizes her. When Mozelle warns of impending doom because of a vision, for instance, Roz forbids the children from going outdoors all summer. Only within the home, she believes, can she protect them.

Although Roz is quite beautiful, she appears in bed only when she comforts the children after Louis's death. The image of the newly widowed Roz is stunning; she sits, surrounded by her children, who protect her from harm like a fortress. In this instance we are reminded how motherhood allows her to maintain the inaccessibility of the colored lady's body.

Throughout the film Roz either suffers her husband's behavior in strained silence or throws shrill tantrums. Performing as a true colored lady, she never considers retaliating by taking a lover. Roz confesses that she married because she desired a "normal" middle-class life. During a walk along the water with Mozelle, she explains her attraction to her husband: "I was just wondering what happened with that woman. I suppose he fixed it. He knows how to fix things. When I first met Louis I watched him set this boy's leg who'd fallen out of a tree and I said to myself, 'Here's a man who can fix things. He's a healer. *He'll take care of me.*' So I leave my family and I moved to this swamp and to find out, *he's just a man*" (emphasis added). Disappointed when she realizes Louis's humanity and embarrassed by his faults, Roz reluctantly becomes a frustrated colored lady with an unfaithful husband, sublimating her own ambitions and desires.

Roz expects Louis to live up to her ideal of marriage by being the man to "take care of her" financially and emotionally. She unquestioningly embraces the myth of a classic American marriage. Uncritical of the marriage contract, Roz falls victim to naïve beliefs; she becomes a beautiful, respected, honored woman trapped in a gilded cage. The fantasy of a normal middle-class family proves disastrous for her. She understands that to challenge Louis would risk her position within the community and threaten her "perfect" family. In order to maintain her status as a colored lady, she finds herself in the same position as white middle-class housewives before the second-wave era. Normalization requires her to sacrifice her sense of self. Despite her husband's flaws, Roz maintains a facade of normalcy because upholding their social position for her children, community, and race is more important than personal happiness.

Throughout the film Lemmons questions the notion of the colored lady. Even Eve's conversation with her father evokes this impossible standard of womanhood:

> LOUIS: Daddy loves you very much.
> EVE: I know. You love Mama?
> LOUIS: Your Mama is *the most beautiful perfect woman* I ever met. Your Mama is a *lady* and I'll always love her. Always. Understand? [emphasis added]

In both Louis's and Eve's imagination the perfect Roz represents a colored lady with impeccable morals and flawless beauty. Louis delivers this message to Eve in a hushed, reverent tone that denotes the intensity of his love and respect for Roz despite his infidelities.

The exchange between father and daughter is especially poignant because it occurs right after Eve has discovered her father with Matty. Louis's comments nearly suggest that he is unfaithful *because* Roz is a colored lady; a lover could never be the mother of his children nor hold the position of wife. Although it refers to the trite dichotomy between the virgin madonna and the whore, nevertheless it is a privilege for a black woman to occupy the role as the virgin mother or even pampered homemaker. Just as Louis ensures Roz's position, Roz ensures his role "as the most respected colored doctor in all Louisiana." She represents the type of woman Louis hopes their daughters will emulate—colored ladies, not "imperfect" women like his lovers.

Like the gravity of the sexually harassed Anita Hill and the dead Janeen in *Long Time since Yesterday*, the tragic ending of *Eve's Bayou* suggests that the desire to maintain middle-class respectability by concealing ugly sexual issues leads only to devastation. When the Batiste women gather behind closed doors to discuss the latest scandal concerning Louis—a lover's pregnancy—the children hover outside, eavesdropping. The matriarchy's clandestine meeting confirms that the problems are important, but they merit concealment not exposure. Sexual secrets continue to plague the Batiste family. Instead of acting like a proper young colored lady who accepts the fictions of middle-class black society, however, Eve rebels. When she questions her father about the rumors she aligns herself with Aunt Mozelle within the family discourse.

Mozelle is anything but a conventional colored lady. Her reddish hair, expressive eyes, and saucy speech distinguish her from the decidedly prim, reserved Roz. Mozelle models for her nieces an atypical, uncommon style of womanhood that moves beyond the colored lady. She uses neither decorporealization nor normalization to maintain class status; rather, she embraces her sexual life and romantic entanglements. Fortunately for her, Mozelle's membership in a prominent family exempts her from the kind of scrutiny that Matty suffers. The eccentric Mozelle is the only woman who smokes (she even allows Eve an opportunity to puff on a cigarette), and, like Elzora, her work as a psychic counselor places her outside normative boundaries for proper colored ladies. As a respected spiritual healer she doctors the spirit like her brother heals the body. She does not work for financial reasons; psychic counseling, Louis remarks, is "something the family lets her do."

Indisputably, Mozelle's work marks her as a spiritual descendent of the matriarch Eve. Both are closely aligned with the supernatural. Although it is a typical strategy, Mozelle's emphasis on the spiritual world does not place her outside the corporeal. For most of the film she operates in the spiritual, not the physical, realm despite multiple marriages and a penchant for affairs. Moreover, hoodoo and visions dominate her landscape and foreground her spirit at the expense of her body. Yet Mozelle still radiates a sensuousness that the repressed Roz lacks.

Mozelle refuses to abide by her middle-class family's expectations. Louis dismisses his eccentric sister as one who is not "unfamiliar with the inside of a mental institution."[17] Mozelle's refusal to succumb to the misfortune of widowhood or become more conservative also mark her as different from her sister-in-law and expand the notion of the middle-class black woman. After Mozelle's third husband, Harry (Branford Marsalis), dies in an automobile accident, she temporarily capitulates to the community's label of black widow and concentrates solely on her work as a psychic counselor. Instead of remaining a long-suffering widow for the rest of the film, however, she becomes engaged yet again. Although she is childless, Mozelle is gratified by her role as aunt and especially close to the precocious Eve. A romantic character, Mozelle carries her tragedies as a badge of honor. Her three dead husbands lend her an air of mystery.

The gift of sight does not allow Mozelle to predict or thwart her own misfortunes, but she provides the family with a tie to their past. In *Symbolizing the Past* Sandra Grayson explains that Mozelle's storytelling honors the oral tradition and preserves the Batiste family history.[18] Not only do Mozelle's stories link the Batistes' past and present but they also unite the film's plot. Much like her prophecies, her accounts of the past provide narrative signposts. In retelling her experiences, Mozelle relives them and allows Eve to learn from her mistakes. When Mozelle describes her complicated love life as well as their maternal ancestor's relationship with General Batiste, she reveals the dangers black women must navigate as they explore sexual options. Mozelle's unconventional work and troubled personal life do not undermine her influential role as the repository of family history.

Mozelle rejects the expectation that colored ladies should promote racial uplift through comportment and instead models for her nieces an atypical style of womanhood that moves beyond the role of colored lady. She also defies other cinematic representations of middle-class black women in that she is highly sexual; unlike the women in popular romantic comedies she has no trouble finding love. In one of the most riveting scenes in the film, Mozelle, standing before a mirror, tells Eve about taking a lover, Hosea (Marcus Lyle Brown) when married to her second husband, Maynard (Leonard L. Thomas). Instead of portraying the affair with Hosea as a mistake, Mozelle describes it as an intense and highly sexual relationship quite different from her more dispassionate marriage. Not only is she willing to acknowledge herself as a sexual being but she also chooses lovers for their ability to "light a fire within her." Far from Roz's plan to marry a man who can "take care of her" financially and socially, Mozelle prioritizes passion and romance. Only after her seemingly stable and respectable husband challenges Hosea does Mozelle realize she loves him.

In the mirror, both Eve and Mozelle observe Maynard confront Hosea. Mozelle steps into the flashback to stand beside Maynard in the mirror and lives through Hosea murdering him yet again. In this scene Lemmons uses a mirror for the third time as a device for characters to revisit the past. The visitations always involve either Eve or Mozelle, the only women in the family who possess the gift of second sight. The mirror signifies how observation, scrutiny, and surveillance govern the behavior and appearance of the middle-class black woman's body and identity. The mirror also signifies the past—both the past that lends itself to revisionism and the past that haunts the black middle-class subject.

The history of sexual objectification and abuse haunts all black women, but the figure of the colored lady also haunts middle-class black women and continues to influence their behavior and sensibility. Gran Mére's comments at the opening of the film position her as an authority and allude to a broader southern middle class that has little respect for "fast" women. Like the Trees, who haunt the suicidal Janeen in Gibson's *Long Time since Yesterday*, the Batiste family matriarch establishes the parameters of proper conduct for ladies with equally domineering authority. In several key scenes Gran Mére advises Roz that her children "should be seen but not heard" and provides her daughter-in-law counsel when it is rumored that Louis may have fathered a child out of wedlock.

From the landscape of southern ladies around them Cisely and Eve learn that to gain male favor women must be either seductive like Louis's lovers or compliant like their mother. Although her behavior is innocent, Cisely begins to lavish her father with attention as she competes with Roz for Louis's affections. At times Cisely treats her father like a spouse. She waits up for him at night, pours his evening scotch, sits on his lap, plants kisses on his lips, and massages his shoulders after a hard day. Cisely's nascent sexuality (which she marks by cutting off her long ponytail and styling her hair in a fashion resembling her mother's) begins to make the manner in which she interacts with her father suspect. In retrospect, Cisely and Louis's dance in the opening scene takes on heightened significance. Cisely's attempts to supplant Roz destabilize the boundaries between father and daughter. The film never makes explicit whether Louis attempts to molest his daughter or whether Cisely initiates the incursion, but something occurs that crosses the line of propriety. As a consequence Cisely suffers a breakdown. Like Roz, she insists on silence regarding the incident, and this begins Cisely's final indoctrination into the code of the colored lady. She knows the importance of decorum; for her, the consequences of being on the margins, like Elzora or Matty, are unbearable. The sisters share the secret, but when Louis and Roz send Cisely away after her breakdown she signals to Eve, a finger over her lips, not to protest or reveal anything.

Whether Louis initiated an incestuous kiss is unclear, but the girls initially believe that he transgressed his paternal role and act on this belief. Neither informs their mother because Roz, a colored lady, is, they think, too weak to protect them; Eve therefore tries to enlist Mozelle to help avenge Cisely.

The trust that exists between aunt and niece allows for mutual confidences. Mozelle is the only adult in whom Eve confides; when she tells her about her father's infidelity with Matty, Mozelle reciprocates by revealing that she witnessed her lover murder her second husband. Mozelle's revelations about her sexual infidelities allow the precocious Eve to imagine a life that troubles the boundaries of middle-class propriety. Instead of adopting the role of the long-suffering wife or celibate widow, Mozelle has forged a unique path. She insists on her own rules. Although her sexual choices and work as a psychic counselor place her outside the expectations of the black middle class, like Matty and Elzora, Mozelle still manages to earn the respect and trust of her community and family. Some consider her peculiar, but Mozelle negotiates her status as both an insider and outsider. At the end of the film she demonstrates bravery and independence by defying the black widow curse and agreeing to marry for the fourth time. She disregards conventional notions of propriety while managing to maintain her identity as a colored lady.

Mozelle's connection to the spiritual world offers her solace in tragedies and a link to her past. Spirituality also helps her imagine a future. She resists expectations of a sexless widowhood and maintains sexual agency. After Matty's cuckolded husband murders Louis, Mozelle consoles Eve with another story: "Last night I had a dream that I was flying. It was such a fine feeling. But from the corner of my eye, I saw a woman drowning in the very same air that was keeping me afloat. And I knew without looking that it was me. Should I save her? Then I heard Louis's voice saying, 'don't look back.' So I kept on flying . . . and I let her drown. When I woke up, I told Julian I would marry him. . . . He wouldn't have it any other way. Maybe God will be kind and allow me to go with him. So tired of being left alone."

Unlike Roz, Mozelle accepts the inevitability of loss. She survives because she refuses to embrace the victimization that comes with the prescribed role of colored lady. The drowning figure in her dream not only represents her past but is also a rejection of that role and codes that suffocate and stifle the spirit. Mozelle allows the colored lady to drown and models a defiant middle-class black womanhood for Eve and Cisely. Her life includes tragedy and misfortune, but, like Gibson's Laveer, Mozelle's refusal to stop flying suggests that a black woman can fashion her life in creative and liberating ways.

Eve, more than any of the women in the family, comes closet to autonomy and emulates Mozelle when she defends her older sister's honor, body, and sexuality by using her powers to destroy the man who violates her. Yet when Mozelle refuses to teach Eve how to use voodoo, Eve turns to Elzora. In doing so, Eve establishes an identity independent of her mother and aunt. Stepping outside her immediate family, but drawing on her ancestral and spiritual traditions, she reveals her determination to assert self-sufficiency and agency.

Eve's Bayou challenges assumptions about black middle-class respectability and southern gentility by illustrating that despite efforts to sublimate desire, the middle-class black female body retains its signification as a site of danger and contamination. Although Roz and Mozelle are quite different, Lemmons presents both women as isolated and untouchable. Roz, although stunningly attractive, remains unimpeachable, modest, and pure. Mozelle, the doomed, barren "black widow," conveys a sexual potency that devours every man who loves her. These narrative positions initially strip both women of agency, yet Mozelle's reluctance to tolerate the restrictions of her social position allows for her humanity. Among all the Batiste women she is the most similar to the Louisiana bayou—powerful, dangerous, and beautiful.

Lemmons grants her audience a nostalgic vision of black life in the southern United States. Like other artists she redefines the South for African Americans and reclaims what is useful about the region. She casts it not only as a site of pain and horror but also as a place of culture, history, myth, and mysticism. *Eve's Bayou*'s depiction of a South absent whiteness, poverty, racial violence, and civil rights activism is troubling, but Lemmons's strategy allows her to deliver a complex and rare portrayal of middle-class black sexuality.

DAUGHTERS OF THE DUST

In Julie Dash's poetic *Daughters of the Dust* the tasteful decor of the Batiste home gives way to the rustic cabins of the Peazant family. As in *Eve's Bayou*, the southern landscape resonates as a character in its own right. Expansive white sand beaches, the blue sea, lush fields, and dramatically crooked trees provide a serene but potent, almost sacred backdrop. Dash features an enchanting landscape, and, like Lemmons, populates the film with gorgeous black women. As she confessed, one of her objectives was to "show black families, particularly black women, as we have never seen them before."[19] The women in the cast, most of whom are dark-skinned, wear natural hairstyles and dress in lovely, rich white fabrics that adorn their ample frames. Also like *Eve's Bayou*, *Daughters of the Dust* challenges dominant notions of beauty that privilege whiteness by casting black women as undeniably desirable.

This first nationally distributed feature film directed by an African American woman addresses the issue of black middle-class sexuality indirectly. *Daughters of the Dust* does not portray a financially and socially secure black family. Instead, Dash situates her narrative within the tensions between Gullah culture, West African–inspired spirituality, and the Victorian notions of respectability and propriety espoused by the black middle class. The film is set on a day in 1902 when the Peazant family plans to migrate from their ancestral home on the Sea Islands to the mainland and life in the North. They spend the day celebrating their departure, negotiating their connection to each other, and mourning the inevitable losses the journey necessitates. The women are particularly cognizant of the dangers their new world may present to their bodies and notions of self.

Daughters of the Dust presents two ways for black women to assure survival and understand black female sexuality. Women must either embrace Victorian values and pious Christianity in order to achieve colored-lady status, or, in a more radical or subversive tactic, claim their worth as an essence, something derived from their ancestors that cannot be destroyed no matter what kind of experiences slavery and the antebellum period brought. This juxtaposition is played out through two cousins who have come back home to chaperon the family's migration north: Viola Peazant (Cheryl Lynn Bruce), a Christian missionary, and her cousin, Yellow Mary Peazant (Barbara O. Jones), a prostitute. Yellow Mary and Viola, who have thrived away from the island, both cross from the mainland to celebrate the family's departure and offer advice influenced by their experiences. The ideological battle between what these two women symbolize plays out before the family and allows the other women to imagine how their lives may change after migrating.

Other than Viola and Yellow Mary, the film uses an array of diverse personalities to tell unfamiliar stories about black womanhood. Another principal character, Eula Peazant (Alva Rogers), is a rape victim. Knowledge of the rape not only haunts Eula but also torments her husband, Eli (Adisa Anderson). That Eula's violation came by the hands of a white man evokes the family's recent slave past and reminds them that their home on Ibo Landing contains their roots but does not offer complete safety. Eula's unborn child, much like Anima/Animus, the spirit of the dead child in Jackson's *WOMBmanWARS*, is a major presence. Unborn Child (Kai-Lynn Warren) unites the past and future with voice-overs and appearances at key moments that add to the film's mystical quality. She knows that it is her duty to help her family make the transition to the mainland, and she also knows that because she is her father's child and not a product of the rape her arrival will restore the bond between her parents. The Unborn Child is also a bridge between the story's African-centered nonlinear narrative, its magical realist elements, and the film's belief in family as a balm for healing.

Eighty-eight-year-old Nana Peazant (Cora Lee Day), the family matriarch, represents spirituality, the family's connection to ancestors, culture, and the earth. Nana tries to instill in her offspring the lessons she learned growing up on Ibo Landing. She explains the importance of the bottle tree as a way of remaining close to "old souls" who protect the family from "evil and bad luck." Nana asks her children to consider what it means to abandon their ancestral roots, traditions, and home. When she visits her husband's grave, she reminds Eli that "it's up to the living to keep in touch with the dead." By stressing the importance of the family's history on Ibo Landing she underscores the family's African past as well as its ties to the land they have occupied for generations. She embraces the fragments of African spirituality that she has retained despite slavery, and her non-Christian faith is in stark contrast to Viola's religious beliefs. Some dismiss Nana as living in the past and praise the migration for its promise of class ascension, even though Viola's repressed manner and Yellow Mary's allusion to sexual exploitation call that promise into question.

Embracing a different set of values, Viola represents the proper colored lady who embraces the future and new beliefs. She brags to Mr. Snead, the photographer she has hired to document the family's historic crossing, that she "sees this day as their first steps towards progress, an engraved invitation . . . to the culture, education, and wealth of the mainland." The relationship between Viola and Mr. Snead best illustrates her transformation during that day, although nothing could be less apparent at the start. Mr. Snead's standing as a gentleman is represented by the fact that his first name is never revealed. Dash refers to Snead in the script as a "Philadelphia Negro," a term based on the W. E. B. Du Bois study of urban African Americans in the late nineteenth century and which came to describe upstanding, respectable, middle-class blacks. Although both parties are unmarried there is never a hint of impropriety in Snead and Viola traveling together without a chaperon. The proper photographer operates as a symbol of Viola's sophistication and class position, and she is the proper colored lady whose status is enriched by being a missionary. She incorporates the strategy of decorporealization even more than Roz Batiste does. As Angeletta KM Gourdine suggests, her clothing illustrates her repression. Viola's "A-line skirt has a taut waistband, which along with the billow of the skirt both accentuates and conceals her body's natural curves . . . the constricting clothing displaces her rigid sexuality onto her religious convictions."[20] It more than clothing, however, that contributes to her conservative performance. Viola wears her hair in a tight bun, carries herself with restraint, and keeps her hands folded in her lap. As the unimpeachable colored lady, she is adamant that the family should depart from the island, which she considers backward. She pleads with them to accept Christian values and relinquish their beliefs.[21] Ironically, Viola's ideological rival, Yellow Mary, dons a St. Christopher medal that also links her to Christianity; it is the patron saint of travelers who ushers Yellow Mary to Ibo Landing. Unbeknown to both women, their homecoming will grant them opportunity address their disparate sexual histories.

Both Nana Peazant and Viola worry about the threat of further ruination that awaits black women outside the island enclave, but the two advocate different survival strategies. The family's response to Yellow Mary and her mysterious companion Trula (Trula Hoosier) indicates that the Peazants harbor fears about the mainland and the moral challenges life in the North may present. Yellow Mary left the island to work as a wet nurse for a white family, but the husband's harassment forced her to "fix the tit" in order to be released from their employ.[22]

Eula's rape, like Yellow Mary's subjugation, is another residue of slavery, a theme that arises once again. Being a wet nurse allowed Yellow Mary the freedom to travel, yet that occupation trapped her in domestic service where she was vulnerable to abuse. The finery in which she arrives on the island demonstrates that Yellow Mary, like Viola, has obtained a measure of success. While she has material goods, she nevertheless seems spiritually and psychically bereft. Like the ancestor Eve who bore her former master sixteen children, Yellow Mary's body pays a high price for freedom.

The narrative links Eula and Yellow Mary because both have been sexually victimized. The family considers Eula an innocent victim, but Yellow Mary's life disturbs them. The Peazant women must accept them both if they are to envision themselves as whole and fully human. At Nana Peazant's farewell ceremony the matriarch calls on the family to embrace its past and culture. Sensing a rift caused by Yellow Mary's presence, Eula breaks into a frantic monolog: "As far as this place is concerned, we never enjoyed our womanhood.... Deep inside, we believed that they ruined our mothers, and their mothers before them. And we live our lives always expecting the worst because we feel we don't deserve any better.... There's going to be all kinds of roads to take in life.... Let's not be afraid to take them. We deserve them, because we all good 'omen."

As the innocent one, Eula invites the family to consider how it experiences its worth. Her passionate speech raises an uneasy issue that particularly influences the lives of black women. Eula defends Yellow Mary, the woman in the family whose chosen road marked her as an outsider and as impure. She implores the Peazant family—especially its women—to believe that "we are all good women." A victim of rape by a white man herself, Eula's plea suggests that despite violation black woman can embody goodness and remain untainted. Eula posits a transformative belief, especially considering that these descendents of slaves were taught to believe that African Americans are property and that black women are vulgar. Eula's appeal is raw. Coming at the end of the film it emphasizes the lengths to which black women must go in order to convince the world, even their own families, of their worth. She wants the family to understand that if the Peazant women want to "love yourselves then love Yellow Mary cause she a part of you just like we part of our mothers." To accept and embrace Yellow Mary is to accept the contradictions inherent in being a black woman in the new world.

Dash uses an excerpt from *The Gnostic Gospels*, "Thunder Perfect Mind," to underscore the contradictions that black women confront and the dichotomy between the black middle-class ideal for women and their real experiences. Yellow Mary's voice-over lays bare the irony of black womanhood in a haunting but defiant tone: "I am the whore and the holy one. / I am the wife and the virgin. / I am the barren one, and many / are my daughters."

Black women have difficulty bridging the chasm between Mary, mother of Jesus, and Mary Magdalene, the alleged prostitute. Dash's film evokes other powerful images of black women with characters like Eula, the wife; Viola, the virginal woman; and Yellow Mary, the barren one.[23] The Peazant women consider the legacy of sexual abuse that marks them as "ruint." Indeed, the way in which the family sets Yellow Mary apart allows them to maintain some sense of propriety and sacredness. Dash, however, proves the weakness of this strategy; scapegoating Yellow Mary only reveals their anxiety about their own inherent value.

Unwilling to present a neat tale, Dash shows how migration fragments the black family when some of the daughters choose not to cross to the mainland. Yellow Mary's decision to stay on the island signals the need for black women to embrace their history and community so they can survive assaults on their psyches. Those who decide to migrate are changed by the afternoon's events. Even Viola, who repeatedly insists that the family relinquish its "old ways" as it departs for the mainland, finds herself transformed, and she begins to recognize the value of what she left behind on Ibo Landing.

Dash defends romanticizing black history in an extensive quote that begins the film: "At the turn of the century, Sea Island Gullahs, descendants of African captives, remained isolated from the mainland of South Carolina and Georgia. As a result of their isolation, the Gullah created and maintained a distinct, imaginative, and original African American culture." This prolog signals the audience that it is about to be immersed in a culture it knows little about. Some viewers complained that the characters spoke a Gullah dialect, but the film includes that element because Dash expects her audience to want to know the culture and because she is invested in showing the connection between "African" culture and the lure of the future. By the end of the film, the person who most represents the future, with his camera and kaleidoscope, is Mr. Snead. He has become fascinated by the family's history, Gullah culture, and the island's mythical qualities. Mr. Snead's kiss shocks

Viola, but it is his expression of desire and her slow acquiescence that mark her departure from middle-class decorum and free her. She is thus able to reconnect with her family's culture and history and her own sexuality. Viola allows her hair, which throughout the film remains in a tight bun, to fall free. The loosened hair, a symbol of Viola's repressed sensuality and status as a colored lady, calls into question the overdetermined narrative in feature films whereby middle-class black women are unable to find love.

Although *Daughters of the Dust* romanticizes the African American southern past it also reclaims the site of black women's victimization as one of regeneration and hope. This film joins Lemmons's middle-class black family narrative in exposing for African American women the limits of conventional middle-class morality. Placing issues of female sexuality at the center of these films is an important intervention in black film. In her conversation with Houston Baker, Dash rightly acknowledges the timidity of many independent black filmmakers with regard to presenting sex, and she applauds Spike Lee's controversial and groundbreaking *She's Gotta Have It* (1989):

> I think one of the most magnificent things that Spike reintroduced into black film was sex. Because the rest of us were making these righteous films, like: no sex, none of that. And he introduced all this sex and sensuality and eroticism and it's just like: 'Oh yeah, we have a sex life, too. Why can't we show ... ?' I think most of the filmmakers were so afraid to depict anything sexual because we were trying to stay away from the black exploitation films of the early 1970s. And so our films became very dry, and very didactic and so on.[24]

The gratuitous depictions of the black body in American iconography as well as Blaxploitation Era films justify the reluctance on the part of black directors to represent black sexuality. They appear to be even more hesitant about depicting middle-class blacks as sexual.

Dash's *Daughters of the Dust* and Lemmons's *Eve's Bayou* unapologetically render black sexuality. By bringing multiple representations of southern colored ladies to the screen, Dash and Lemmons reveal that the perception of the black body as harshly sexual is a lie; their soft and gentle renderings allow audiences to envision middle-class black women beyond the asexual stereotype. Although few opportunities exist for African American women to direct feature films, filmmakers such as Cheryl Dunye, Darnell Martin, Leslie Harris, and Sanaa Hamri have joined Lemmons and Dash with complex narratives that allow for a broader range of African American characters. They continue to prioritize compelling, realistic, and nuanced depictions of black women who have sexual agency.

PART 2

Refashioning the Black Female Self

4

Narrating Sexuality in Contemporary African American Autobiography

Anita Hill's memoir *Speaking Truth to Power* provided a platform from which the embattled law professor attempted to set the record straight about her character. Hill spends considerable time establishing herself as a proper middle-class woman. Hers is similar to many autobiographies by the African American middle class who desire to set the record straight because they are a segment of the black community that is often regarded as deficient, self-interested, and racially inauthentic. Many late-twentieth-century autobiographies reveal how some black middle-class women have developed an array of strategies to negotiate the restrictions and expectations society places on them. Lorene Cary's *Black Ice* (1991) and Jill Nelson's *Volunteer Slavery* (1993) concern their response to the changing racial and sexual boundaries of the 1960s, when African American middle class began a historic expansion.[1] In *Shifting* (2003) Charisse Jones and Kumea Shorter-Gooden observe that black women, because of the persistence of racial and gender discrimination, employ as a survival strategy something they label "shifting"; much like the culture of dissemblance, shifting is "a sort of subterfuge" that allows them to perform in ways that "serve and satisfy others." It enables black women to "hide their true selves to placate White colleagues, Black men, and other segments of the community."[2]

The compelling stories that Cary and Nelson share support Jones and Shorter-Gooden's claim about the necessity of such subterfuge, but their subsequent revelations about sexual experiences question the long-term viability of such concealment. Both autobiographies reveal that strategies of silence and concealment, the hallmarks for performance of black middle-class respectability and womanhood, ultimately fall short. Further, because Cary and Nelson each make their sexual development integral to their autobiographies, they broaden notions of a black middle-class womanhood. While Anita Hill downplayed her sexual development and Roz Batiste of *Eve's Bayou* desexualizes herself to play what she regards as the role of a doctor's proper wife, Cary's and Nelson's narratives suggest that understanding and asserting themselves as sexual beings is pivotal to constructing and appreciating black middle-class identity.

Black middle-class autobiographies, especially ones that proliferated during the 1990s, recall numerous antebellum slave narratives that appeared at the end of the nineteenth century.[3] Scholars such as William Andrews and Robert Stepto maintain that the narratives not only represented black Americans' desires for literacy and liberty but also demonstrated the ability of texts to rally the nation against chattel slavery by exposing the consistent indignities and horrendous crimes of the institution. Autobiography allowed former slaves to assert their humanity, claim "I am" in a society that viewed them as possessions, and insert their presence into the American literary landscape. Much like the slave narrator, contemporary autobiographies by middle-class African Americans describe and humanize their lives during the post–civil rights era.[4]

The narratives help redefine blackness beyond suffering, so stories about being part of the black middle class are considered normative. Instead of accepting criticisms of the black middle class as inauthentic, the books suggest that boarding schools, vacation homes, and professional careers are as authentic and genuine as experiences conventionally discussed in African American literature. In her preface to *Black Ice*, "June 1989," Cary explains that she "began writing about St. Paul's School when I stopped thinking of my prep-school experience as an aberration from the common run of black life in America.... The narratives that helped me, that kept me company, along with the living, breathing people in my life, were those that talked honestly about growing up black in America.... I am writing this book to become part of that unruly conversation, and to bring my experience back to the community of minds that made it possible."[5] Cary conceives of her story within a tradition of African American autobiography and suggests normalizing the black middle-class experience.

Not only do memoirs like Cary's celebrate triumphs of middle-class life but they also insist upon a place for middle-class women within the overdetermined notions of blackness. *Black Ice* and *Volunteer Slavery* rewrite the sexual script for black women because they discuss sexual matters in detail and posit sexual experiences as being integral to African American autobiography and black women's life stories. Cary and Nelson convey their sexual experiences not simply as moments of loss, pain, or disappointment (although some of the episodes are rife with those sentiments), but their narratives are compelling because they convey these moments as fundamental to understanding themselves as black, female, and middle class. Their autobiographies join a growing trend of books that defend the black middle-class experience and showcase middle-class aspirations while contextualizing, historicizing, and commemorating each individual's economic and professional accomplishments.[6]

Stephen Butterfield posits in his landmark text *Black Autobiography in America* that "the genre of autobiography lives in two worlds of history and literature, objective fact and subjective awareness."[7] Therefore, readers and critics often consider African American autobiography as sociological and historical as well as literary. Black feminist scholars such as Joanne M. Braxton, Frances Smith Foster, bell hooks, and Nellie McKay contextualize the particular role black women's autobiography plays in African American literature and history.[8] McKay maintains that "the narratives of black women present a more complicated dilemma than those of their male counterparts" because their lives, prescribed by gender as well as race and social station, encourage creative solutions to life choices.[9]

Although the genre provides a space for black women to assert themselves, bell hooks expresses the difficulty inherent in writing her life story and speaks of a need to "kill the self"—a notion far from what is considered the tradition of African American autobiography. Telling her past allows hooks to reconstruct her identity and "be rid of" a previous, tormented self, not to "forget the past but to break its hold."[10] To further distinguish black women's autobiography, Braxton suggests that unlike the impulse in traditional American autobiography to foreground the individual, the black female "autobiographer incorporates communal values into the performance of the autobiographical act, sometimes rising to function as the point of consciousness of her people."[11]

Autobiographies by members of an oppressed community also reveal how those outside of the dominant culture experience its changing ideals, cultural values, and sexual mores. In *Voice Lessons,* Nancy Mairs suggests that autobiographers operate both as individuals and representatives of their particular community: "I want my 'life,' in reporting the details of my own life, to recount, at the level beneath the details, the lives of others."[12] Yet the responsibility of representing all African American women presents quite an imposition and plays into notions of a monolithic black experience. To expect an autobiography to illuminate the lives of the entire black female community obscures particularities and challenges among the different geographic regions, time periods, and socioeconomic classes. Although it is true that black female autobiographers speak as members of a community, Cary's and Nelson's work expands the parameters of African American autobiography with the particular and distinctive experiences of black middle-class women and by revealing intimate sexual matters. Because Cary and Nelson render their sexual experiences in different ways, the autobiographies disrupt conventional notions and monolithic visions of black middle-class womanhood.

Examining the lives of black middle-class women in isolation may reinforce the marginalization of working-class black women, but Carolyn Heilbrun rightfully argues against the inclination to ignore the problems and issues plaguing "privileged" women. In her examination of the trends in the autobiographical writing of upper-class women in England and America in the early twentieth century, Heilbrun shows that "voicelessness and oppression are linked among the privileged as well as among those oppressed by race and class."[13] Similarly, narratives by black middle-class women present many of the sexual experiences and obstacles that define, shape, and circumscribe the development of young black women in general. African American middle-class autobiography, for example, reveals that many issues considered specific to working-class black women not only transcend the barrier of class but are also amplified because of a woman's social and economic standing. If one of the aims of authors is to bear witness, then Cary and Nelson do so to the lives of black middle-class women.

The autobiographies present two distinct renderings of sexual development as they navigate what they perceive to be the expectations of the dominant culture and the black community and their families. In *Volunteer Slavery*, Nelson's sexual conquests help her avoid the constraints of black middle-class life; in *Black Ice*, Cary carefully renders her sexuality in order to be a part of the middle class. Neither considers herself to be the hopeless, tragic, black middle-class woman such as the one depicted in P. J. Gibson's *Long Time since Yesterday* or the lonely, frustrated figures in black romantic comedies, but they do understand that they must navigate the shoals of race, class, and sexuality. Much like Hill, both Cary and Nelson are victims of inappropriate sexual discourse, but they suffer that harassment in relative obscurity. Even in private battles, their narratives suggest that black middle-class women are acutely aware of the significant role they play in the maintaining and upholding a positive public perception of African American sexuality. They also recognize that their strategies for dealing with inappropriate sexual behavior or language reveal self-consciousness about the precarious position they occupy in African American culture.

Cary's and Nelson's books illuminate other unsettling similarities between contemporary black middle-class autobiography and slave narratives. Nelson's postmodern satirical title makes ironic reference to the Peculiar Institution and places her autobiography directly in relation to slave narratives. As Frances Smith Foster explains, slave narratives revealed the horrendous circumstances black women endured, and the genre aided in slavery's abolition by detailing sexual abuses and violations experienced by the formerly enslaved woman.[14] The dictates of the era and the delicate procedure of revealing harsh treatment often called on writers to conceal descriptions of actual sexual assaults. Contending with sexual exploitation and racial stereotypes remain prominent themes for black female autobiographers. The act of writing about their sexual experiences, however, has freed black women writers then and now from the silence imposed around sexual matters, especially among women in the middle class. The desire to find emancipation from narrow expectations is evident in Cary's and Nelson's autobiographies; they narrate their most significant sexual experiences and share how they came to understand their sexual identities. Unlike slave narratives, contemporary black middle-class autobiography can describe the writer's actual sexual experiences more openly. Yet these texts illustrate how concerns about recalcitrant sexual stereotypes and shame about sexual violations continue to plague black women despite their determination to portray themselves as having intelligence, pride, and sexual agency.

Nelson and Cary work in a genre more self-revealing than feature film or theater so they must determine how to represent their sexual choices, experiences, and desires. Unlike Hill's memoir, they do not obscure sexual matters but represent their lives and intervene in larger debates about the role of sexuality in feminism, class, and race. Mary Burgher remarks, "If any form of literature is capable of aiding in the Black woman's attempts to correct the record, it is autobiography, for nowhere does one find literature as a celebration of life more than here."[15] *Black Ice* and *Volunteer Slavery* demonstrate that black middle-class women are discovering ways to complicate their sexual representation despite racism, sexism, and internalized stereotypes.

Both autobiographies depict the experiences of young black women coming of age during the 1960s in the northeastern United States. Cary recounts a traditional tale of ascension, whereas Nelson explodes the success narrative by exposing the cost that career and family exact. Each book, however, is in dialog with the trend of heterosexual women reclaiming sexuality as a salient component of feminism. Considerations of race and class further complicate the difficult sexual development for a young woman in American culture. These stories disrupt expectations about black middle-class subjectivity by discussing how the authors negotiated sexual development, sexual identity, and sexual expression.

Much like the variety of characters in *Long Time since Yesterday*, the autobiographies demonstrate vastly different ways of representing black middle-class sexuality.[16] Cary demonstrates how understanding her sexuality helped her appreciate the responsibility that came with a changing class position, and Nelson uses sexual bravado and experimentation to undermine moralistic expectations. Both distance themselves from the chaste black middle-class femininity that Anita Hill exemplified, and their self-conscience narratives reveal how African American women forge sexual identities in relation to the world's appraisal.[17]

Looking through Black Ice

Black Ice, a 1992 American Library Association Notable Book, recounts novelist Lorene Cary's youth in suburban Philadelphia during the 1970s and her experiences at a New England boarding school, first as a student, than as a teacher, and finally as a trustee. Cary, bright and ambitious, entered New Hampshire's prestigious St. Paul's School—an institution attended by such figures as newspaper publisher William Randolph Hearst and U.S. Senator John Kerry—and found that boarding school created major alterations in her life. Cary's determination, along with her parents' influence, helps foster a strong sense of racial and gender identity that allows negotiating a new class status. What makes her autobiography so compelling is how the narrative ties Cary's sexual awakening to her class mobility, thereby linking class ascension to sexual awareness. Cary even uses sexual terms to describe being recruited to St. Paul's by an older African American student: "It had been just that confidence that had seduced me, the poise that passed my understanding and made me think that if I were where he'd come from, I, too, would emerge young, gifted, and black for all to admire" (45). The language of seduction links class ascension with sexuality. Leaving the safe harbor of her parents' home, which she considered middle class until being exposed to those of more privilege, for prep school means entering an environment in which she is unsure of her value. Being nervous about her place among the elite makes Cary hypervigilant about her sexual conduct; any missteps may mark her as an out-of-place black girl.

Despite being third-generation black middle class, Cary recognizes that most consider her boarding-school experience as outside the African American cultural norm. Her grandparents "belonged to clubs whose members were the old, genteel black Philadelphia" (33), and her parents, a teacher and a homemaker, are "part of the generation who profited from opportunities for educational and economic advancement due to progressive New Deal programs."[18] Cary depicts the black middle class at a time when affirmative action altered many lives.[19] Although a beneficiary of federal and local policies that resulted from political agitation for greater educational and occupational equality, those benefits had troubling psychological consequences for Cary and others who entered the black middle and upper-middle class. Her empathy with less-privileged African Americans contests the assumption that middle-class blacks focus only on their own interests.[20]

Cary enjoys her new opportunities and expanding privileges but recognizes the parameters of life as a black girl. Changing class position makes her increasingly ambivalent about the nature of privilege: "What did these white people say in a hundred ways but that we were somehow different from the common run of black people out there in America? What did they say but that we were special, picked out for a special destiny? I was ashamed even to consider the possibility, but it was hard not to believe it sometimes" (78). It is difficult for her to feel she deserves good fortune, and she recognizes the insidious paternalism that accompanies it. She also feels shame for occasionally embracing the notion of "specialness" because of her ability to take advantage of an educational opportunity and endures recurring "survivor's guilt" while navigating the demands of her new sexual universe.

Cary seems to suffer from what Patricia Williams identifies as the enduring racial and class guilt that permeates much of black middle-class life:

> The black middle class is filled with the histories of remarkable "strivers" whose fortunes have always very directly relied upon the sacrifices of those not-so-middle-class kin and friends as well as upon the affirmative disposition and action of powerful institutions to make real opportunity available. ... The awareness of connection is perhaps one of the saddest social losses of the current climate of relentless exceptionalism, in which the black middle class is understood, and not infrequently understands itself, as a fragmented band of "escapees," refugees rather than relatives of those whose struggle for survival is barely seen until it is taken to the streets.[21]

Williams confirms that the angst, guilt, and isolation Cary experiences powerfully shape the psyche of the black middle class.

Enrolling in boarding school sets Cary apart from her middle-class community and family. Frustrated, she ponders, "I was leaving behind girls who were intelligent and loving and strong. They were my best friends. How was it that I should have this opportunity and they should not?" (35). She refuses to assume that she has the opportunity to attend St. Paul's because she is special or superior to other blacks. Although she realizes the nearly arbitrary nature of her good fortune, Cary understands the expectations that accompany her new life. Much like what Dwight McBride, Mary Pattillo-McCoy, and Melvin Oliver and Thomas Shapiro articulate in their work, middle-class African Americans recognize the precariousness of their position within the middle class because they rarely inherit transformative assets and often share resources with an extended family of predominantly working-class or poor relatives.[22] Transformative assets allow the beneficiary to profit from "unearned, inherited wealth" that has the capacity "to lift a family economically and socially beyond where their own achievements, jobs, and earnings would place them."[23] Instead of money or real property, Cary's transformative asset is the knowledge her mother passes down about the importance of a black woman's sexual conduct.

Black Ice presents Cary's nascent sexuality as an impediment to her new social status. The responsibility of being one of the first blacks at St. Paul's influences her sexual development and decisions. Realizing the stigma associated with the black poor and working class, she tries to avoid being stereotyped as oversexed. From her mother, she learns that a black woman's sexual conduct legitimates her place in the middle class. "Protect yourself," her mother admonishes, reminding her, "I haven't talked to you about how to protect yourself, because you're smart enough to figure that out. You'll do better off staying just as you are. Intact, do you hear me? You're going up there for an education, not for any of that other stuff" (40).

Aware of the "stuff" her mother wants her to avoid, Cary recounts the story of an assault on a neighbor who failed to protect herself from the dangers awaiting young girls. Her burgeoning self-esteem, Cary assumes, will safeguard her from such disastrous consequences. She recognizes that she has too much to lose. Her mother's advice establishes her middle-class family's expectations and exemplifies the pressures Cary feels while isolated from other African Americans at boarding school. Knowing that her sexual and reproductive choices will largely dictate her life chances helps her make decisions based more on professional ambition than transitory desires.

Cary ensures her place in the black middle class not only by competing successfully for top academic honors but also because she abides by the strict sexual code her mother has imparted: no casual sex, no out-of-wedlock pregnancies, and no multiple sexual partners. Unfortunately, however, her first sexual encounter is a life-defining incident, although whether it is consensual or an incidence of date rape is unclear. In either case she is deeply troubled by the experience. Cary's first boyfriend, Ricky, visits her at boarding school, and they spend the night together in her room. Despite his reassurances that he will honor her choices, she is awakened by his body on hers. "Then I knew what was happening, and I strained to see his face. This facelessness was too awful with the pushing and pushing in the dark. Suddenly, I didn't like his smell. I searched in my mind for a word, as if a word would save me from this stupidity, the dull, dark, stupid feeling... I didn't want it like this. I didn't want it. I hated myself" (108). The lack of clarity in this passage—Is she permitting intercourse or being forced?—allows Cary to continue to maintain the stance of a proper middle-class teen. Her anger and self-hatred arise in part from her sense of responsibility. She recognizes that as one of the few blacks in a privileged environment she should act appropriately. An overwhelming feeling of "stupidity" resonates because it represents the very thing against which a bright black middle-class girl is measured: an uneducated, promiscuous black girl.

After her first sexual encounter with Ricky, who has a child from a previous relationship, Cary is panicked that she may become pregnant and imagines devastating consequences for her individual future and her community if that is the case. "And what was I? I thought, trying, but unable to keep from thinking it. What would I be next month if I turned up pregnant? I imagined myself big-bellied and barefoot, teeny-weeny little pickaninny braids sticking off my head, walking around the green lawns of a New England college somewhere asking: 'Y'all seen mah Ricky anywheres? I's lookin' all over for mah man, me an' de little one what's a comin'" (111). Cary's sense of herself as a black middle-class girl is contingent on her sexual choices, so she is painfully aware that she can instantly lose her new class privilege and squander the main transformative asset her family has provided. She finds it impossible to imagine being an unwed mother and a college student and pictures instead her middle-class identity destroyed by an unwanted child. Instead of entering college as a young, innocent freshman struggling to assimilate, Cary envisions herself as lost and abandoned, an ignorant black pickanniny. No longer the brilliant young lady with a bright future, she morphs into the dehumanizing stereotype of a pickanniny, not altogether unlike Gorilla in Judith Alexa Jackson's play *WOMBmanWARS*.

In both instances, the black middle-class woman's identity disintegrates into a figure more intelligible to others. As a pickanniny, Cary's imagined unkempt hair, bare feet, use of the vernacular, and protruding belly signify not just an unwelcome pregnancy but racial and gender stereotypes about black female promiscuity as well. It is striking that she accompanies her physical deformation with a loss of language. As a hypervisible St. Paul's student, she understands that this sexual misstep may not only cost her a place in the black middle class but may also mar her mind and body. Giving birth to a child out of wedlock also contradicts Cary's self-perception about being different from less-fortunate girls.[24]

Immediately after the unprotected sexual encounter with Ricky, Cary considers the incident as a public spectacle that evokes racial and class stereotypes. While trying to compose herself she confesses, "In the mirror I looked, as my mother would have said, like the wild woman of Borneo. I dared not think what else she would have said. My hair had shot up on the back of my head like turkey tail feathers, and my eyes were swollen and red. Sex goddess! I taunted myself and then replaced my flannel nightgown as if to shield me from further damage" (109). Envisioning herself as wild and animalistic increases her fears of turning into a stereotypical exotic, primitive, hypersexual black female. By admonishing herself as a "sex goddess," she accepts the blame and shame for her situation.

Cary dramatizes how black middle-class women become aware of their visibility in the social, political, and sexual landscape. Her revelations indicate that she perceives sex as an activity limited by her race, class, and gender. Although it was an era of sexual experimentation among many young people, Cary realizes that her sexual choices resonate for her entire community and perhaps other African American girls will bear the burden of her mistakes and lose the opportunity to attend St. Paul's.

Black Ice illustrates how middle-class African American women lack the opportunity to discuss their common struggle in the contemporary sexual universe across class lines and social boundaries. Sexual vulnerability foregrounds Cary's racial vulnerability and erases the distance boarding school creates between herself and other black teens. Cary and the young girl who gave birth to Ricky's child are both victims of a patriarchal double standard that taints sexually active girls. As Cary's life in boarding school comes to a close she remains acutely aware of her relative privilege compared with the mother of Ricky's child: "All I could think about was that somewhere in his neighborhood . . . a young woman was buying diapers while we planned smugly for medical school. Somewhere in the park where he wanted to kiss and I let him, because there seemed no way not to, a girl my age would be rolling a stroller while I was filling out my applications to a careful selection of Ivies" (163).

Once again Cary experiences guilt about her privilege, but she also understands that privilege is relative. She and the teenage mother have no way to communicate about similar experiences or different options and opportunities. While Cary proceeds to the next phase of her life, a college student who has more sexual knowledge, the young single mother carries the social stigma of being a sexually active teenager. As a middle-class girl who has luckily avoided pregnancy, Cary lays down another layer of residual guilt for her survival—this time as a sexual victim instead of strictly a racial one. She feels a clear link to the nameless unwed mother but has no public connection to the girl Ricky calls a "slut." Cary acknowledges that her life would have been different, or perceived differently, had she become pregnant. She and her family would probably have arranged for a quiet termination so her hope of becoming a physician would not have been lost; the mother of Ricky's child, it is assumed, had little chance at a productive future.

Another moment that shows how class identity shapes Cary's sexual development occurs one summer when she works as a waitress and one of the restaurant's cooks, an African American, sexually harasses her. When she rejects his advances he is insulted and accuses her of believing she's "too good" for him. Cary realizes that her class position gives her more options with which to negotiate the sexual terrain. Unlike her behavior with Ricky, she does not become a victim. Instead, she reports the cook for locking her in the freezer and accosting her, and their boss takes Cary's side because he considers her a respectable young lady. The politics of respectability work to her advantage just as they did for Mike Tyson's victim, Desiree Washington. Cary's education provides a certain clout and credibility with those in authority. She never feels responsible for the harassment, nor does she regret taking action against the cook. Althoughs she reacts to Ricky's transgression by hating herself, in this later instance she focuses her feelings outward. She emerges from the ordeal with the language and courage to defend her body and assert herself.

The altercation with the cook marks a turning point in Cary's autobiography that leads her to explore black life outside of her middle-class community and the universe of the boarding school. She matures into a self-assured young woman. Her maturity is evident in the decision to terminate her unsatisfying relationship with Ricky and begin dating the restaurant's other cook, Booker, a young black man from outside her social and educational circle. "My mother," Cary admits, "understood more quickly than I that I wanted a date, a normal, local, friendly, working-class date" (165).

Although her initial experience with a working-class man teaches her about a side of black life about which she never knew, she describes their one date fondly but without romanticizing working-class African Americans. While the limited experience with Booker never completely overshadows her harrowing experience with the cook who assaulted her, it does counter her experiences with Ricky. Although Ricky attends prep school, he treats her like an object. Moreover, Cary admits that their relationship "lived like a haunt in my soul" and that the lesson she learned from dating him was to "trust no man" (185). Even as she matures sex is a dangerous element that must be contained and controlled to ensure success.

Although she dates another student at St. Paul's until graduation, Cary never discusses whether she engaged sexually with anyone else, including that student. This foregrounds her interactions with Ricky and the two cooks but leaves unclear whether she remained celibate for the rest of her time in prep school.

The final chapter details Cary's reunion with prep school classmates. Even when recounting her adult memories, she never discloses more details about her intimate life. She reveals that she had a daughter with her second husband, a white man, but says nothing about her first marriage. The reader is left to decide whether her interracial marriage resulted from her difficult experiences with African American men. Even when she relives old memories with her boyfriend from St. Paul's the account fails to evoke a discussion about intimacy.

Cary ends the autobiography by explaining that she now better understands her choices. She embraces the changes that attending St. Paul's school brought and maintains that boarding-school experiences shaped a new identity that she hopes gives the "image of wholeness" (23). Although she finds that her black middle-class upbringing in Philadelphia actually prepared her well for some aspects of New England education, she explains that "I did not want to be trapped in one world. I wanted to be black, to be part of our group, to draw nourishment from it and give back, and yet I wanted to be free to come and go" (150). She appreciates the freedom to occupy several communities that her class position affords.

The lack of joyful sexual experiences in the narrative, however, raises questions about the anxiety created when class identity is linked to sexual behavior. Cary illustrates how she maintained self-respect, but the autobiography never celebrates the pleasures of sexual experimentation or the sexual liberation of the 1970s, probably because of her overwhelming concern to make use of her transformative assets. Even though she is no longer a vulnerable young black female in a world of privilege, Cary ends the book with a silence about sexual matters. The elisions suggest that the complexities of middle-class identity still silence discussions about the pleasures of female sexuality. The narrative demonstrates the difficulty, particularly for middle-class black girls, of exercising sexual agency, especially as they comprehend their role as keepers of a racial and class legacy.

Like the front produced by Anita Hill's stoic performance, conservative garb, and self-serving description of romantic relationships, Cary presents the proper middle-class face to readers. *Black Ice* is a conventional middle-class autobiography that seeks to write the middle class into the larger African American literary tradition, whereas Jill Nelson's *Volunteer Slavery* upends that tradition through a rendering of black female sexuality.

Sexual Liberation and Volunteer Slavery

Set alternately in several major metropolitan cities and on Martha's Vineyard, Nelson's autobiography provides a provocative contrast to Cary's relatively subdued narrative. The title, *Volunteer Slavery*, reveals Nelson's ironic view of black middle-class life and willingness to toy with sacred topics in African American culture. By comparing the hustle for success with chattel slavery she subverts noble stories of black upward mobility that are predominant in African American autobiography. Her journey toward an "authentic" self includes, with raucous disregard of black middle-class ideas and ideals, various sexual exploits. The autobiography contradicts the normalizing or protective impulse. Instead, with brash revelations about intimate encounters and constant questioning of middle-class goals, *Volunteer Slavery* breaks entirely with the black middle-class moral standards that *Black Ice* upholds.

The Noble Press's jacket for the book advertises Nelson's best-selling autobiography as an account that "names names and takes no prisoners."[25] She focuses on the late 1980s, when she shifts from working as a freelance journalist who concentrates on social issues to being the only black female staff writer on the *Washington Post*'s inaugural Sunday magazine. While she primarily documents the frustrations of navigating the *Post*'s conservative culture and Washington's social and racial politics, she also revisits critical moments from her childhood in New York. Nelson uses each episode to justify her ambivalence toward black middle-class ideals, especially those concerning sexuality and success.

As was true of *Black Ice*, *Volunteer Slavery* sets out to reform notions of authentic blackness, but Nelson ultimately refines blackness on different terrain by expanding notions of authentic blackness and middle-class identity. She uses her aggressive sexuality to redefine expectations of middle-class black women. In her world, respectability comes from political convictions, not sexual choices. Her radical politics and ease with black culture shatters the stereotype of middle-class African Americans as inauthentic, self-interested people who feel awkward and uncomfortable among less-affluent blacks.

Nelson alludes to the social construction of race throughout her autobiography by self-consciously questioning whether an event "is an authentic Negro experience." The tone of the book points to the artificiality of racial identity and ridicules America's refusal to acknowledge the experiences of the black middle class as being "real." As Nelson explains in frustration, "As always, I was looking for the authentic Negro experience, which of course my own wasn't, since being bourgeois somehow negated being black."[26] Instead of proudly recounting successes, Nelson constantly scrutinizes professional encounters in order to unearth the racial misconceptions beneath the surface. She also spends a great deal of time claiming her right to black culture and history.

Instead of apologizing for her class status, Nelson establishes a rightful claim to black culture as a black middle-class subject. She begins the narrative by asserting, "Papa wasn't a rolling stone, he was a dentist, Mommy was a businesswoman and librarian, we were solidly upper-middle-class. Besides, I remind myself, this is the 1980s. The day of the glorification of the stereotypical poor, pathological Negro is over. Just like the South, it is time for the black bourgeoisie to rise again, I am a foot soldier in that army" (5). Written during a period when both popular culture and academic discourse contended that the African American community was in crisis, Nelson's autobiography is in dialog with several topics articulated by social critics of the time. In the late 1980s America witnessed a resurgence of the idea, first put forth in the U.S. Department of Labor report *The Negro Family: The Case for National Action* (1965), that the black family's instability is caused by an aberrant black matriarchy.[27] Many argued that solving the black community's problems meant paying increased attention to the plight of African American males.[28] It was also, however, a time of black middle-class expansion. The backlash against feminism and increased sentiment against affirmative action led to a belief that successful black women were one of the main reasons for the difficulties black men faced.

The lack of available male partners for black middle-class women became yet another topic that arose in response to the hysteria about black male "endangerment." The burgeoning black middle class increased the discouraging drop in marriage rates and further complicated the highly charged issue.[29] As Robert Staples and Leanor Boulin Johnson assert, "Black women who have graduated from college are the least likely to have married. Among those who do marry, especially those who have five or more years of college, their divorce rate is higher and their remarriage rate is lower than for Black women with less education."[30] Much like the scrutiny of underclass black women, single middle-class black women became increasingly analyzed and visible because of their difficulty in finding husbands.[31]

A divorcee and single mother who enjoys casual sex, Nelson rejects invisibility and seeks to undermine middle-class sexual standards. Unlike Cary, who works to rid herself of behavior that could be construed as sexual or morally inappropriate, Nelson revels in breeching middle-class social etiquette. Her autobiography confounds the contradictory stereotypes of black female hypersexuality and middle-class propriety with vivid accounts of sexual experiences.

Nelson discusses divorce, addiction, and mental illness and presents herself as a black middle-class woman who unapologetically explores sexuality with little regard for what her behavior may signify to others. She epitomizes the single woman negotiating the social landscape after the sexual revolution. As Lynne Segal explains, "It was indeed, overwhelmingly heterosexual women who gained greater control over their sexuality, and more room for manoeuvre, from the sexual reforms of the 1960s."[32] Nelson describes how she took advantage of those changes, including more effective birth control and legal abortion.

Greater reproductive freedom and economic independence, however, makes black middle-class women a threat. They find themselves punished for professional success and ambition by being the African Americans least likely to marry. Single women threaten middle-class norms with their financial and sexual independence. Nelson, however, presents this independence as costly. As Carole Vance reminds us, "The juxtaposition of pleasure and danger has engaged the attention of feminist theorists and activists in both the nineteenth and twentieth centuries, just as it has been an ongoing subject in the lives of individual women who must weigh the pleasures of sexuality against its cost in their daily calculations, choices, and acts."[33] *Volunteer Slavery* demonstrates how Nelson weighs sexual choices and pays various costs as a black woman.

In their exploration of human sexuality in the United States, John D'Emilio and Estelle Freedman report that in the later twentieth century "the marketing of sex, new demographic patterns, and the movements of women and homosexuals for equality all fostered a substantial revision in attitudes and behavior."[34] Nelson, like Cary, runs up against lingering attitudes about black women as hypersexual. Sexual agency is not an uncontested right for them. Hazel Carby's analysis of African American migration during the late nineteenth and early twentieth century suggests that unless she is monitored or controlled, a black female is considered suspect and "degenerate." Moreover, "The unpoliced black female body is characterized or variously situated as a threat to the progress of the race; as a threat to the establishment of a respectable urban black middle class; as a threat to congenial black and white middle class relations; and as a threat to the formation of black masculinity in an urban environment."[35] Carby's theory also applies to the era Nelson discusses. Unattached heterosexual women with a modicum of financial independence who make sexual liaisons still find themselves without societal sanction. Nonetheless, Nelson seems to relish her role as a threatening figure. Her brazen experiences take on heightened resonance in light of black women's lower statistical chances for finding love, marriage, or sexual partnerships.

Nelson details her adamant refusal to take on the comfortable trappings of a "proper" middle-class existence, and avoiding marriage is central to her strategy. She disparages her parents' failed marriage and ridicules her own attempt at matrimony as further evidence of the fragility and impossibility of the American Dream: "Mostly I try to forget the Ex-Husband, to whom I was married for fifteen unhappy months in the early 1980s. Having broken most of the black bourgeois rules—having a daughter at twenty without benefit of marriage, making it through college and graduate school as a single parent, and then building a successful career—at thirty I temporarily regressed, deciding to go straight and have it all, and I married a plump, economically solvent wannabe" (149). Nelson dedicates only two paragraphs to her former husband's influence on her life. Indeed, it is his acceptable pedigree and financial stability that finally lead her to reject him. Middle-class black masculinity appears sterile and boring to Nelson, and she rarely mentions marriage in the rest of the autobiography. Finding a long-lasting, monogamous relationship is discussed neither as a priority nor an objective.

Nelson is also ambivalent about the narrowness of race and class identity. "I wanted to be a street sister by night," she confesses, "black princess by day" (5). Although she does not explain why she labels her former husband a "wannabe," the use of that pejorative term indicates her discomfort with traditional black middle-class identity. The autobiography argues that the black middle class is as genuine as any other segment of black life, but she falls into the same trap as those who view blacks in general as monolithic when she describes other middle-class people as "wannabes" or "sell-outs." If her decision to follow the accepted route by marrying is a mistake, she replicates it when she seeks to resolve her professional anxieties by accepting the *Washington Post* job.

Several moments in *Volunteer Slavery* prove that Nelson includes her ideas about sex for more than shock value. She undercuts the traditional demure style that characterizes the middle-class narrative and describes her thoughts after her going-away party, parading her sexuality like Tina Turner onstage: "On the real side, I was also looking for sex, which I have always had a tremendous ability to enjoy, regardless of the partner. Of course, it helped that the Mortician was a good lover, and fine. Whenever he did or said something stupid, I'd think about the pure ego feed it always was to look up into his handsome face when he fucked me. Then I'd seduce him again" (23).

Nelson's sense of sexual empowerment pervades the text. She flippantly describes conquests to explode the myth that daughters of the bourgeoisie do not enjoy sex and undercuts dire assumptions about the condition of middle-class women by discussing various sexual partners and boyfriends. The autobiography also disputes the belief that black middle-class women must value monogamy and marriage in order to reject societal stereotypes.

Nelson's book questions the notion of middle-class morality. She problematizes the dichotomy of good and bad behavior by relating an insult suffered at a National Association of Black Journalists (NABJ) annual meeting, an event described as "a mass psychotic episode, in which over a thousand African-Americans meet annually to purge our collective repressed rage and to affirm one another's visibility" (106). She revels in memories of past meetings and jokes about the sexually charged atmosphere. Then, suddenly, a disturbing conversation with a candidate for the association presidency ruins the convention:

> He gives me a look of exaggerated exhaustion. "Jill, if I had to lick the pussy of every woman in NABJ to get their vote, my tongue would be dry before I got halfway through," he says. And then he laughs. LAUGHS!
>
> Me, I just stand there, half-drunk from the sun, the rum, righteous indignation, not believing my ears. Wickham grins naughtily, like a little boy who's just told a dirty joke to his enamored parents. Before I can recover and rip his balls off with my bare hands, he spies other potential votes and moves away. (110)

Nelson responds with shock and "righteous indignation," and never takes responsibility for the incident despite her flirtatious manner or provocative discourse.

Subsequently, when several black female journalists believe his version of events she feels betrayed and garners other female support during the convention to lodge an informal complaint. When she and her colleagues confront the nominee, however, he explains that the nature of his relationship with Nelson allows for that type of verbal exchange. Nelson denies this, but the refutation reveals the social irony of sexually aggressive single black women. She finds herself a victim of the sexist double standard that women must negotiate.[36] Although her response lacks perspective and self-reflection, it can also be read as a refusal to accept communal norms. In addition, the incident demonstrates the difficulty of consistently maintaining a sense of sexual empowerment and rewriting the rules of black middle-class behavior and conduct.

Nelson's most significant romantic and sexual relationship shifts the autobiography's tone from flippant to reflective. Her relationship with a younger man, Michael, a personal trainer with whom she begins a long-distance affair, further expands the representation of black middle-class women's sexuality. Their relationship starts while she is working for the *Washington Post* and he is struggling to start a business in Harlem. In these chapters the reader glimpses the author's more contemplative side.

Nelson meditates on the sexual tension of a long-distance relationship and celebrates the "phone sex, held after the rates go down" (184). She describes the excitement of her newly found delayed gratification: "Hanging up the phone and snuggling under the covers feeling damp and throbbing, nipples tight and aching to be sucked, considering masturbation but deciding against it. I opt instead for the exquisite torture of caressing every part of him with my mind while my body represses itself" (184). Although she is still explicit about her sexual desires, their bond allows Nelson to address her difficulty with intimacy beyond sex. The relationship with Michael bridges the divided self that she experiences with other partners. She describes their first encounter as a "slow dance of sex" that feels different. Once naked with Michael, she realizes that "this time there is no ceiling Jill, no running commentary, no squeezed-shut eyes, after a time no words at all" (186). Because she feels secure, Nelson attempts to integrate all parts of herself in order to become whole. Her experience with Michael allows her to imagine a sexual relationship that does not require distancing physical being from spirit. Integrating her sexual and emotional selves helps her also understand her ambivalence about being part of the middle class.

The relationship allows Nelson to admit to enjoying a life of relative privilege, and she also realizes that exemption from some burdens makes her a target for others. She complains that many blacks she encounters treat her differently because she is middle class. For most of the narrative she describes her class position as a barrier to forging friendships with blacks outside her social group. In rebellion, she expresses "authentic blackness" through sexual activity.[37] The relationship with Michael, however, disrupts that pattern, and Nelson begins to assess her new lover's intentions:

> My various traps do not seem so inescapable with Michael because he is so young, smart, unformed, and free.... He is not the ideal bourgie professional man who makes more money than I do, drives an expensive car, has a gold card, and is emotionally unavailable just as I am not the trophy girlfriend/wife. ... Michael loves me without artifice. Not because I am a latter-day Harriet Tubman, or a Vineyard girl, or have nice legs, "good" hair, a good job with white folks, one-fourth inheritance of a house in Oak Bluffs. Without all that, he still likes me. I begin to see that "all that" is weighing me down. (188)

She believes Michael is disinterested in her middle-class status and that his love is unconditional. The appraisal also implies that the elements of her life that represent her status impede her ability to find and accept love or bond with other blacks.

Although Michael ultimately fails as the ideal romantic partner, it is during the relative safety of this relationship that Nelson faces her drinking problem, dysfunctional family, and professional discontent. She feels secure enough to acknowledge her pain and confesses, "[W]hen I finally let go, I do very quietly, methodically, without screaming or yelling or stamping my feet. I flip out neatly" (227). Contending with the responsibilities of work, activism, and motherhood causes her to suffer a nervous breakdown. She depends on Michael's emotional support to nurse her back to health even though their relationship ends.

Insofar as Nelson's relationship with Michael does not lead to the altar it makes a significant statement about black men and women supporting each other. Curiously, after sharing many intimate sexual details of her life to this point, she fails to explain in any detail why this one good relationship ends. In the Epilogue, Nelson shares that her association with Michael still continues, thus foregrounding the fact that lasting friendships are as important to the survival of the African American community and black middle-class women as lasting marriages. She may not challenge all notions about black middle-class women and what they may desire, but Nelson's autobiography does represent one black single woman's content without a monogamous sexual partnership. Unlike Anita Hill, who as a proper black lady conceals the details of her love life except when she must discuss it in order to prove her accusations against Clarence Thomas, Nelson describes her sex life to establish her authentic black female self. Her notion of womanhood, like Laveer's in P. J. Gibson's *Long Time since Yesterday* and Mozelle's in Kasi Lemmons's *Eve's Bayou,* lays claim to her sexuality as part of herself, regardless of other people's understanding of black middle-class identity.

* * *

Nelson and Cary tell their stories of sexual development to an audience that includes black women who are also attempting to refashion a sense of self in light of a crippling discourse that disregards their humanity and denies their sexuality. These autobiographies show how class anxiety influenced expression of black female sexuality in the late twentieth century. Although their narratives illustrate what it means to be African American, female, and middle class, they do not construct a template for how to behave. Both Cary and Nelson seem acutely aware of the role of others' expectations in forming their identities and demonstrate how ideas about racial authenticity are linked to sexual conduct. Just as Lemmons and Gibson have grappled with the political and social ramifications of representing black female sexuality, Cary and Nelson suggest that black women must tell their stories in order to defy the popular discourse. It is important to set the record straight for the broader society and for each other as well. The autobiographies of black middle-class women not only link contemporary women to the past by helping to reconstruct a common history but also provide a map that may help others like them navigate the future.

As bell hooks divulges, the genre of autobiography intrigued her because she "wanted not to forget the past but to break its hold." Cary and Nelson undermine the power of their individual pasts through autobiography, which, hooks says, presents "a unique recounting of events not so much as they have happened but as we remember and invent them."[38]

Black Ice and *Volunteer Slavery* document the lives of black women who came of age after the era of civil rights. Their revelations about sex not only explain the tenor of the times but also indicate how notions of sexuality shore up dominant beliefs about black middle-class women. The sexual choices of Cary and Nelson came in response to notions of blackness, and many of the problems they encountered arose from negotiating sexuality. Both women describe encounters that involved a measure of sexual "abuse." Cary suffers manipulation by a trusted boyfriend, and Nelson struggles being misperceived by colleagues. Mary Burgher insightfully concludes that "the uniqueness of the autobiographical literature of Black women is its powerful and poignant portrayal of both the anguish and the joy of Black life in a largely white world, and its poignant portrayal of what it feels like, inside, to be a woman in such a world."[39] *Black Ice* and *Volunteer Slavery* contribute to African American autobiography by recounting the stories of two middle-class women who celebrate ambition and triumph without apology but also cast individual success in relation to the difficulties of negotiating expanding perceptions of race, class, and sexuality.

5

Sex, Travel, and the Single African American Girl
Andrea Lee's Sarah Phillips

In 1961 Hazel Scott, the glamorous expatriate jazz and classical pianist, published, "What Paris Means to Me," an essay lauding her life in France after leaving behind American bigotry. "I'm not going to say that France is paradise," the outspoken entertainer confided, "but I will say this: You can live anywhere if you've got the money to live. You can go anywhere if you've got the money to go and whomever you marry or date is your business."[1] Scott bemoaned segregation's tedious indignities that not only determined where one lived but also, more important, one's choice of lover.

While Scott's desire for autonomy from the social barriers imposed on African Americans led the musician to a 1950s Paris that promised cultural and racial freedom, Andrea Lee's first novel, *Sarah Phillips* (1984), presents a young black woman who travels to France during the 1970s to avoid the social dictates and expectations of the black middle class. Much like Lorene Cary's autobiography *Black Ice*, Lee's coming-of-age story challenges the assumption that the black middle class is racially inauthentic, and, like Jill Nelson's *Volunteer Slavery*, the novel fractures the particularly unflattering portrait of middle-class women in African American literature as frigid, romantically frustrated, or asexual.[2] *Sarah Phillips* destabilizes traditional notions of black middle-class identity with a heroine whose sexual and geographic explorations allow her to challenge the restrictions of class position, racial identity, and womanhood. The trope of travel allows Lee to critique conventional notions of race, tourism, and sexuality as she inserts an idiosyncratic middle-class heroine into the African American literary tradition.

In recent years African American women novelists have more frequently presented black female protagonists who focus on personal development and what Barbara Christian calls "the commitment to self-understanding," which allows them to explore how the "self is related to the world."[3] Christian also notes the tendency of black female writers to create characters who undermine racial and gender stereotypes and ensure a variety of black female sexual representations. Although Christian focuses on the ways lesbian themes diversify sexual expression, Sarah, in *Sarah Phillips,* is a heterosexual middle-class heroine who significantly shifts and challenges established sexual norms and class expectations.

Lee's work does not stand alone. Beginning in the 1990s, several novels have contributed to contemporary fictive representations of black middle-class heroines.[4] In "Roots of Privilege: New Black Fiction," a review of *Sarah Phillips,* Ntozake Shange's *Betsey Brown* (1985), and Gloria Naylor's *Linden Hills* (1985), Sherley Anne Williams acknowledges a developing body of fiction focused on black middle-class women. This is not a new phenomenon. During the Harlem Renaissance, many writers showcased the lives and dilemmas of the urban middle class, but the Harlem portraits were not necessarily flattering. As Williams explains, "By the mid-1930s, with the increasing emphasis on the lives of average, workaday blacks in literature, Afro-American writers more often treated the black bourgeoisie as the object of scorn, deriding them for intellectual superficiality and conspicuous consumption, as well as for their shame of the slave past, of the culture that spawned blues and jazz, and of physical features that linked them to Africa."[5]

The tendency by African American writers to reject the black middle class while celebrating the working class as authentically black continued well into the 1980s. Many African American novels depict a middle class without a significant connection to the broader African American community because of a commitment to "alien" values.[6] In addition, because middle-class women were and are considered the doyennes of black culture and decorum, they have been continually presented as particularly troubled. As others have argued, in African American literature the black middle-class woman resembles the tragic mulatto. Both are doomed to unhappiness and failure.[7]

If the mulatto figure is torn between blackness and whiteness, the middle-class character also lives at the intersection of two worlds—one defined by class, the other by race. Several celebrated contemporary writers—Marita Golden, Paule Marshall, Toni Morrison, Alice Walker, Gloria Naylor, and Ntozake Shange—have constructed troubling accounts of disenfranchised black middle-class women. Many of their female characters also suffer from warped sexual lives and have little or no expectation of romantic fulfillment.[8]

The novels of Morrison and Naylor, with sustained narratives about middle-class families and communities, provide the most consequential images of black middle-class women in contemporary literature.

In Morrison's *The Song of Solomon* the fate of middle-class black women is discouraging at best.[9] First Corinthians and Magdalene Dead cannot find husbands because of their family's prominence in the community and their own dispositions. Trapped by their class position, the sisters are destined to spend their lives alone. Even more disturbing is their deranged mother, Ruth, a "pale but complicated women given to deviousness and ultra-fine manners."[10] Her deviousness includes a ghoulish relationship with her father, inappropriate intimate contact with her son, and a sexless marriage with her husband. Although it is unclear whether Ruth is sexually deviant, it is obvious that she does have problems negotiating appropriate intimate boundaries. The women in *Song of Solomon* are classic tragic black middle-class heroines destined to live in hopeless isolation and sexual frustration.[11]

Likewise, Naylor's *Linden Hills* is a resounding critique of black middle-class shallowness and greed. Based loosely on Dante's *Inferno*, *Linden Hills* follows the disintegration of a black middle-class neighborhood led by Luther Nedeed, a mortician and landlord, who rules his wife, Willa, and his community with a stern hand. Naylor implies that the community becomes twisted when it repudiates traditional African American values of church, family, and community. The novel also deploys sexual perversion as a way to prove the deeply troubled nature of the black middle class.[12] After Willa conceives, she endures a sexless marriage, as generations of Nedeeds did before her. Naylor doggedly illustrates the price for middle-class success: professional and economic attainment destroys intimacy and perverts desire.[13] Morrison, Naylor, and other African American novelists of this era depict middle-class black women as even more tragic and troubled than the characters found in contemporary movies.

Despite this long-standing tradition, by the late twentieth century popular fiction writers began featuring middle-class black women whose fates were not necessarily tragic. Increasingly, authors such as Connie Briscoe, Bebe Moore Campbell, Benilde Little, Karin V. Siplin, Trisha R. Thomas, and Terry McMillan have depicted the middle class as a normal segment of black life. Even novels by Jill Nelson and Lorene Cary depict the experiences of middle-class African American women.[14] These novels more often than not chronicle the romantic and sexual lives of black female professionals.

The shift in sexual representation in African American literature has occurred very subtly because writers now depict the sexual experiences of black middle-class female characters in a matter-of-fact manner. The current trend toward presenting love, sex, and romance in popular fiction must assuredly derive from McMillan's phenomenal success with *Disappearing Acts* (1989), *Waiting to Exhale* (1992), and *How Stella Got Her Groove Back* (1996).[15] While McMillan's achievements may provide momentum for the genre, the notoriety of these books is also due to a growing middle-class African American reading audience who enjoy seeing their experiences reflected in literary form.

Thulani Davis speaks for some when she bemoans the fate of contemporary black literature, what she labels "Bup art," for its "self-involvement, a narrow focus on the struggling individual, and in some cases a narcissism downright unusual for African American literature," but some black feminist critics have begun revising their reading of the black middle class in African American literature.[16] For instance, Mary Helen Washington notes, "The image of the middle-class black woman as a coldly self-centered snob, chattering irrelevantly at bridge club and sorority meetings, was as much a mask as the grin on the face of Stepin' Fetchit."[17]

Washington and other black feminist critics such as Hazel Carby, Cheryl Wall, and Ann duCille acknowledge the sociopolitical enterprise of early writers, including Jessie Fauset, Pauline Hopkins, and Nella Larsen, whose representations were of black middle-class women struggling with issues such as passing and sexuality.[18] In *The Coupling Convention* duCille contends that early-twentieth-century black female novelists were successful at "problematizing female identity and sexuality, and critiquing both gender conventions and power relations." Further, duCille credits Fauset and Larsen as the first to "depict openly sensual black female subjects." Their characters, however, often faced devastating consequences because of sexual relationships.[19] Still, in the dominant literary and filmic depiction of black middle-class heroines, sexual pleasure and experimentation leads to physical punishment, social exile, or both.

In a reversal of that conventional theme, Lee's Sarah decides upon her own brand of social exile when she becomes an American expatriate who makes sexual experimentation a part of her travels. *Sarah Phillips* mimics a long-standing but narrowly examined aspect of African American literature, the travel narrative. Farah Jasmine Griffin, Cheryl J. Fish, Carole Boyce Davies, and others have advanced the analysis of African American travel literature by complicating the critical lens used to discuss black tourists, travelers, and migrants. In *Black Women, Writing and Identity,* Davies explains the challenges that travel poses for black women's narratives since "escape/flight/

movement is embedded in various ways" that are markedly different from those texts about African American men. Davies uses a theoretical apparatus that considers "a series of modalities—time, age, space, education, language ability, family, location and so on."[20] Griffin and Fish's anthology, *A Stranger in the Village,* has collected the writing of various blacks who have traveled and lived abroad. As they explain the various reasons African Americans give in to the impulse to leave "home," "African American mobility is often connected to the impulse for increased opportunities and the desire to find a home or homeland as well as for the purpose of pilgrimage, exile, and pleasure; thus, it is both unique and typical of the urge that many people have had throughout history in the quest for improvement and the claim for new dwelling places."[21]

Sarah exemplifies the theory that middle-class African Americans traveled after the civil rights era not because of racism but from the desire to find pleasure in escape and independence in the role of the exile. Traveling provides Sarah with many distractions and allows her to escape the narrow confines of her existence in Philadelphia. Lee explores the impulse to remake and redefine the black middle-class self by traveling across geographic and sexual boundaries. Travel to France affords her heroine access to sexual freedoms and pleasures that she cannot enjoy in the United States because of her parents' scrutiny and the stifling nature of conventional race relations.

The sexual experiences of African American travelers, especially women, have received little critical attention. Although Jessie Fauset, Hazel Scott, Juanita Harrison, and Gwendolyn Bennett have described their experiences as black women in Europe, these narratives rarely discuss sexual matters. *Sarah Phillips* is unique in illustrating the ways that travel allows a means to examine, question, and redraw sexual boundaries. Lee, an expatriate who resides in Italy, wrote her own travel narrative, *Russian Journal* (1979), which details the year she spent in that country while her husband completed doctoral work. Although he is white, *Russian Journal* barely mentions race. Lee spends most of the book describing daily life under communism and very little time discussing her experiences as an African American in an interracial marriage in the Soviet Union. *Interesting Women* (2002), her collection of short stories, features both white and black women who live in Europe and grapple with love, sensuality, and sexuality. Similarly, *Lost Hearts in Italy* (2006) depicts the demise of the marriage between Mira Ward, a Harvard-educated African American travel writer, and her WASP husband. Similar to Sarah, Mira is from "a clan of teachers and lawyers rooted in Philadelphia for generations, set in their ways and their neighborhoods as only middle-class mulattos can be" who leaves the States because she refuses to embrace traditional notions of black middle-class decorum.[22]

Beyond the Black Lady

Like *Black Ice* and *Eve's Bayou*, *Sarah Phillips* challenges the rendering of middle-class women as tragic, inauthentic, and sexually repressed members of the African American community. Lee repositions them as humans who are neither perfect nor inherently flawed. Her novel focuses on a woman struggling to discover what Lynne Segal calls "liberated sex" and new notions of romantic love.[23] Instead of asserting sexual agency solely in response to gender oppression, Sarah pursues sexual relationships as a means of challenging the confines of race and class. Much like Jill Nelson's behavior in *Volunteer Slavery*, her sexual activities outside the sanction of marriage or a monogamous relationship disrupt traditional notions of acceptable behavior.

Set in the late 1960s and early 1970s, during the movements for sexual liberation, feminism, and civil rights, Lee's novella (first published as a series of short stories in *The New Yorker*) traces Sarah's life through a series of locations that mark her development. She grows up in the Philadelphia suburbs; attends prep school, summer camp, and college in New England; and then travels in Western Europe. Sarah's spatial movement counterbalances the social movements that destabilize the world. As Valerie Smith explains in the foreword to the 1993 reprint, this unique historical moment during Sarah's adolescence "problematizes the meanings of resistance and accommodation in the post-integration era."[24]

While trying to grasp this new terrain she must also negotiate her parents' overbearing racial and class legacy. Sarah's father, a minister who is a proponent of civil rights, and her socially proper mother, hope their children will inherit their racial politics and conduct themselves in ways that reflect their middle-class background. Sarah's parents are an important part of the novel. Much like the training Lorene Cary receives at home, Sarah learns about black middle-class womanhood from her mother:

> My mother, Grace Renfrew Phillips, had been brought up with all the fussy airs and graces of middle-class colored girls born around the time of World War I. There was about her an endearing air of a provincial maiden striving for sophistication, a sweet affectation of culture that reminded me, when I was older, of Emma Bovary. She and her cluster of pretty, light-skinned sisters grew up in a red-brick house with marble steps in South Philadelphia. They all

played the piano, knew a bit of French and yards of Wordsworth, and expected to become social workers, elementary school teachers, or simply good wives to suitable young men from their own background—sober young doctors, clergymen, and postal administrators, not too dark of complexion.[25]

Sarah becomes aware of the rules, unspoken and spoken, of black middle-class decorum, including sexual restraint, by observing her mother, who—initially—seems possessed of the restrained sexuality of a proper middle-class woman. Several times Sarah observes the loose breasts of other women she encounters and compares them to her mother's "well-contained bosoms" (43).

Lee complicates notions, however, because her characterization of Sarah's mother allows for slippage and inconsistencies. Mrs. Phillips is described as someone with a "lasting attraction to the bizarre side of life," and "beneath a sometimes prudish exterior, she quivered with excitement in the same way her children did over newspaper accounts of trunk murders, foreign earthquakes, Siamese twins, Mafia graves in the New Jersey pine barrens" (32). As a young girl Mrs. Phillips even belonged to political organizations that "dismayed her family." Her odd fascinations disturb the idea of a black middle-class woman imprisoned by the boundaries of her role as a minister's wife and make her seem multifaceted as she tries to grapple with the changes in her community and family. In significant ways her fascinations with dark and dangerous things allow for the possibility of Sarah's rebellion.

The historical moment, with its change in racial politics and the advent of more birth control options, complicates Sarah's ability and desire to be a proper young woman in her mother's image. The relationship between the sexes is also altered, and Sarah, part of the first generation exploring the new landscape, makes sexual choices counter to the status quo. New racial boundaries as well as new codes of sexual behavior help define one of the social and ethical difficulties for the largest black middle class in American history. Sarah symbolizes a new black middle-class woman who recognizes herself as a pioneer confronting an altered racial universe. Her sexual choices challenge traditional notions. Moreover, the intersection of travel and sexuality allows for a new black middle-class figure who is ambivalent about African American history, culture, and politics. The chapters "Negatives" and "In France" delineate Sarah's experiences in college and in Europe and show how travel both destabilizes and reifies black middle-class identity.

At Harvard, Sarah champions the social milieu that expects her to have a lover of another race because doing so carries panache. She admits that "a few years earlier it might have been possible for me to find the necessary thrill simply by going out with white boys, the forbidden fruit of my mother's generation; but in the arty circles I frequented at Harvard, such pairings were just about required, if one was to cut any dash at all" (97). Sarah's desire to raise eyebrows among her social set through her choice of lovers also allows her to undercut her parents' hopes and expectations.

The Phillipses have failed to anticipate that success would place their children in a world they can neither approve nor comprehend. Both Sarah and her older brother, Matthew, break with social tradition by defying their parents and choosing white mates. Sarah confides that tension reigns whenever Matthew brings his Jewish girlfriend home from Swarthmore for weekends. During one such weekend he responds to his mother's visible intolerance with a poignant tirade: "'You are just incredible! You and Daddy spend all of your lives sending us to white schools and teaching us to live in a never-never land where people of all colors just get along swell, and then when the inevitable happens you start talking like a goddam Lester Maddox!'" (64). Lee points to one of the ironies of racial integration when she has Matthew call attention to the hypocrisy of his parent's vision of a future with racial equality that forbids interracial relationships.[26] Naively, Sarah's parents fail to anticipate that their children's privilege will make it almost inevitable that they will choose whites as friends and lovers.

Sarah, like Matthew, is uninterested in conventional romantic pairings. Her closest experience with an African American man underscores her ambivalence about being middle class. Unlike Nelson, who takes pride in her black middle-class roots, Sarah is less comfortable with her link to that community. Her romantic relationships reflect a rebelliousness rooted in fascination and fetishization of racial difference. Her exploration of racial others begins in the United States and continues during her year abroad. Although in college Sarah dates men of various racial and ethnic backgrounds, including a Chinese law student, a Norwegian graduate student, and various whites, Lee dedicates an entire chapter, "Negatives," to a relationship she decides not to pursue.

In rekindling the relationship with a family friend, Curry Daniels, Sarah is forced to confront her desire for a man from a similar racial and class background. She confides that a photograph of Curry kept her "awake and restless through a few starry May nights" in adolescence (87). When Sarah encounters him in college she is still enamored and admits to admiring his "abstruse intellectual manner" (91). They now spend their time together trading quips and avoiding their mutual attraction. Boredom one afternoon leads

Curry to want to photograph Sarah, and at his suggestion she poses nude. During the photo session Sarah feels clumsy. Although she admits that "the poses we tried were amusing or acrobatic rather than erotic: neither of us quite knew what to do with my naked body" (93). Although she poses as a subject, she feels more like an exposed, naked lover than an artistic nude. As an object of the black male gaze Sarah feels violated, awkward, and on display. The interaction speaks to their difficulty in confronting the black middle-class body. Recognizing their desire for each other embarrasses them, and they are driven by corporeality of the moment to acknowledge uneasiness with black middle-class sexuality and irrevocably redefine their attachment to one another.

While Sarah admits to feeling naked and exposed during the photo session itself, it is later, when she and Curry develop the photos, that her discomfort grows:

> In the red light his gold-rimmed glasses gleamed rosily, and his green plaid shirt looked black. The open neck of the shirt showed the tender-looking skin that stretched over his knobby collarbones, and for the first time since I had know him, with what was less a conscious thought than an impulse of my flesh, I was curious about how it would feel to touch his throat, his chest. At the same time I wondered briefly and coldly why Curry and I had never become lovers. The answer was fairly clear, as we stared at each other with eyes almost alike enough to be those of siblings, into faces that for *each of us symbolized the unbearably familiar things of life*. (93–94, emphasis added)

Although she imagines the possibility of them becoming lovers, Curry seems too vulnerable and far too familiar. It is at this moment that his body becomes visible to her. Sarah does not know what to do with his exposed flesh any more than he knows what to do with hers. For each, familiarity breeds contempt; it is not comforting, but "unbearable." Only difference arouses her desire because it offers a distance from insular black middle-class identity. Sarah confesses that she feels "strange irritation and grief" while in the darkroom with him. Her brief, cold consideration of Curry is similar to her ambivalence toward traditional black middle-class life.

This passage also emphasizes the consequences of Sarah's estrangement from African American culture. By not becoming sexually involved, Sarah and Curry forfeit the opportunity to redefine the black middle class. By repudiating their respective families' politics, heritage, and social ideals, they miss the opportunity for a fuller understanding of what it means to be a member of the African American middle class in the post–civil rights era. Unlike the generation of middle-class African Americans whom Trey Ellis describes in "The New Black Aesthetic" who celebrate exposure to and affinity for white and black cultural influences, Sarah is estranged from all her background represents. When she recognizes how Curry resembles her, "with his lean face that showed almost an evenly balanced mixture of black, white and Indian blood" (88), it is so disturbing that it obliterates all sexual attraction. Instead, both opt for white lovers, as does Sarah's brother. Their commonalties could shed light on the experiences unique to their generation, but they deny their attraction. Defeated by the familiarity of her mirror image, Sarah rejects Curry and a part of herself.

Yet Lee portrays Sarah as a girl too sophisticated for self-loathing. She seems mildly enchanted by the white women around her but maintains a playful appreciation of her own appearance. She describes herself as "tall and lanky and light-skinned, quite pretty in a nervous sort of way" (4). Sarah renders Curry's girlfriend in ambivalent language: "Phillipa was a blond from New York, undeniably beautiful, but a little faded and monotone in coloring, a fine-arts major with feminist ideas that she expressed with an incongruous wispy, little girl's voice" (90). Her disinterested, dismissive tone nonetheless reveals some appreciation. Sarah realizes her desirability compares unfavorably with that of the white females who dominate her world, and she confesses that while attending prep school she hoped to be "transformed by some magical agency into a Shetland-clad blonde with a cute blip of a nickname" (56). The fact that Curry chooses someone like Phillipa instead of Sarah has ramifications for the middle class.

The skirmishes between Sarah, Curry, and their parents signify the need to reestablish or reinvent black middle-class culture and politics for a changing, expanding, intricate society. Sarah explains to her mother that the combination of "a nice colored girl and a nice colored boy [is] . . . a little too boring" (90). Curry acknowledges that when he debates with his father, exploiting "long quotations from Marcuse and Che Guevara," he is displaying behavior that is "naughty and perverse" (89). They both accentuate the difference between their world of privilege, with its diverse influences, and their parents' more limited one. Without marriages between people like Curry and Sarah, the traditional black middle-class family cannot survive, and Lee provides no indication of what will replace it.

Their interracial liaisons, however, are not necessarily tragic. Although somewhat precocious, Curry's and Sarah's behavior, as well as that of their white lovers, derives from their position as a unique generation experiencing a sexual revolution concurrent with a movement for racial equality. In their rapidly evolving culture, old enemies are now lovers of choice. Sarah willingly questions traditions and race loyalty and does not replace them with uncomplicated alternatives. In doing so Lee refuses to romanticize an authentic African American past. Indeed, while in Europe Sarah rejects "the hermetic world of the old fashioned black bourgeoisie" as she forges sexual liaisons with white men exclusively (4).

The chapter "In France" reveals how Lee uses spatial movement to more fully address Sarah's sexuality. After her father's sudden death, she graduates and leaves the United States "to study French literature in Lausanne, intending never to come back" (4). Travel gives Sarah hope that she will finally free herself from what she considers the dictates and indignities of traditional black middle-class life. Going to Europe will allow her to live not necessarily as a white person but as someone free of the bonds of personal history and the burden of race. In his analysis of travel writing, Paul Fussell suggests that travel "triggers the thrill of escape" and that "the escape is also from the traveler's domestic identity, and among strangers a new sense of selfhood can be tried on, like a costume."[27] It is true that Sarah tries on a new persona, but the traveler Fussell describes is a white male of means. For a young middle-class black woman, exchanging identities presents more difficulty. A "new" self initially allows Sarah to ignore her racial and personal history, but over time her strategy collapses. The trip to France provides a brief escape from the United States, but once the thrill diminishes Sarah realizes the difficulties of escape for African American women.

The African diaspora was initially created out of forced travel to the West. Therefore, the notion of travel resonates in complicated ways for American blacks; Lee uses it as an ironic trope that symbolizes Sarah's search for identity. Often the treatment and representation of the other in traditional travel narratives is fraught with ethnocentrism and racist imaginings. Travel writing allows African Americans to juxtapose experiences outside the United States with lives at home and does not result in a simplistic recounting of positive and negative experiences. Instead, relating encounters abroad illustrates the complexities of "blackness" both nationally and internationally. Lee questions the possibility of black women remaking and redefining the self by crossing geographic and sexual boundaries.

Travel figures prominently in *Sarah Phillips* because Europe allows Sarah to explore "vague literary aspirations, and [a] lively appetite for white boys" without her parents' scrutiny and judgments (4). Just at the time when the black middle class begins what Griffin calls a "countermigration" to the southern United States for a return to a romanticized past or homeland, Sarah finds herself venturing to Europe. France's position in the African American imagination makes it an ideal location. For many disillusioned black Americans throughout the nineteenth and twentieth centuries France symbolized a certain freedom and acceptance that was lacking in the United States.[28] Several prominent authors moved to France, most notably James Baldwin, Jessie Fauset, Countee Cullen, and Richard Wright. The freedom they found is evident in expatriate Baldwin's remarks in "Equal in Paris" that he had to think of himself differently, as an "American" instead of as a "despised black man."[29]

At first, life in France supports how Sarah envisions herself outside the accepted categories allowed in America. She arrives at just the moment, however, when Europeans were beginning to regard Africans as a nuisance, so other racial tensions erupt in her life.[30] Here, Mary Pratt's formulation of a contact zone provides a useful framework. As Pratt defines it, a contact zone is "the spatial and temporal copresence of subjects previously separated by geographic and historical disjunctures, and whose trajectories now intersect."[31] While Pratt uses the term to discuss the "colonial frontier," *Sarah Phillips* inverts the frontier with a heroine who is from a marginalized racial category and trying to conquer, through sex, former colonists on their own terrain. Lee's inversion of this model speaks to the tradition of Western women traversing the sexual landscape of various former European colonies in Africa, Asia, and the Caribbean.[32]

Until recently, the role of black female travelers within sex tourism has been relatively unexplored, although Paulla Ebron discusses the complicated presence of African American women within sex tourism in Africa and the Caribbean nations. In "Traffic in Men," Ebron complicates the relationship of gender, race, and transnational travel through an examination of European women's stories about sexual interactions with native men in The Gambia by extending the study to include the experiences of black American female travelers. She concludes, "African American women in The Gambia are engaged in a search for African culture, a culture that will help them alter their own U.S. predicament... African American women's attempts to reach out to build a bridge of cultural knowledge in The Gambia are insistently and repetitively reinterpreted as promiscuity."[33] Ebron's project illustrates some of the problems African American women encounter when visiting Africa in search of their "imaginary" homeland. Unfortunately, along with expectations for a cultural homecoming the travelers bring the history of subjugated black female bodies, and, as Ebron explains, are read as sexually available, aggressive, and immoral in several African countries.

The representation of sex tourism for African American women in African American literature is most notable in Terry McMillan's popular novel *How Stella Got Her Groove Back* (1996). Both McMillan's and Lee's middle-class heroines expand their sexual experiences with foreign men. McMillan's text points to some of the assumptions of African American tourists in the Caribbean. The protagonist, Stella, travels to Jamaica to relax. Excited about the prospect of a single woman exploring the island alone, Stella's sister exclaims, "Way to go. Take plenty of condoms with you and get some from all those young Jamaican boys with big flapping dicks—do one a day if you can handle it, girl—and oooooh I wish I could go with you."[34] The comment echoes a typical stereotype about black male sexuality. Stella's sister considers the "native" Afro-Caribbean men as others. *How Stella Got Her Groove Back* implies that travel allows African American women to consider engaging in sexual activities that they hesitate to perform at home.[35] Travel to another country gives them a perception of anonymity accompanied by sexual freedom. With little examination of the economic imbalance that creates the atmosphere of sex tourism, Stella falls in love with a young Jamaican who fulfills both her romantic dreams and sexual fantasies. Sarah's adventures, however, do not allow for such a simple conclusion.

Sarah Phillips complicates the idea of sex tourism by crossing unconventional racial and class borders. The novel subverts the traditional travel narrative by recasting the expected roles in sex tourism. Although traditional travel narratives interpret the other from the viewpoint of the Western visitor confronting a new and dangerous landscape, Sarah travels to France, one of the centers of the Western world. Contemporary scholars argue that much of the discourse describing expeditions was framed in terms of sexual conquest.[36] Although colonial explorers uncovered the developing world's hidden, "dark," mysterious terrain, Sarah conquers Europeans. The novella undermines traditional ideas of nation and history by inserting a black woman in the place of the white male traveler and a white man in the place of the "native" woman of color.

In Europe, Sarah attempts to relinquish her specifically black middle-class identity in order to emerge as a nonspecific citizen of the world. Unlike many Africans who immigrate to Europe hoping to find work, she "loafed around the apartment or rambled through the Louvre" (7). France promises a life unfettered by history and America's over-determined notions of blackness. Although she considers herself black, she primarily identifies herself as others do, an "American girl." Relieved to be away from Philadelphia, she feels guilty about not writing home. She goes on to explain that while traveling she "kept a sharp lookout in London for certain types of tourists; prosperous black Americans, a little overdressed and a bit uneasy in hotel lobbies, who could instantly identify where I came from, and who might know my family" (8). She distances herself not only because she is worried that they might inform her family but also because she fears being like them. Sarah's desire to disassociate herself entirely from her old black middle-class life is overwhelming. She complains, "I had grown up in the hermetic world of the old-fashioned black bourgeoisie—a group largely unknown to other Americans, which has carried on with cautious pomp for years in eastern cities and suburbs . . . I found that my lifelong impulse to discard Philadelphia had turned into a loathing of everything that made up my past" (4). For Sarah, there is nothing more worthy of disdain than the pedestrian appetites and insecurities of the black middle class, and she wants to distance herself from its oppressive expectations and outdated mores.

Sarah's journey draws attention to the way class permits certain types of geographical mobility whereas race contains and defines travel. Moving to Europe allows her to reimagine her life, but the strategy collapses when racism erupts and reinforces the limits of racial and gender identity. Although she is an "American," the moments with the greatest significance arise when her national identity evaporates and she is seen as simply a black girl.

"In France" details Sarah's expatriate life in Europe. The relationship with her lover, Henri, begins with a presumption of equality because they are young, single, and educated. Sarah's desire for independence and assertion of agency is most evident in their relationship. Determined to remain independent, she does not allow Henri to purchase clothing for her; assuming the role of a true bohemian, she wears garments that are tattered. While Sarah's descriptions of college relationships are tame, her sexual exploits in France are detailed and more transgressive. Henri is her boyfriend, yet she insists on a measure of sexual freedom and sleeps with all her housemates, enjoying their attention. She compares herself to the heroine of Francois Truffaut's film *Jules and Jim* (1962) in which a young white woman sustains simultaneous affairs with a French and a German student. Unlike Anita Hill, who goes to great pains to sanitize her romantic relationships so she appears as unimpeachably middle class, Lee's character relishes a promiscuity that marks her as cosmopolitan and more sophisticated than what she considers the "old-fashioned black bourgeoisie" (4). Clearly interested in defying traditional black middle-class values, Sarah casually explains that she sometimes has sex with one flatmate while in bed next to the other.[37]

For a young black woman to find herself the lover of several European men recalls dominant myths of unrestrained black female sexuality. Because Sarah chooses this arrangement of her own accord, however, it suggests that she ignores troubling racial histories in order to relish her own sexual choices. The novel subverts sexual stereotypes by casting European men as foreigners who provide a sexual and emotional distraction for an African American woman of relative privilege. Sarah enjoys the attentions of white men as well as getting away from what she considers a claustrophobic existence at home.

Sarah's international travel magnifies the ways in which racially liminal bodies are always scripted as "public" and spectacular in that they are made into objects of desire through the gaze. Despite Sarah's privileged status as an American girl who selects lovers among European boys, she ultimately finds herself on display in France. Although she tries to distance herself from racial objectification in the United States, she nevertheless becomes an objectified other. Echoing the experiences of the Hottentot Venus (Sara Baartman) and Josephine Baker, Sarah displays herself for the pleasure of a European audience.[38] She confides that she and her housemates, when bored, "played a game called Galatea, in which I stood naked on a wooden box and turned slowly to have my body appraised and criticized" (6–7). Their game reveals her companions' difficulty with acknowledging her beauty. In Greek mythology Galatea is the standard of female perfection created by Pygmalion, a misogynist, to illustrate what other women lack.[39] To his surprise, he falls in love with his creation and is nearly destroyed by desire for her. The unimpeachable loveliness of Galatea, so integral to the myth, falls apart when applied to a black female figure. When Sarah's companions "create" a vision of her through their objectifying gaze, she is far from an ideal maiden. Ironically, although their appraisal is both punitive and appreciative, Sarah feels none of the self-consciousness or discomfort she experienced when posing for Curry.

Sarah's performance as Galatea also evokes the image of Baartman and Baker onstage. Sarah's objectified body becomes exploited by her flatmates' gawking, andobjectification translates into a more complicated set of exchanges. Basing their preferences on conventional heterosexual and racial politics that eroticize the other, the young men judge what is good about her body. "They told me I was beautiful and showed me off to their friends at cafés and discos and at the two Drugstores" (7) Sarah explains in another scene. Like Baartman and Baker, she entertains and amuses white men. All their bodies become fascinating icons of savage, pure, and exotic sexuality. Unlike Baker or Baartman, however, whose performances were part of stage acts for which they were paid, Sarah considers herself beyond the pettiness of race and in control of her image because class privilege allows her presence to be voluntary. Nonetheless, there is never a moment when the men find themselves on display. Her sexual antics lose their charm when she realizes the unsettling racial anxieties about black bodies that actually do exist abroad.

While Sarah briefly engages in liberal sexual play, the recognition of Europe's racial limitations prompts her to return to the United States: "Henri and I were in foul moods ourselves, mainly because the mutual fascination that had joined us suddenly and profoundly three months before had begun to break down into boredom and suspicion" (8). Her hope for racial transcendence collapses once her rejected racial identity resurfaces in interracial sexual encounters. Travel allows Sarah to dismiss her past only temporarily. The ugliness of racism inserts itself as the men's tone changes during one of the games. In a particularly scathing exchange, Sarah's lover insinuates that her clothes make her "look like a prostitute" (10). Taking his cue from Henri, Roger exclaims, "Sarah, ma vielle, you're certainly pretty enough, but why don't you put your hair up properly? Or cut if off? You have the look of a savage!" (10). Roger evokes the notion of the primitive black savage, much like the image of the wild women of Borneo that haunts Lorene Cary after her boyfriend assaults her. The young men continue to disparage Sarah's family by accusing her mother of being an Irishwoman who was "raped by a jazz musician as big and black as King Kong, with sexual equipment to match" (10–11). The comments made by her flatmates and her lover signal their own anxieties about racial purity and sexual fascinations and not only mark Sarah's body as a site of racial betrayal and contamination but also disclose how transatlantic racial and sexual stereotypes influence their perceptions.

Most critics call attention to Sarah's racial ambivalence but fail to mention how she fetishizes whiteness.[40] The novel does not cast Sarah as only a victim but rather illustrates that she is equally guilty of racial fetishism. The sexual liaisons are based as much on mutual curiosity as romance: "Throughout our short romance we remained incomprehensible to each other, each of us clutching a private exotic vision in the various beds where we made love.... He couldn't begin to imagine the America I came from, nor did I know, or even try to find out, what it was like to grow up in Lorraine, in a provincial city, where at school the other boys gang up on you, pull down your pants, and smear you with black shoe polish because you have no father" (5).

Sarah is uninterested in Henri's origins. Although he adopts many racist notions from the West, his personal history also influences his understandings of identity and marginalization. Henri's unknown parentage makes him a victim and literally a "marked" other. Because he does not know the identity of his father, Henri symbolizes blackness in his home village; the violations he suffers at the hands of other students put him on display. The blackness with which his schoolmates mark his body suggests that he fathoms the horrors of marginality far more accurately than Sarah. Her admission of holding to her own "private exotic vision" suggests that in her imagination Henri is also an other whose body she enjoys. Once Sarah acknowledges that her relationships with European lovers are based on mutual fetishization and objectification she finds herself reeling between the past and an uncertain future. Ambivalence only obscures, it cannot obliterate, her racial identity. Sarah's class privilege, which gives her the means to travel, makes her as myopic as McMillan's Stella.

Sarah's response to Henri's tale of miscegenation also reveals her naïveté. Although similarity thwarts her connection with Curry, difference prevents enjoying a successful relationship with Henri. Their disparate racial, national, and class histories frustrate any desire to realign sexual and racial boundaries, even in a new age of possibilities. She is unable to articulate her feelings about their insults but concedes that she must return home and confront her past.

Structurally, the circular narrative of *Sarah Phillips*, which begins with Sarah's present in France and then transitions to her childhood in Philadelphia and her college years in Cambridge, forces an open reading of the text. The return to America remains uncharted and unscripted. Sarah resigns herself to returning when, after a devastating fight with Henri, she realizes "with blinding clarity the hopeless presumption of trying to discard my portion of America" (15). She abandons hopes of reinvention and accepts that "my days in France had a number, that for me the bright, frank, endlessly beckoning horizon of the runaway had been, at some point, transformed into a complicated return" (15). Like other African American expatriates in the past, she returns home with a keener sense of race and sexuality across national boundaries and contact zones.

The return is complicated for several reasons. Sarah's troubled relationship with home stems from her rejection of stifling black middle-class values and disdain for American racism. During her time away, however, she has failed to reconcile her ambivalence. Indeed, despite her social position she comes back with more questions about the burden of race. Sarah's journeys destabilize her because she cannot reconcile an identity that contains multiple meanings at home and abroad. The notion of blackness in the postmodern era requires the subject to move beyond W. E. B. Du Bois's notion of duality. Much like the African American women in Ebron's study, Sarah remains trapped in a master racial and sexual narrative that defines her despite her attempts to assert agency in the contact zone.

The narrative begins and ends with Sarah planning for a journey, and travel ensures that her identity remains in flux. Although *Sarah Phillips* questions the idea of middle-class African Americans finding a home, Lee does expand the African American literary tradition because she allows a black middle-class heroine to be ambivalent about race but remain anchored to an African American culture.

In her foreword to the paperback edition of *Sarah Phillips,* Valerie Smith mentions that many of her students "disapproved of the book because it resists certain generally unspoken constructions of black women's lives" and because of the novel's "unwillingness . . . to conform to conventions of representing 'blackness' and 'black womanhood'" (x). I have experienced similar responses to the novel in both graduate and undergraduate courses. I gather that *Sarah Phillips* disturbs students because it calls into question the pivotal role middle-class black women play in representing black respectability and morality. Just as Jill Nelson and Anita Hill redefined their relationship to the politics of black respectability, Lee's heroine also distances herself from traditional expectations. Much like Lorene Cary's *Black Ice* and P. J. Gibson's *Long Time since Yesterday, Sarah Phillips* suggests that black middle-class identity hinges too completely on the sexual behavior of women. Moreover, the tragedies depicted in *Long Time since Yesterday, Daughters of the Dust,* and *Eve's Bayou* all call attention to the gravity and importance of sexual representation for African American women.

Epilogue

In June 2008 my play *Single Black Female* opened off-Broadway at the Duke on 42d Street.[1] The irreverent show, originally billed as a new comedy about sex, love, and shopping, depicts the frustrations faced by middle-class black women as they encounter bad dates, abrasive gynecologists, and insensitive relatives. Rendering the lives of SBF 1 and SBF 2 as they help each other survive the narrow odds of finding partnership in an unfriendly landscape gave me the opportunity to create characters who complained, "We did what we were suppose to do! We earned ourselves law degrees, Ph.D.s, IRAs, and 401Ks. We bring all this to the table and Tiger Woods marries a nanny? We could have avoided all those student loans if that's all men want."[2] Throughout the show the duo humorously express the ambivalence, hope, and desires of many single, middle-class, African American women in the post–civil rights era.

Written in response to the material I unearthed while researching representations of middle-class African American women when I was a doctoral student in modern thought and literature at Stanford University, *Single Black Female* became my dissertation's alter ego. After spending the day in the library, I would spend my evenings giving voice to those silenced and invisible in the media. The two-woman show about unmarried African American urban professionals was my reaction to what I considered unsophisticated depictions of blacks in contemporary popular culture. I hungered for adequate representations of middle-class black women navigating the quandaries of race, gender, and sexuality that preoccupied me and the other women I knew and respected.

Most portrayals are inadequate to reflect the lives of black women. Where were the witty, quirky, and clever African American characters? For that matter, where were the representations of black women suffering existential angst? Where were the stories of middle-class women that neither focused on nor completely ignored racial issues? The women I know are smarter, more sophisticated, and lead more complicated lives than what popular culture conveys. Moreover, most middle-class women understand their unique place within African American culture, but many in the current generation no longer want to accept traditional expectations about proper behavior.

Beyond the Black Lady emerged from my desire to discuss how middle-class black women challenge antiquated norms in literature and film at the end of the twentieth century. Undoubtedly, watching Anita Hill testify before the Senate in October 1991 also inspired both *Single Black Female* and *Beyond the Black Lady*. I wondered how the American public would have reacted if Hill had had a very different past—one with less defensible sexual and romantic choices. My answer to that question chilled me. I doubted that the political left would have defended Hill with the same vigor. I also felt that the conservative right would have relied even more on racial stereotypes in order to disparage her character. I was most troubled by the thought that neither the right nor the left seemed to know exactly what to make of Hill. Clearly, she was an anomaly to those who had never encountered an Ivy League–educated African American woman. At the time of the hearings I had just completed my master's degree in African American studies at UCLA and was working as a part-time research assistant for the legal scholar Kimberlé Crenshaw. I recall the surreal feeling I had watching Crenshaw among the group of supporters who entered the Senate chamber behind the very apprehensive Hill. I knew that Crenshaw and the rest of the team would provide the kind of precise, complex theorizing that would help Hill survive the spectacle with a new perspective on race and gender in America, but I also understood that the events that were about to unfold would leave new, enduring bruises to the image and psyche of black women.

More than fifteen years after the Thomas-Hill hearings and despite the outcry about Hill's treatment before the Senate, African American women continue to find themselves embattled in highly publicized national scandals, many of them involving sex. From President Clinton's firing of U.S. Surgeon General Jocelyn Elders in 1994 because of her views on preventing teenage pregnancy to the 2006 Duke University lacrosse party scandal, black women remain at the center of discussions about American racial ethics and sexual morality. When legal scholar Lani Guinier lost her bid for a place in President Clinton's cabinet as the first black woman to head the Civil Rights Division of the Department of Justice, her legal opinions on voting rights were called into question in a fashion that evoked images of black women as sexually rampant. By calling Guinier a "quota queen," her critics called to mind the image of the welfare queen (a term customarily used to disparage single mothers with multiple children), thereby linking her ideological position with black female sexual excess. As with Anita Hill, the spectacles surrounding these women generated publicity beyond the scope and significance of the particular incident in which they were involved. In each instance, the women found themselves defending against attacks that portrayed them as buffoons, prudes, harlots, or quota queens, attacks that revived dehumanizing stereotypes about black women in American culture.[3]

Even now, I am troubled by dominant depictions of middle-class black women's sexuality in popular culture. Since entering the international stage, First Lady Michelle Obama has been subjected to unprecedented media coverage about her body; only time will tell how her presence in the White House will alter perceptions of black womanhood.[4] Will examinations of cultural productions such as film and literature change the material conditions of black women? As Michelle Wallace asserts, "I am also well aware that I lay myself open to charges of elitism when I proceed as though cultural criticism were as crucial as health, the law, politics, economics and the family to the condition of black women. But I am convinced that the major battle for the 'other' will be to find voice, transforming the construction of dominant discourse in the process. Only with those voices—written, published, televised, taped, filmed, staged, cross-indexed and footnoted—will we approach control over our own lives."[5] I agree with Wallace's suggestion that a powerful connection exists between artistic representations of and by African American women and their ability to control their lives. Images of African American womanhood need to reflect diversity in sexuality, class, geographic region, and age. Until black women are recognized as a diverse group who play myriad roles within and for the black community, African Americans in general will continue to be seen as a monolith.

This volume (and its literary alter-ego, *Single Black Female*) is intended to prompt reconsideration of the proper role of middle-class black women and the representation of sexuality in African American culture. The late-twentieth-century literary and dramatic texts I have described here represent a unique historical moment for middle-class African American women who no longer want to silence their sexual histories and desires in order to "better" the race. Recognizing the toll that outdated expectations take on black women also encourages broader understanding of their available contemporary roles.

Notes

Introduction

1. Throughout the book I use the terms *black* and *African American* interchangeably to signify U.S. citizens of African descent.

2. The *Washington Post*'s executive editor, Leonard Downie Jr., complained, "*The Boondocks* strips in question commented on the private life of the national security adviser and its relationship to her official duties in ways that violated our standards for taste, fairness and invasion of privacy." For a discussion of the newspaper's stance, see Michael Getler, "Putting 'The Boondocks' in the Dock," *Washington Post,* Sunday, Oct. 19, 2003, B6.

3. For an extensive discussion of respectability and African Americans, see Victoria Wolcott, *Remaking Respectability: African American Women in Interwar Detroit* (Chapel Hill: University of Carolina Press, 2001), and Candice M. Jenkins, *Private Lives, Proper Relations: Regulating Black Intimacy* (Minneapolis: University of Minnesota Press, 2007).

4. Helen Cooper, "Dance of Diplomacy Is Grist for the Gossip Mill," *New York Times,* Sept. 13, 2006, A10.

5. Marcus Mabry, *Twice as Good* (New York: Modern Times, 2007), xxxiii, 87–91; Elisabeth Bumiller, *An American Life: A Biography* (New York: Random House, 2007), 69–72.

6. "Modern-day Sally Hemmings" is from the title of blogger Liza Sabater's November 18, 2004, online article, posted on culturkitchen.com: http://www.culturekitchen.com/archives/000647.html (Jan. 9, 2007). Another example of media's interest in Bush and Rice is a cartoon parody of the Bush administration, *Lil' Bush.* The cartoon first aired in September 2006 on Amp'd Mobile and became a short-lived series on Comedy Central a year later. The cartoon features elementary school versions of

Bush, Richard Cheney, Donald Rumsfeld, Karl Rove, and Condoleezza Rice. In the pilot, Lil' Condi pines for her thick-headed classmate Lil' Bush, who is in love with the new kid, a plump bookworm named Laura, and only seeks to exploit Condi's talents.

7. Deborah Schoeneman, "Armani's Exchange . . . Condi's Slip . . . Forget the Alamo," *New York*, April 26, 2004, http://nymag.com/nymetro/news/people/columns/intelligencer/n_10245/ (Dec. 8, 2006); Laura Kipnis, "Condi's Inner Life," *Slate.com*, April 26, 2004, at http://www.slate.com/id/2099516/ (Jan. 15, 2005). Rice claimed in one interview that she "doesn't believe she ever made the slip." Marcus Mabry, *Twice as Good* (New York: Modern Times, 2007), xxxvii.

8. For an insightful analysis of the role of race, class, and sexuality in performance, see E. Patrick Johnson, *Appropriating Blackness: Performance and the Politics of Authenticity* (Durham: Duke University Press, 2003). Johnson articulates how the trope of performance allows for racial appropriation and maintains that "performance is dynamic and generative, enabling difficult and controversial stances and poses that ultimately help us better to articulate our objects (and subjects) of inquiry" (6–7).

9. Deborah Gray White, *Too Heavy a Load: Black Women in Defense of Themselves, 1894–1994* (New York: W. W. Norton, 1999), 106.

10. For a useful discussion about the origins and persistence of these stereotypes in American culture see Deborah Gray White, *A'rn't I a Woman? Female Slaves in the Plantation South* (New York: W. W. Norton, 1985); Donald Bogle, *Toms, Coons, Mulattoes, Mammies, and Bucks: An Interpretive History of Blacks in American Films* (New York: Viking Press, 1973); and Patricia Hill Collins, *Black Feminist Thought: Knowledge, Consciousness, and the Politics of Empowerment* (Boston: Unwin Hyman, 1990), 67–90.

11. Daphne Brooks, *Bodies in Dissent: Spectacular Performances of Race and Freedom, 1850–1910* (Durham: Duke University Press, 2006), 7.

12. Many have argued about the connection between racist violence and sexual violation. African American men were lynched for alleged sexual slights against white women, and lynchings often included castration. Eric Foner, *A Short History of Reconstruction, 1863–1877* (New York: Harper and Row, 1990); Leon F. Litwack, *Been in the Storm so Long* (New York: Vintage Books, 1979).

13. Darlene Clark Hine, "Rape and the Inner Lives of Black Women: Thoughts on the Culture of Dissemblance," in *Hine Sight: Black Women and the Re-Construction of American History* (Bloomington: Indiana University Press, 1994), 37.

14. For an analysis of black female sexuality in early African American literature see Claudia Tate, *Domestic Allegories of Political Desire* (New York: Oxford University Press, 1992). In addition, see Hazel V. Carby, *Reconstructing Womanhood: The Emergence of the Afro-American Novelist* (New York: Oxford University Press, 1987); and Kevin K. Gaines, *Uplifting the Race: Black Leadership, Politics, and Culture in the Twentieth Century* (Chapel Hill: University of North Carolina Press, 1996).

15. Charles Nero, "Toward a Black Gay Aesthetic: Signifying in Contemporary

Black Gay Literature," in *Cornerstones: An Anthology of African American Literature*, edited by Melvin Donalson (New York: St. Martin's Press, 1996), 977.

16. For other early examples of the presentation of the black middle class see Frances E. W. Harper's novel *Iola Leroy; or, Shadows Uplifted* (1893, repr. New York: Oxford University Press, 1988); Frank J. Webb's novel *The Garies and Their Friends* (1857, repr. Baltimore: Johns Hopkins University Press, 1997); and Angelina Grimke's play *Rachel* (1920, repr. College Park: McGrath, 1969).

17. This style of sexual representation repeatedly foregrounds the difficult romantic predicaments experienced by middle-class black women who are able to pass for white, linking the tragic mulatto figure to the middle-class black woman. Jessie Fauset, *The Chinaberry Tree* (New York: Frederick A. Stokes, 1931); Jessie Fauset, *Plum Bun* (1929, repr. Boston: Beacon Press, 1999); Jessie Fauset, *Comedy American Style* (1933, repr. Lebanon, N.H.: Northeastern University Press, 1989); Nella Larsen, *Quicksand* (1928, repr. New York: Penguin Books, 1987); Nella Larsen, *Passing* (1929, repr. New York: Penguin Books, 1997); Dorothy West, *The Living Is Easy* (1948, repr. Old Westbury: Feminist Press, 1982).

18. Hazel Carby maintains that "racist sexual ideologies proclaimed the black woman to be a rampant sexual being; in response, black women writers either focused on defending their morality or on displacing sexuality onto another terrain" (*Reconstructing Womanhood*, 174).

19. Ann Petry, *The Street* (Boston: Houghton Mifflin, 1946); Ann Petry, *The Narrows* (1953, repr. Boston: Beacon Hill Press, 1988); Gayl Jones, *Corregidora* (1975, repr. Boston: Beacon Press, 1987); Gayl Jones, *Eva's Man* (1976, repr. Boston: Beacon Press, 1987).

20. Many artists and activists argued that blacks who adopted American middle-class values and wanted to assimilate were a detriment to black liberation. Stokely Carmichael and Charles V. Hamilton, *Black Power: The Politics of Liberation in America* (New York: Vintage Books, 1967); Larry Neal, "The Black Arts Movement," in *Within the Circle: An Anthology of African American Literary Criticism for the Harlem Renaissance to the Present*, edited by Angelyn Mitchell (Durham: Duke University Press, 1994), 184–98.

21. E. Franklin Frazier, *The Black Bourgeoisie: The Rise of a New Middle Class in the United States* (New York: Free Press, 1957); Nathan Hare, *The Black Anglo-Saxons* (London: Collier Books, 1965). Frazier suggests that "having abandoned their social heritage and being rejected by the white world, the black bourgeoisie have an intense feeling of inferiority, constantly seek various forms of recognition and place great value upon status symbols in order to compensate for their inferiority complex" (*Black Bourgeoisie*, 111).

22. Amiri Baraka, *The Dutchman* (New York: HarperCollins, 1964); Alice Childress, *Wine in the Wilderness* (New York: Dramatists Play Service, 1969); Toni Morrison, *The Bluest Eye* (New York: Alfred Knopf, 1970); Ann Petry, *The Narrows* (1953, repr. Boston: Beacon Press, 1988). I discuss the genealogy of this trend in African Ameri-

can fiction in chapter 5, "Sex, Travel, and the Single African American Girl: Andrea Lee's *Sarah Phillips*."

23. See Trey Ellis, "The New Black Aesthetic," *Callaloo* 12 (Winter 1989): 233–46, as well as responses by Tera Hunter, "It's a Man's Man's Man's World: Specters of the Old Re-Newed in Afro-American Culture and Criticism," and Eric Lott, "Response to Trey Ellis's 'The New Black Aesthetic,'" in the same issue.

24. Isaac Julien uses the term *cultural policing* to signify how certain members of the African American community (often the elite) monitor the behavior of others so that lines of proper conduct are seldom breached. Julien, "Black Is, Black Ain't: Notes on De-Essentializing Black Identities," in *Black Popular Culture*, edited by Gina Dent (Seattle: Bay Press, 1992), 258.

25. Wahneema Lubiano, "Black Ladies, Welfare Queens, and State Minstrels: Ideological War by Narrative Means," in *Race-ing Justice, En-gendering Power: Essays on Anita Hill, Clarence Thomas, and the Construction of Social Reality*, edited by Toni Morrison (New York: Pantheon Books, 1992). Morrison also uses the term *black lady* in her introductory essay in the same volume.

26. Wolcott, *Remaking Respectability*, 6.

27. Anna Julia Cooper, "Womanhood: A Vital Element in the Regeneration and Progress of a Race," in *The Voice of Anna Julia Cooper*, edited by Charles Lemert and Esme Bhan (Lanham: Rowan and Littlefield, 1988), 64, 70.

28. Lubiano, "Black Ladies, Welfare Queens, and State Minstrels" (quotation on 335); Cathy Cohen, "Punks, Bull Daggers, and Welfare Queens: The Radical Potential of 'Queer' Politics," *GLQ* 3 (1997): 437–65. I discuss this concept further in chapter 1, "Anita Hill and the Problem of Innocence."

29. Rice rarely loses an opportunity to remind audiences about her background. When she spoke at the Republican National Convention in 2000, for example, she made her southern middle-class roots a cornerstone of the speech. Excerpts of the speech are in "The Republicans; Rice's Comments on Bush: 'Uncommonly Good Judgment,'" *New York Times,* Aug. 2, 2000, A20. Rice also made a point of mentioning her family in an opening statement to the Senate Foreign Relations Committee on January 15, 2005, as part of her confirmation hearings. www.senate.gov/~foreign/testimony/2005/RiceTestimony050118.pdf (March 2, 2007).

30. Elisabeth Bumiller, *An American Life: A Biography* (New York: Random House, 2007); Glenn Kessler, *The Confidante: Condoleezza Rice and the Creation of the Bush Legacy* (New York: St. Martin's Press, 2007); Marcus Mabry, *Twice as Good: Condoleezza Rice and Her Path to Power* (New York: Modern Times, 2007).

31. Antonia Felix, *Condi: The Condoleezza Rice Story* (New York: Pocket Books, 2002), 36.

32. Mabry, *Twice as Good*, 35.

33. When Rice departs from the script it garners excessive commentary. When she wore a long black coat and towering, knee-high boots with slender heels on a visit to Wiesbaden Army Airfield, for example, the *Washington Post* reported on her "sexy"

attire. Robin Givhan, "Condoleezza Rice's Commanding Clothes," *Washington Post*, Feb. 25, 2005, C1.

34. Mabry, *Twice as Good*, 58.

35. Roderick A. Ferguson, *Aberrations in Black: Toward a Queer of Color Critique* (Minneapolis: University of Minnesota Press, 2004), 145.

36. Hortense Spillers, "Interstices: A Small Drama of Words," in *Pleasure and Danger: Exploring Female Sexuality*, edited by Carole Vance (Boston: Routledge and Kegan Paul, 1984), 74. Here I am thinking about work by theorists such as Michel Foucault, who virtually ignores the issue of race or pays it scant attention. Foucault, *The History of Sexuality: An Introduction*, vol. 1 (1978, repr. New York: Vintage Books, 1990).

37. Carby, *Reconstructing Womanhood*, 174; see also Deborah McDowell, *'The Changing Same': Black Women's Literature, Criticism and Theory* (Bloomington: Indiana University Press, 1995).

38. Evelyn Hammonds, "Toward a Genealogy of Black Female Sexuality: The Problematic of Silence," in *Feminist Genealogies, Colonial Legacies, Democratic Futures*, edited by M. Jacqui Alexander and Chandra Talpade Mohanty (New York: Routledge, 1997), 175.

39. Other black feminist critics who theorize about black female sexuality include Ann duCille, Sharon Holland, Deborah McDowell, Valerie Smith, and Michele Wallace.

40. Spillers, "Interstices," 79.

41. Another form of labor was that of black middle-class women (beginning with free blacks in the antebellum period) responsible for representing the race as chaste, moral, and honorable.

42. Spillers, "Interstices," 79.

43. bell hooks, *Black Looks: Race and Representation* (Boston: South End Press, 1992), 62.

44. For other discussions of black women negotiating the gaze see Michele Wallace, *Invisibility Blues: From Pop to Theory* (London: Verso Press, 1990).

45. hooks, *Black Looks*, 69.

46. Gayle Wyatt, *Stolen Women: Reclaiming Our Sexuality, Taking Back Our Lives* (New York: John Wiley, 1997); Tricia Rose, *Longing to Tell: Black Women Talk about Sexuality and Intimacy* (New York: Farrar, Straus and Giroux, 2003).

47. Wyatt, *Stolen Women*, 7.

48. Ibid., 29.

49. Wyatt's observation continues to reverberate when one thinks of then–National Security Advisor Condoleezza Rice's testimony before the 9/11 Commission in 2004 as well her confirmation hearings before other Senate committees.

50. Wyatt, *Stolen Women*, 38. One troubling aspect about the over-reliance on black middle-class performance is the presumption that behaviors commonly associated with less priviledged black women justify sexual stereotypes and mistreatment.

51. Collins, *Black Feminist Thought*, 77; see also Cathy Cohen, *The Boundaries of*

Blackness: AIDS and the Breakdown of Black Politics (Chicago: University of Chicago Press, 1999); and Lubiano, "Black Ladies, Welfare Queens, and State Minstrels."

52. Ann Snitow, "The Front Lines: Notes on Sex in Novels by Women, 1969–1979," in *Women—Sex and Sexuality*, edited by Catherine R. Stimpson and Ethel Spector Person (Chicago: University of Chicago Press, 1980), 87–105.

53. Among the popular fiction published in the United States during the late 1960s and early 1970s were Erica Jong, *Fear of Flying* (New York: Holt, Rinehart, and Winston, 1973), Jacqueline Susann, *Valley of the Dolls* (New York: B. Geis Associates distributed by Random House, 1966), and Helen Gurley Brown, *Sex and the Single Girl* ([New York]: B. Geis Associates distributed by Random House, 1962). That trend toward celebrating female sexual desire continued in theoretical writing and other modes of cultural production.

54. Evelyn Hammonds, "Black (W)holes and the Geometry of Black Female Sexuality," *Differences: A Journal of Feminist Cultural Studies* 6, nos. 2–3 (1994): 138.

55. Barbara Christian, "The Race for Theory," *Feminist Studies* 14, no. 1 (1988): 68.

56. Lynne Segal, *Straight Sex: Rethinking the Politics of Pleasure* (Berkeley: University of California Press, 1994), 266.

57. John D'Emilio and Estelle B. Freedman, *Intimate Matters: A History of Sexuality in America* (1988, repr. Chicago: Chicago University Press, 1997).

58. Deborah Tolman and Tracy Higgins, "How Being a Good Girl Can Be Bad," in *"Bad Girls/Good Girls": Women, Sex and Power in the Nineties*, edited by Nan Bauer Maglin and Donna Perry (New Brunswick: Rutgers University Press, 1996), 205, emphasis added.

59. hooks, *Black Looks*, 65.

60. Even defining the middle class more broadly proves difficult. In "Without Health Benefits, a Good Life Turns Fragile," *New York Times*, March 5, 2007, A1, Robert Pear notes, "While the government does not have an official definition of 'middle class,' one commonly used point of reference is the median household income, which was $46,326 in 2005."

61. Bart Landry, *The New Black Middle Class* (Berkeley: University of California Press, 1987); Melvin Oliver and Thomas M. Shapiro, *Black Wealth/White Wealth: A New Perspective on Racial Inequality* (New York: Routledge, 1997).

62. Landry suggests that the latter part of the twentieth century witnessed a rise in the racial composition of the middle class: "[B]etween 1960 and 1970, the black middle class doubled in size, achieving a growth rate of 106.8 percent. Between 1970 and 1980, its rate of growth declined to 61.9 percent" (*The New Black Middle Class*, 194). More recent reports also present data that reflect the extent to which the black middle class lags behind whites. According to one study, "black household income averaging $25,050 in 1997, compared with $38,972 for white households, but it has narrowed as black household income has risen six times faster than that of whites between 1989 and 1997." John Simons, "American Opinions: Black Middle Class Gains

Ground, but Still Finds Its Situation Shaky," *Wall Street Journal*, Dec. 10, 1998, A10. In *Black Wealth/White Wealth*, Oliver and Shapiro map differences between the white and black middle class by measuring wealth instead of income. Their findings indicate that U.S. blacks, because of slavery, discrimination, and institutional racism, have had a brief time to accumulate assets and more difficulty in doing so (e.g., through financial assets and real estate) than whites. Thus middle-class status is relative. Suffering from what the authors term "sedimentation of racial inequality," the disparity between black achievement and reward challenges the idea of the middle class as a segment of the black population that has escaped racism (5).

63. Mary Pattillo-McCoy, *Black Picket Fences: Privilege and Peril among the Black Middle Class* (Chicago: University Chicago Press, 1999), 22; see also Mary Pattillo, *Black on the Block: The Politics of Race and Class in the City* (Chicago: University Chicago Press, 2007).

64. Landry, *The New Black Middle Class*; Pattillo-McCoy, *Black Picket Fences*.

65. In *Black Picket Fences*, for example, Pattillo-McCoy explains the complex workings of a black middle-class Chicago neighborhood that includes the city's top gang leader, a drug dealer, and a politician, all of whom are black. Although the residents do not escape crime, they do employ an informal network of checks and balances (68–90).

66. Oliver and Shapiro, *Black Wealth/White Wealth*, 8. To further explore the precarious position of the black middle class see Martin Carnoy, *Faded Dreams: The Politics and Economics of Race in America* (New York: Cambridge University Press, 1994); Reynolds Farley and Walter Allen, *The Color Line and the Quality of American Life* (New York: Oxford University Press 1989); and Alphonso Pinkney, *The Myth of Black Progress* (New York: Cambridge University Press, 1984).

67. Ellis Cose, *The Rage of a Privileged Class* (New York: HarperCollins, 1993); Joe R. Feagin and Melvin P. Sikes, eds., *Living with Racism: The Black Middle-Class Experience* (Boston: Beacon Press, 1994).

68. Karyn Lacy, *Blue-chip Black: Race, Class, and Status in the New Black Middle Class* (Berkeley: University of California Press, 2007); Martin Summers, *Manliness and Its Discontents: The Middle Class and the Transformation of Masculinity, 1900–1930* (Chapel Hill: University of North Carolina Press, 2004). For more analysis of black middle-class disappointments and frustrations see Lawrence Otis Graham, *Member of the Club: Reflections on Life in a Racially Polarized World* (New York: HarperPerennial, 1995). Critiques of the black middle class have not disappeared, and among them is Michael Dyson's *Is Bill Cosby Right? Or Has the Black Middle Class Lost Its Mind* (New York: Basic Books, 2005). Dyson not only lambastes the popular comedian's tirade about dysfunctional behavior within the black community but also criticizes "upper-middle-class blacks and black elite who rain down fire and brimstone upon poor blacks for their deviance and pathology, and for their lack of couth and culture" (xiii–xiv). While Dyson acknowledges that working-class blacks also echo many of Cosby's complaints, he only criticizes those he labels the "Afristrocacy" for what he

considers uncharitable beliefs. In *Come on People* (Nashville: Thomas Nelson, 2007), written with Alvin Poussaint, Cosby provides what can be considered a rebuttal to Dyson and continues to comment on black self-reliance, personal responsibility, and respectability.

69. Larry Tye, *Rising from the Rails: Pullman Porters and the Making of the Black Middle Class* (New York: Henry Holt, 2004); Michele Mitchell, *Righteous Propagation: African Americans and the Politics of Racial Destiny after Reconstruction* (Chapel Hill: University of North Carolina Press, 1991); Wolcott, *Remaking Respectability*.

70. Other texts about middle-class black women include Veronica Chambers, *Having It All? Black Women and Success* (New York: Harlem Moon, 2003); Charisse Jones and Kumea Shorter-Gooden, *Shifting: The Double Lives of Black Women in America* (New York: HarperCollins, 2003); and Elizabeth Higginbotham, *Too Much to Ask: Black Women in the Era of Integration* (Chapel Hill: University of North Carolina Press, 2001).

71. Stephen David Ross, "The Limits of Sexuality," in *The Philosophy of Sex: Contemporary Readings,* 2d ed., edited by Alan Soble (Totowa: Rowman and Littlefield, 1980), 159–75.

Chapter 1: Spectacle of the Respectable: Anita Hill and the Problem of Innocence

1. Other than the November 11, 1991, *People* magazine cover story featuring his wife, Virginia Thomas, Justice Thomas has rarely offered his reflections about the matter. Hill's continued relevance is clear from the number of major news outlets seeking her response to Thomas's memoir. In his editorial Frank Rich reported, "CBS News was the only one of the three broadcast news divisions that did not seek her reaction to the latest Thomas salvos." Rich, "Nobody Knows the Lynchings He's Seen," *New York Times,* Oct. 7, 2007, 14.

2. Clarence Thomas, interview by Steve Kroft, *60 Minutes,* CBS, Sept. 30, 2007.

3. Clarence Thomas, *My Grandfather's Son: A Memoir* (New York: HarperCollins, 2007) 171, 244.

4. Thomas, *My Grandfather's Son,* 252–53.

5. Hill wrote an editorial for *The New York Times* in response to the publication of Thomas's autobiography and used the editorial to advance the conversation about sexual harassment further by asking "how we will resolve the kinds of issues my testimony exposed. My belief is that in the past sixteen years we have come closer to making the resolution of these issues an honest search for the truth, which, after all, is at the core of all legal inquiry. My hope is that Justice Thomas's latest fusillade will not divert us from that path." "The Smear This Time," *New York Times,* Oct. 2, 2007, 25.

6. Hill has also appeared on programs such as *The Today Show, Meet the Press,* and *Good Morning America.* Her story was linked to Lewinsky's in various publications,

and the hearings are considered the turning point for the current climate of sexual scandal in politics. Anita Hill, "Insider Women with Outsider Values" (editorial), *New York Times,* June 6, 2002, A31; Anita Hill, "In Politics, Still a Man's World" (editorial), *New York Times,* Feb. 11, 2000, A31; Anita Hill, "Some Warnings on Calling Witnesses" (editorial), *Boston Globe,* Jan. 25, 1999, A15; Anita Hill, "Thomas vs. Clinton," *New York Times,* May 29, 1994, 4:11, and Anita Hill, "The Lewinsky Affair: Whose Story Is It Anyway?" *Village Voice,* Feb. 3, 1998, 38. Versions of many of Hill's editorials also appear in newspapers with smaller circulation such as the *Palm Beach Post, News Tribune* (Tacoma, Wash.), *Durham Herald, Star Tribune* (Minneapolis), *Plain Dealer* (Cleveland), *Houston Chronicle,* and *Phoenix Gazette.* That alone allows her to reach a broad audience of readers and stay in the public sphere on the national and local level.

7. Dru Sefton, "'I Have a Dream': In a Century of Speeches, Certain Words still Soar," *USA Today,* Dec. 30, 1999, 8D. Two researchers surveyed 137 academics who chose Hill's speech based on "impact, rhetorical artistry, organization, style and presentation of arguments" (8). Martin Luther King Jr.'s "I Have a Dream" was first.

8. Toni Morrison, ed., *Race-ing Justice, En-gendering Power: Essays on Anita Hill, Clarence Thomas, and the Construction of Social Reality* (New York: Pantheon Books, 1992); Jane Flax, *The American Dream in Black and White: The Clarence Thomas Hearings* (Ithaca: Cornell University Press, 1998); Timothy M. Phelps, *Capitol Games: Clarence Thomas, Anita Hill, and the Story of a Supreme Court Nomination* (New York: W. W. Norton, 1992); "Clarence Thomas and Anita Hill: Public Hearing, Private Pain," the *Frontline* documentary (1992). Other texts include Geneva Smitherman, ed., *African American Women Speak Out on Anita Hill–Clarence Thomas* (Detroit: Wayne State University Press, 1995); and Robert Chrisman and Robert L. Allen, eds., *The Black Scholar*'s collection, *Court of Appeal: The Black Community Speaks Out on the Racial and Sexual Politics of Thomas vs. Hill* (New York: Ballentine Books, 1992). Much like the hearings themselves, the material produced in response usually presents one side more favorably than the other; former Senator John C. Danforth, also a principal in the scandal, has written about the hearings in *Resurrection: The Confirmation of Clarence Thomas* (New York: Viking Press, 1994). For a balanced assessment of Thomas's cultural significance, see Kevin Merida and Michael A. Fletcher, *Supreme Discomfort: The Divided Soul of Clarence Thomas* (New York: Doubleday, 2007).

9. Anthony B. Pinn, *Terror and Triumph: The Nature of Black Religion* (Minneapolis: Fortress Press, 2003); Eric Lott, *Love and Theft: Blackface Minstrelsy and the American Working Class* (New York: Oxford University Press, 1993); James Allen, ed., *Without Sanctuary* (Santa Fe: Twin Palms Publishers, 2000); Philip Dray, *At the Hands of Persons Unknown: The Lynching of Black America* (New York: Modern Library, 2002).

10. On the evening of October 11, 1991, in prepared remarks Thomas declared, "From my standpoint, as a black American, as far as I am concerned, it is a high-tech lynching for uppity blacks who in any way design to think for themselves." Anita

Miller, ed., *The Complete Transcripts of the Clarence Thomas–Anita Hill Hearings, October 11, 12, 13, 1991* (Chicago: Academy Chicago Publishers, 1994), 118.

11. Stephen L. Carter, "Two Good People" (editorial), *New York Times*, Oct. 13, 1991, 4:15; Sharon LaFraniere, "'It Is an Unpleasant Issue': Accuser Explains Her Decision to Come Forward," *Washington Post*, Oct. 8, 1991, A1; Ruth Marcus, "Allegation Clouds Vote on Thomas: Nominee's Supporters Question Credibility of Former Aide Charging Sexual Harassment," *Washington Post*, Oct. 7, 1991, A1; Mary McGrory, "A Day That Shouldn't Have Been," *Washington Post*, Oct. 13, 1991, C1; Ann Devroy, "Path to Confirmation Became 'Slippery Slope': White House Damage Control Efforts Failed to Quell Rising Doubts in Senate," *Washington Post*, Oct. 9, 1991, A6; Tom Wicker, "In the Nation; Blaming Anita Hill," *New York Times*, Oct. 10, 1991, A27; David Margolick, "At the Bar; In a Confirmation Battle Filled with Yalies, the Law School's Dean Is Caught in the Crossfire," *New York Times*, Oct. 11, 1991, B7; Patrick E. Tyler, "The Thomas Nomination: New Witness Says She Is Willing to Corroborate Accusations by Professor," *New York Times*, Oct. 11, 1991, A16. The most detailed of all the articles is Carter's editorial, which describes Hill as "a person of integrity, compassion and deep spiritual substance. She is not a political activist. She is not vindictive. She is not a publicity hound. She does not seek controversy. She is warm. She is smart. She is funny. She is, perhaps, a little shy" ("Two Good People," 15).

12. Nell Irvin Painter, "Hill, Thomas, and the Use of Racial Stereotype," in *Race-ing Justice, En-gendering Power: Essays on Anita Hill, Clarence Thomas, and the Construction of Social Reality*, edited by Toni Morrison (New York: Pantheon Books, 1992), 209.

13. I comment on the backlash against black women further in chapter 2, "Staging Black Female Desire: The Drama of Race and Class." In addition, see Ron Karenga, "Under the Camouflage of Color and Gender: The Dread and Drama of Thomas-Hill," in *Court of Appeal: The Black Community Speaks Out on the Racial and Sexual Politics of Thomas vs. Hill*, edited by Robert Chrisman and Robert L. Allen (New York: Ballantine Books, 1992), 125–35.

14. Painter, "Hill, Thomas, and the Use of Racial Stereotype," 209.

15. Julianne Malveaux, "No Peace in a Sisterly Space," in *Court of Appeal: The Black Community Speaks Out on the Racial and Sexual Politics of Thomas vs. Hill*, edited by Robert Chrisman and Robert L. Allen (New York: Ballantine Books, 1992), 143–47. Malveaux notes that "some black women's resentment against Professor Hill was resentment that she fought when they could not. Indeed, because the black women's burden is lightened by class, educational status, and generation, many black women could distance themselves from the achieving Hill, depicting her as 'other' even in the community of black women" (145). See also Orlando Patterson, "Race, Gender, and Liberal Fallacies," in the same volume (160–64).

16. Earlier examples of the black lady include such public figures as Ida B. Wells, Mary Church Terrell, Pauline Hopkins, and Frances Harper. These women epito-

mized the regal, modern, elegant, and educated woman emulated by members of the nineteenth-century black women's national club movement. Evelyn Brooks Higginbotham, *Righteous Discontent: The Black Women's Movement in the Black Baptist Church, 1880–1920* (Cambridge: Harvard University Press, 1993); Deborah Gray White, *Too Heavy a Load: Black Women in Defense of Themselves, 1894–1994* (New York: W. W. Norton, 1999); Shirley J. Carlson, "Black Ideals of Womanhood in the Late Victorian Era," *Journal of Negro History* 77, no. 2 (1992): 61–73.

17. Lubiano, "Black Ladies, Welfare Queens, and State Minstrels," 335.

18. For discussion of how black women are criticized for undermining the black family and black males, see Daniel Moynihan, *Negro Family: The Case for National Action* (Washington: Department of Labor, Office of Policy, Planning and Research, 1965); and Paula Giddings, *When and Where I Enter: The Impact of Black Women on Race and Sex in America* (New York: William Morrow, 1984), 299–357.

19. Jill Smolowe, "She Said, He Said," *Time*, Oct. 21, 1991, 36.

20. Nancy Gibbs, "An Ugly Circus," *Time*, Oct. 21, 1991, 35.

21. Gloria Borger et al., "Judging Thomas," *U.S. News & World Report*, Oct. 21, 1991, 36.

22. Eloise Salhouz, "Thomas and Hill: Mentor or Tormentor?" *Newsweek*, Oct. 21, 1991, 29.

23. Smolowe, "She Said, He Said" (emphasis added).

24. Newspaper reports of Hill's testimony presented her in much the same way as news magazines did. *The New York Times* described Hill as "his accuser" whose testimony was "equally moving and, to her evident distaste, far more specific [than Thomas's]." "Her Story, and His" (editorial), *New York Times*, Oct. 12, 1991, 1:28. See also Anna Quindlen, "Public and Private: An American Tragedy," *New York Times*, Oct. 12, 1991, 1:29; and Ann F. Lewis, "The Feminists Will Strike Back," *New York Times*, Oct. 16, 1991, A25. Similarly, the *Boston Globe*, *Los Angeles Times*, and *Washington Post* categorized Hill's allegations as believable.

25. For the history of black sexual stereotypes see George M. Fredrickson, *The Black Image in the White Mind: The Debate on Afro-American Character and Destiny, 1817–1914* (New York: Harper and Row, 1971); Calvin C. Hernton, *The Sexual Mountain and Black Women Writers: Adventures in Sex, Literature and Real Life* (New York: Anchor Press, 1987); and Deborah Gray White, *Ar'n't I a Woman? Female Slaves in the Plantation South* (New York: W. W. Norton, 1985).

26. Miller, ed., *Complete Transcripts*, 294. In fact, during Hill's Senate statement, Alvarez characterized the Hill she knew at the EEOC as "a hard, tough woman. She was opinionated. She was arrogant. She was a relentless debater. And she was the kind of woman who always made you feel like she was not going to be messed with, like she was not going to take anything from anyone. . . . she definitely came across as someone who was ambitious and watched out for her own advancement" (294–95). See also Elsa Barkley Brown, "Imaging Lynching: African American Women, Com-

munities of Struggle, and Collective Memory," in *African American Women Speak Out on Anita Hill–Clarence Thomas*, edited by Geneva Smitherman (Detroit: Wayne State University Press, 1995), 100–124.

27. Miller, ed., *Complete Transcripts*, 41.

28. Jürgen Habermas, *The Structural Transformation of the Public Sphere*, translated by Thomas Burger (Cambridge: MIT Press, 1989).

29. Nancy Fraser, "Rethinking the Public Sphere: A Contribution to the Critique of Actually Existing Democracy," in *Habermas and the Public Sphere*, edited by Craig Calhoun (Cambridge: MIT Press, 1992), 110–11.

30. Although U.S. citizens passively watch television programming, viewers assert their will through ratings and written responses to the networks about shows. ABC's *Designing Women*, for example, aired an episode about Hill-Thomas hearings in which characters were divided in their opinions about witnesses, a situation that mirrored viewing the actual hearings. The program took advantage of public furor over the hearings to increase ratings and allowed viewers to further process the scandal. The FOX comedy sketch series *In Living Color* also did an episode depicting Thomas as a brash buffoon repeating the most scandalous line from the hearings. Many viewers discuss what they watch on television and interpolate television programs into their lives. Raymond Williams, *Television, Technology and Cultural Form* (New York; Schocken Books, 1975).

31. Fraser, "Rethinking," 112.

32. Bipartisan female lawmakers and voters made it known to the Senate that they needed to delay their vote on Thomas's confirmation after Hill's charges were explored. E. J. Dionne Jr., "GOP Women Divided over Thomas Charges; Many Join Democratic Colleagues in Assailing Senate's Handling of Sexual Harassment Issue," *Washington Post*, Oct. 10, 1991, A19; Michael K. Frisby, "Women Bring Their Issues to the Fore; the Thomas Nomination," *Boston Globe*, Oct. 10, 1991, 1; Borger et al., "Judging Thomas"; Margaret Carlson, "The Ultimate Men's Club," *Time*, Oct. 21, 1991, 50; Barbara Ehrenreich, "Women Would Have Known," *Time*, Oct. 21 1991, 104; "Finally, a Proper Hearing" (editorial), *New York Times*, Oct. 10, 1991, A:26.

33. I am here thinking of how activists reshaped the debate around the AIDS health crisis and how Jesse Jackson was able to influence the terminology used to describe black people.

34. Fraser, "Rethinking," 123.

35. Nancy Fraser, "Sex, Lies and the Public Sphere," in *Feminism, the Public and the Private*, edited by Joan B. Landes (New York: Oxford University Press, 1998), 325.

36. For examples of black women addressing Thomas's nomination see "Roundtable: Doubting Thomas," *Tikkun* 6, no. 5 (1991): 23–30, in which UCLA law professor Kimberlé Crenshaw dominated the discussion with Peter Gabel, Catherine A. MacKinnon, Gary Peller, and Cornel West. See also the essays in Morrison's *Race-ing Justice, En-gendering Power*; Smitherman, ed., *African American Women Speak Out*; and Elise Washington, *Uncivil War*.

37. Michael Dawson and others contend that the black counterpublic has tremendous usefulness. Dawson, "A Black Counterpublic? Economic Earthquakes, Racial Agenda(s), and Black Politics," in *The Black Public Sphere: A Public Culture Book*, edited by the Public Sphere Collective (Chicago: University of Chicago Press, 1995). In the introduction to *The Black Public Sphere* the Collective asserts that "the black public sphere is also an answer insofar as it is a transnational space whose violent birth and diasporic conditions of life provide a counternarrative to the exclusionary national narratives of Europe, the United States, the Caribbean, and Africa. Thus the public sphere is one critical space where new democratic forms and emergent diasporic movements can enrich and question one another" (1). They do not, however, separate or acknowledge the different aspects of the black counterpublic along gender and class lines.

38. Dawson, "A Black Counterpublic?" 201.

39. Deborah White, *Too Heavy a Load*, 16.

40. Ibid., 17.

41. Nellie Y. McKay, in *Race-ing Justice, En-gendering Power: Essays on Anita Hill, Clarence Thomas, and the Construction of Social Reality*, edited by Toni Morrison (New York: Pantheon Books, 1992), 289.

42. Fraser ("Rethinking," 124) further notes that "subaltern counterpublics have a dual character. On the one hand, they function as spaces of withdrawal and regroupment; on the other hand, they also function as bases and training grounds for agitational activities directed toward wider publics. It is precisely in the dialectic between these functions that their emancipatory potential resides. This dialectic enables subaltern counterpublics partially to offset, although not wholly to eradicate, the unjust participatory privileges enjoyed by members of dominant social groups in stratified societies."

43. Barbara Ransby, "A Righteous Rage and Grassroots Mobilization," in *African American Woman Speak Out on Anita Hill–Clarence Thomas*, edited by Geneva Smitherman (Detroit: Wayne State University Press, 1995), 46.

44. In a fashion similar to Ida B. Wells's antilynching campaign, these women attempted to influence public sentiment.

45. Advertisement, African American Women in Defense of Ourselves, *New York Times*, 17 Nov. 1991, 53. Hill applauds the ad, considering the intervention "a clarion call for African American women to introduce our narratives into the discourse that ultimately defines the normative universe in which we reside." Anita F. Hill, "Marriage and Patronage in the Empowerment and Disempowerment of African American Women," in *Race, Gender, and Power in America: The Legacy of the Hill-Thomas Hearings*, edited by Hill and Emma Coleman Jordan (New York: Oxford University Press, 1995), 271–91 (quotation on 287).

46. Ransby, "A Righteous Rage," 49.

47. Ibid., 46.

48. For a discussion of black feminist organizations and class tensions see Kim

Springer, *Living for the Revolution: Black Feminist Organizations, 1968–1980* (Chapel Hill: Duke University Press, 2005).

49. The theory of intersectionality demonstrates how the circuits of oppression work together to illuminate differences, but it is not always possible to weight each component equally. Kimberlé W. Crenshaw, "Demarginalizing the Intersection of Race and Sex: A Black Feminist Critique of Antidiscrimination Doctrine, Feminist Theory and Antiracist Politics," *University of Chicago Legal Forum* (1989): 139–67.

50. Miller, ed. *Complete Transcripts*, 66.

51. Anita Hill, *Speaking Truth to Power* (New York: Doubleday, 1997), 6. Further citations to this work appear in parentheses.

52. James Olney, *Metaphors of Self: The Meaning of Autobiography* (Princeton: Princeton University Press, 1972), 50.

53. For a discussion of African American autobiography, see Edward J. Blum, *W. E. B. Du Bois, American Prophet* (Philadelphia: University of Pennsylvania Press, 2007); Stephen Butterfield, *Black Autobiography in America* (Amherst: University of Massachusetts Press, 1974); David L. Dudley, *My Father's Shadow: Intergenerational Conflict in African American Men's Autobiography* (Philadelphia: University of Pennsylvania Press, 1991); and V. P. Franklin, *Living Our Stories, Telling Our Truths: Autobiography and the Making of the African-American Intellectual Tradition* (New York: Oxford University Press, 1995).

54. Hill's strategy is much like Thomas's testimony during the hearing. He made a grand gesture during his second appearance before the committee that suggested his motivation for participating in the hearings was no longer professional. Thomas complained, "The Supreme Court is not worth it. No job is worth it. I am not here for that. I am here for my name, my family, my life and my integrity" (Miller, ed., *Complete Transcripts*, 117).

55. Ibid., 78.

56. Ibid., 228.

57. Ibid., 229.

58. Ibid., 236.

59. Ibid., 367–72. The testimony of John N. Doggett III (another Yale Law School graduate) was introduced to undermine Carr's statements and Hill's image as a desirable woman, and Doggett used her bookishness and middle-class status against her.

60. William Safire, "The Plot to Savage Thomas," *New York Times*, Oct. 14, 1991; William Safire, "About Men: Cordialities and Crushes," *New York Times Magazine*, Nov. 3, 1991, 18.

61. In the film *Strange Justice* (1999), directed by Ernest Dickerson and written by Jacob Epstein, Hill does not suffer in silence. The film was adapted from the book *Strange Justice: The Selling of a Supreme Court Justice* (New York: Houghton Mifflin, 1994) by *Wall Street Journal* reporters Jayne Mayer and Jill Abramson. Unable to provide a somber rendition, the fictionalized drama fails to portray Hill (Regina

Taylor) as she appeared in the hearings. Instead, the film elects to depict her as extremely emotional. Hill even hums a tune while testifying. In an effort to examine her underlying feelings during the hearings, the film portrays Hill's response to the Senate questioning as seething, angry, and loud. Similarly, Thomas (Delroy Lindo) responds to his former assistant's betrayal with even more melodrama than he exhibited in the actual hearings. At one point, he strips off his shirt and delivers his "high tech lynching" line while using his tie as a noose. Many critics considered the "fictionalization" of the story disturbing. Wendy Williams, "Sex and Politics Make Strange Bedfellows; Showtime Looks at 'Strange Justice' in the Case of Clarence Thomas and Anita Hill," *Boston Herald,* Aug. 29, 1999, 6; Susan King, "Cover Story; a Supreme Showdown," *Los Angeles Times,* Aug. 29, 1999, 3; Margo Jefferson, "Revisions: Television as Storyteller, Shaping History into Legend," *New York Times,* Sept. 6, 1999, E2; Caryn James, "He Said, She Said, and the Whole Nation Listened," *New York Times,* Aug. 27, 1999, E29.

62. Roland L. Freeman, *A Communion of Spirits* (Nashville: Rutledge Hill Press, 1996), xviii.

63. Margot Anne Kelley, "Sisters' Choices: Quilting Aesthetics in Contemporary African American Women's Fiction," in *Quilt Culture: Tracing the Pattern,* edited by Cheryl B. Torsney and Judy Elsley (Columbia: University of Missouri Press, 1994), 49–67.

64. For instance, *Race, Gender, and Power in America,* edited by Hill and Jordan, explores the "emergence of gender discontent among African Americans" and reinserts Hill into the public as a voice that advances African American womanhood, as is noted on the book jacket.

65. Audre Lorde, *Sister/Outsider: Essays and Speeches* (San Francisco: Crossing Press, 1984), 41.

66. Fraser, "Sex, Lies and the Pubic Sphere," 332.

67. Neil A. Lewis, "In New Book, Justice Thomas Weighs in on Former Accuser," *New York Times,* Sept. 30, 2007, 20; Orlando Patterson, "Thomas Agonistes," *New York Times Book Review,* June 17, 2007, 1; interview, *Good Morning America,* Oct. 2, 2007; Ellis Cose, "Still Keeping Score," *Newsweek,* April 30, 2007, 50; Lally Weymouth, "A Justice's Candid Opinions," *Newsweek,* Oct. 22, 2007, 50; John Yoo, "The Real Clarence Thomas," *Wall Street Journal,* Oct. 9, 2007, A17; William Grimes, "The Justice Looks Back and Settles Old Scores," *New York Times,* Oct. 10, 2007, B1–9; "Then and Now: Anita Hill," *CNN.com,* June 19, 2005, at http://www.cnn.com/2005/US/01/03/cnn25.tan.anita.hill/index.html (Jan. 2, 2007).

68. Hill was slow to reenter the public. There are few published interviews with her between autumn 1991 and 1993. Mayer and Abramson maintain (*Strange Justice,* 1) that "for almost two years, she had refused all inquiries from the news media concerning her part in the Senate confirmation hearings of Supreme Court Justice Clarence Thomas. . . . She had largely retreated from the public eye, getting an unlisted phone number at her modest ranch house in Norman, Oklahoma, installing a

security system sensitive to movement, and, when she did go out in public, sometimes rebuking autograph-seekers for violating her privacy."

Chapter 2: Staging Black Female Desire: The Drama of Race, Class, and Sexuality

1. Although more celebrated contemporary playwrights such as Lynn Nottage and Adrienne Kennedy also populate their work with middle-class black women, I hope to help expand the critical archive by discussing the innovative work of two lesser-known African American playwrights.

2. Glenda Dickerson, "The Cult of True Womanhood: Toward a Womanist Attitude in African-American Theater," in *Performing Feminisms: Feminist Critical Theory and Theater*, edited by Sue-Ellen Case (Baltimore: Johns Hopkins University Press, 1990), 110.

3. For a reading of Henry Box Brown's escape and performances see Daphne A. Brooks, *Bodies in Dissent: Spectacular Performances of Race and Freedom, 1850–1910* (Durham: Duke University Press, 2006).

4. Kathy A. Perkins and Judith L. Stephens, eds., *Strange Fruit: Plays on Lynching by American Women* (Bloomington: Indiana University Press, 1998); Judith L. Stephens, *The Plays of Georgia Douglas Johnson: From the New Negro Renaissance to the Civil Rights Movement* (Urbana: University of Illinois Press, 2006).

5. W. E. B. Du Bois, "Krigwa Players Little Negro Theater," *The Crisis* 32 (July 1926): 134–36.

6. Sandra Richards, "Writing the Absent Potential: Drama, Performance, and the Canon of African-American Literature," in *Performativity and Performance*, edited by Andrew Parker and Eve Kosofsky Sedgwick (New York: Routledge, 1995), 65.

7. Richards's observation hints at the lowly position of theater studies in academia. Sue-Ellen Case explains that "theater departments are relatively new to the university. Prior to their founding, the study of theater was located within English departments. This location meant that the study of theater was regarded primarily as the analysis of play texts, isolating them from practice, and employing the devices common to literary studies. When theater departments were founded, the focus was and still is, in training practitioners. As the study of theater within theater departments developed, it was dominated by the history of theater, rather than its criticism." Case, Introduction, in *Performing Feminisms: Feminist Critical Theory and Theater*, edited by Sue-Ellen Case (Baltimore: Johns Hopkins University Press, 1990), 2. This tension is also evident in African American theater itself; see Henry Louis Gates Jr., "The Chitlin Circuit," *The New Yorker*, Feb. 3, 1997, 44.

8. William Branch, "Introduction: The Legacy of the African Grove: from *King Shotaway* to *The Piano Lesson*," in *Black Thunder: An Anthology of Contemporary African American Drama* (New York: Penguin Books, 1992), xxxiv.

9. Historically, African American theater has presented the black middle class con-

fronting various dilemmas from miscegenation to lynching. Performing blackness on the American stage began with white actors portraying blacks in an exaggerated manner. When African Americans began to present and control their image they found it necessary to counter the stereotypes perpetuated by minstrel shows and other degrading iconography. That impulse influenced the type of theater produced. Plays often emphasized racial uplift and sought to illustrate the damaging effects of racism, even among the black middle class. For a discussion of the minstrel tradition in U.S. culture see Eric Lott, *Eric Lott, Love and Theft: Blackface Minstrelsy and the American Working Class* (New York: Oxford University Press, 1993) as well as Marlon Riggs's documentary *Ethnic Notions* (1986).

10. For a comprehensive history of African American theater see Errol Hill, ed., *The Theater of Black Americans,* vols. 1 and 2 (Englewood Cliffs: Prentice-Hall, 1980); Leslie Catherine Sanders, *The Development of Black Theater in America: From Shadows to Selves* (Baton Rouge: Louisiana State University Press, 1988); and Samuel A. Hay, *African American Theatre: An Historical and Critical Analysis* (New York: Cambridge University Press, 1994).

11. For discussions about black arts movement ideology see Addison Gayle, *The Black Aesthetic* (New York: Doubleday, 1971); Carolyn F. Gerald, "The Black Writer and His Role," *Negro Digest* 18 (1969): 42–48; LeRoi Jones, *Home: Social Essays* (New York: William Morrow) 1966; Ernest D. Mason, "Black Art and the Configurations of Experience: The Philosophy of the Black Aesthetic," *CLA Journal* 27 (1983): 1–17; Larry Neal, *Visions of a Liberated Future: Black Arts Movement Writings* (New York: Thunder's Mouth Press, 1989); and Mance Williams, *Black Theatre in the 1960s and 1970s* (Westport: Greenwood Press, 1985).

12. Adrienne Kennedy, *Funnyhouse of a Negro* and *The Ohio State Murders,* in Kennedy, *The Alexander Plays* (Minneapolis: University of Minnesota Press, 1992).

13. To showcase the contributions of black female playwrights, theater critics and artists have assembled important collections since the mid-1980s. Elizabeth Brown-Guillory, ed., *Wines in the Wilderness: Plays by African American Women from the Harlem Renaissance to the Present* (New York: Greenwood Press, 1990); Sydné Mahone, ed., *Moon Marked and Touched by the Sun* (New York: Theatre Communications Group, 1994); Kathy Perkins, ed., *Black Female Playwrights: An Anthology of Plays before 1950,* (Bloomington: Indiana University Press, 1989); Margaret B. Wilkerson, ed., *Nine Plays by Black Women* (New York: New American Library, 1986); and Kathy Perkins and Roberta Uno, eds., *Contemporary Plays by Women of Color* (London: Routledge, 1996) recover the primary material for critically interrogating previously unavailable works. That intervention also ensures the survival of new dramatic texts by black women playwrights. Like contemporary black female novelists, although on a smaller scale, several black female dramatists have received notice for their work that foregrounds the domestic sphere and intimacy and thus alters the African American theatrical tradition.

14. Ntozake Shange, *For Colored Girls Who Consider Suicide When the Rainbow*

Is Enuf (New York: Macmillan, 1977); Ntozake Shange, *A Photograph: Lovers in Motion*, in Shange, *Three Pieces* (New York: Penguin, 1981), 53–108; Aishah Rahman, *Unfinished Women Cry in No Man's Land while a Bird Dies in a Gilded Cage*, in *Nine Plays by Black Women*, edited by Margaret Wilkerson (New York: Mentor, 1986), 197–237.

15. Suzan-Lori Parks, *The America Play and Other Works* (New York: Theatre Communications Group, 1995), 19, 20.

16. As I discuss in the Introduction, the new black aesthetic and the broadening of the black middle class has altered the perception and presentation of the black middle class.

17. Evelyn Hammonds, "Black (W)holes and the Geometry of Black Female Sexuality," *Differences: A Journal of Feminist Cultural Studies* 6, nos. 2–3 (1994): 134.

18. Other plays that depict black middle-class women negotiating issues of sexuality include Lisa Jones, *Combination Skin*, in *Contemporary Plays by Women of Color*, edited by Kathy Perkins and Roberta Uno (London: Routledge, 1996), 215–29; Ntozake Shange, *The Resurrection of the Daughter: Liliane* (also a novel), in *Moon Marked and Touched by Sun*, edited by Sydné Mahone (New York: Theatre Communications Group, 1994), 321–52; and Ntozake Shange, *A Photograph: Lovers in Motion* (1979); Alexis DeVeaux, *Tapestry*, in *Nine Plays by Black Women*, edited by Margaret Wilkerson (New York: Mentor, 1986), 135–95; Sandra Seaton, *The Bridge Party*, in *Strange Fruit: Plays on Lynching by American Women*, edited by Kathy Perkins and Judith L. Stephens (Bloomington: Indiana University Press, 1998), 320–65; and Lisa B. Thompson, *Single Black Female* (1998). Other contemporary plays address the long legacy of black women's sexual oppression within the African American community and society at large: Rita Dove, *The Darker Face of the Earth* (Brownsville, Ore.: Story Line Press, 1994); Elaine Jackson, *Paper Dolls*, in *Nine Plays by Black Women*, edited by Margaret Wilkerson (New York: Mentor, 1986), 347–423; Robbie McCauley, *Sally's Rape* (1992) (an Obie Award winner), in *Moon Marked and Touched by Sun*, edited by Sydné Mahone (New York: Theatre Communications Group, 1994), 211–37; Aisha Rahman, *Unfinished Women Cry in No Man's Land while a Bird Dies in a Gilded Cage*, in *Nine Plays by Black Women*, edited by Margaret Wilkerson (New York: Mentor, 1986) 197–237; Ntozake Shange, *For Colored Girls Who Have Considered Suicide* (1976); Suzan-Lori Parks, *Venus* (New York: Dramatist Play Service, 1998); and Suzan-Lori Parks, *In the Blood* (New York: Theatre Communications Group, 2000).

19. Tanya Modleski, "Feminism and the Power of Interpretation: Some Critical Readings," in *Feminist Studies/Critical Studies*, edited by Teresa de Lauretis (Bloomington: Indiana University Press, 1986), 126.

20. Lynda Hart criticizes Modleski's model for presuming "a stable knowledge, experience, and identity" for both the oppressors and the oppressed. Hart, "Identity and Seduction: Lesbians in the Mainstream," in *Acting Out: Feminist Performances*, edited by Lynda Hart and Peggy Phelan (Ann Arbor: University of Michigan Press, 1993), 119–37.

21. Coco Fusco, "Performance and the Power of the Popular," in *Let's Get It On: The Politics of Black Performance*, edited by Catherine Ugwu (Seattle: Bay Press, 1995), 161, 164.

22. Hill's private and public suffering symbolizes that experienced by many middle-class black women. Condoleezza Rice also experienced fibroids. The similarities between the two women go beyond personal style. Some consider the decline in marriage and birth rates among black middle-class women—the African American elite, if you will—as a catastrophe that threatens the black community's possibilities for survival and advancement.

23. Steven Winn, "*WOMBmanWars* Takes on Black Battle of the Sexes," *San Francisco Chronicle*, Daily Datebook, Feb. 11, 1995, E1.

24. Judith Alexa Jackson, *WOMBmanWars*, in *Moon Marked and Touched by Sun: Plays by African-American Women*, edited by Sydné Mahome (New York: Theatre Communications Group, 1994), 145

25. I am indebted to Patricia J. Williams for formulating these publicly staged sensational events. For discussions of a more recent public spectacle see Patricia J. Williams, "Gigglegate and Gomorrah," and Anita F. Hill, "The Lewinsky Affair: Whose Story Is It Anyway?" both in *Village Voice*, Jan. 28–Feb. 3, 1998, 37, 38.

26. Anna Deavere Smith, *Fires in the Mirror* (New York: Anchor, 1993); Anna Deavere Smith, *Twilight: Los Angeles 1992* (New York: Bantam, 1994). Jackson mostly writes "one-woman performance plays"; her previous unpublished solo works include "N*gg*r Café," "Huhbehah's," "House," and "Origin of a Biscuit." Anna Deavere Smith, Introduction, in *Fires in the Mirror*, xxix. For extensive discussions of Smith's work see Ann Pellegrini, *Performance Anxieties: Staging Psychoanalysis, Staging Race* (New York: Routledge, 1997); Carol Martin, "Bearing Witness: Anna Deavere Smith from Community to Theatre to Mass Media," in *A Sourcebook of Feminist Theatre and Performance* (New York: Routledge, 1996), 81–93; Sandra Richards, "Caught in the Act of Social Definition: On the Road with Anna Deavere Smith," in *Acting Out: Feminist Performances*, edited by Lynda Hart and Peggy Phelan (Ann Arbor: University of Michigan Press, 1993), 35–53; and Tania Modleski, "Doing Justice to the Subjects: Mimetic Art in a Multicultural Society: The Work of Anna Deavere Smith," in *Female Subjects in Black and White: Race, Psychoanalysis, Feminism*, edited by Elizabeth Abel, Barbara Christian, and Helene Moglen (Berkeley: University of California Press, 1997), 57–76. That fascination for the "real" of which Smith speaks is also evident in the popularity of television talk shows, another site of popular performance.

27. Jackson, "Author's Note," in *Moon Marked and Touched by Sun*, ed. Mahone, 151.

28. Jan Breslauer, "Reality Bites," *Los Angeles Times*, July 28, 1996, 9.

29. Jackson, *WOMBmanWars*, in *Moon Marked and Touched by the Sun*, ed. Mahome, 154. Further citations to this work appear in parentheses.

30. Hortense J. Spillers, "Mama's Baby, Papa's Maybe: An American Grammar Book," *Diacritics* 17, no. 2 (1987): 65.

31. As I note in chapter 1, the black lady was and continues to be, even revised, another demeaning stereotype.

32. Toni Morrison, ed., *Race-ing Justice, En-gendering Power: Essays on Anita Hill, Clarence Thomas, and the Construction of Social Reality* (New York: Pantheon Books, 1992), xvi.

33. Nell Irvin Painter, "Hill, Thomas, and the Use of Racial Stereotype," in *Race-ing Justice, En-gendering Power: Essays on Anita Hill, Clarence Thomas, and the Construction of Social Reality*, edited by Toni Morrison (New York: Pantheon Books, 1992), 200–214. Painter states, "Simply to comprehend Hill's identity as a highly educated, ambitious, black female Republican imposed a burden on American audiences, black and white, that they were unable—at least at that very moment—to shoulder" (205).

34. J. Martin Favor, *Authentic Blackness* (Durham: Duke University Press, 1999); Nathan Hare, *The Black Anglo-Saxons* (London: Collier Books, 1965). Hare's work predates those who complain that *The Cosby Show* was not a "real" depiction of African American life.

35. Cheryl Gilkes, *If It Wasn't for the Women: Black Women's Experience and Womanist Culture in Church and Community* (Maryknoll, N.Y.: Orbis Books, 2001), demonstrates that the vital importance of women in black churches belies the posturing of black male ministers as patriarchs.

36. For a discussion of *Cosby* as an icon of the African American middle class see Herman Gray, *Watching Race: Television and the Struggle for "Blackness"* (Minneapolis: University of Minnesota Press, 1995), and Marlon Riggs's documentary about blacks in television, *Color Adjustment* (1991).

37. Charles R. Lawrence III, "The Message of the Verdict: A Three-Act Morality Play Starring Clarence Thomas, Willie Smith, and Mike Tyson," in *Black Men on Race, Gender, and Sexuality*, edited by Devon Carbado (New York: New York University Press, 1999), 212–36. As Lawrence explains, "Tyson could not have been more perfectly cast for the role of the rapist—he fit all the time-honored stereotypes of the violent, sexual, savage, unintelligent, irresponsible, scary black male. The *Sports Illustrated* cover story on the trial described Tyson as 'a single-purpose organism, bred for bad intentions and well maintained for its unique ability to enact violent public spectacles, but entirely unsuited for real life'" (222). Lawrence also offers an explanation for Tyson's demonization in the press and rapid verdict regarding what happened. Jackson, however, makes little comment on the flawless performance of black masculinity that traps Tyson into a dangerous and demeaning racial and sexual script. Also in Carbado's volume see also Kevin Brown, "The Social Construction of a Rape Victim: Stories of African-American Males about the Rape of Desirée Washington," 147–58.

38. Michael Awkward, "'You're Turning Me On': The Boxer, the Beauty Queen, and the Rituals of Gender," in *Black Men on Race, Gender, and Sexuality*, edited by Devon W. Carbado (New York: New York University Press, 1999), 132.

39. Awkward. "'You're Turning Me On,'" 139.

40. Washington's class status was used against Tyson in the rape trial but against Washington in certain public debates, Ironically, among some African Americans Tyson's vastly superior economic status was used only to support notions of his victimization, being that Washington and other women are considered predatory gold diggers.

41. Todd Barrett, "He Started Laughing Like It Was a Game," *Newsweek*, Feb. 10, 1992, 30.

42. Lawrence, "The Message of the Verdict," 224. Lawrence maintains that the criminal justice system and media "allowed [Desire Washington] to play 'Miss Anne'"(224) although casting black middle-class women as white elides the difficulties they face.

43. Kimberlé W. Crenshaw, "Demarginalizing the Intersection of Race and Sex: A Black Feminist Critique of Antidiscrimination Doctrine, Feminist Theory and Antiracist Politics," *University of Chicago Legal Forum* (1989): 406. For further analysis about intersectionality see Crenshaw, "Whose Story Is It Anyway? Feminist and Antiracist Appropriations of Anita Hill," in *Race-ing Justice, Engendering Power: Essays on Anita Hill, Clarence Thomas, and the Construction of Social Reality*, edited by Toni Morrison (New York: Pantheon Books, 1992), 402–40.

44. P. J. Gibson, *Destiny's Daughters: Nine Voices of P. J. Gibson* (New York: First Books, 2002).

45. Gibson, *Destiny's Daughters*, xvi.

46. Neilesh Bose, "A Play of Substance; New Horizon Production Veers from the Mainstream," *Pittsburgh Post-Gazette* May 28, 1999, 21.

47. Wilkerson, ed., *Nine Plays by Black Women*, 425.

48. John Hayes, Philadelphia Post-Gazette.com magazine May 25, 1999, at www.post-gazette.com/magazine.19990525gibson3.asp (Oct. 6, 2005).

49. Alice Childress, "Knowing the Human Condition," in *Black American Literature and Humanism*, edited by R. Baxter Miller (Lexington: University Press of Kentucky, 1981), 9–10.

50. Perkins and Stephens, eds., *Strange Fruit*.

51. Hortense Spillers comments that "the unsexed black female and the supersexed black female embody the very same vice, cast the very same shadow, inasmuch as both are an exaggeration—at either pole—of the uses to which sex might be put." Spillers, "Interstices: A Small Drama of Words," in *Pleasure and Danger: Exploring Female Sexuality*, edited by Carole Vance (Boston: Routledge and Kegan Paul, 1984), 85.

52. Gibson, *Long Time since Yesterday*, in *Black Thunder: An Anthology of Contemporary African American Drama* (New York: Penguin Books, 1992), 211–75. Further citations to this work appear in parentheses.

53. Once her sexual orientation is revealed, Panzi is depicted as the stereotypical predatory lesbian. It is also suggested that lesbianism is the product of her mother's

lack of affection. Although she does try to make the other friends' angry about Panzi's rejection of Janeen, Gibson fails to challenge sexual stereotypes.

54. Janeen's parents' social group, a fictional organization called The Trees, is strikingly similar to the middle-class African American group The Links.

55. Although Laveer has many partners, she no longer criticizes Janeen for her relative lack of them. Laveer assures Janeen: "Three men in your life is not a disgrace. I should be so lucky" (Gibson, *Long Time,* 252). By the time she returns for Janeen's funeral, Laveer has settled down, but she does not regret her racy past.

56. The litany considers each identity as problematic. Labeling Panzi a dyke further reinforces the negative image of lesbianism. Ibid., 273.

57. In both of Gibson's plays sexual encounters are played offstage or are merely suggested by stage directions.

58. Richards, "Writing the Absent Potential," 83.

59. Alain Locke, ed., *The New Negro* (1925, repr. New York: Atheneum, 1969), xi.

60. Performance art pieces such as Eve Ensler's *The Vagina Monologues* (New York: Villard, 1998), for example, celebrate eroticism at the same time they acknowledge gender oppression.

61. Spillers, "Interstices," 74.

Chapter 3: Black Ladies and Black Magic Women: Independent Film and Black Society

1. Condoleezza Rice commented that "the legacy of Mrs. King and her husband is that people like me get to do the things that I'm now doing. Their struggle meant everything to me. The difference between my life in Alabama in 1963 and my life in 1965, post segregation, was profound. As a child I remember seeing her with Dr. King when they would come into the city, but I saw her last when I was national security adviser at an event at The White House. She was so kind and so supportive. She said, 'You're doing great, and we're very proud of you.' I was thrilled to have her say that." Rice's comments attempt to tie her own success to the King legacy. Even George Herbert Walker Bush remarked, "When she wore a veil at forty years old, her dignity revealed the deepest trust in God and His purposes. In decades of prominence, her dignity drew others to the unfinished work of justice. In all her years, Coretta Scott King showed that a person of conviction and strength could also be a beautiful soul. This kind and gentle woman became one of the most admired Americans of our time." Mary Mitchell, "She Dreamed a World," *Essence,* April 2006, 127; "President Honors Coretta Scott King at Homegoing Celebration" at http://www.whitehouse.gov/news/releases/2006/02/20060207.html. (Nov. 20, 2007).

2. Houston A. Baker Jr., *Turning South Again: Re-Thinking Modernism/Re-Reading Booker T.* (Durham: Duke University Press, 2001) 18.

3. For a discussion of black women lives under slavery, see Deborah Gray White, *A'rn't I a Woman? Female Slaves in the Plantation South* (New York: W. W. Norton, 1985).

4. Sarah Warn, "The Right Time: Lesbianism in Middle-Class Black Movies," June 2002 at www.afterellen.com/movies/blackmovies.html (Jan. 26, 2006).

5. Joel R. Brouwer, "Repositioning: Center and Margin in Julie Dash's *Daughters of the Dust*," *African American Review*, 29 (March 1995): 5.

6. Houston A. Baker Jr., "Not without My Daughters: A Conversation with Julie Dash and Houston A. Baker, Jr.," *Transition* 57 (1992): 151.

7. Dash sets the film on Ibo Landing, but the deities she names, Ogun, Osun, and Yemoja, are all Yoruba.

8. Baker, "Not without My Daughters," 163.

9. Mia L. Mask, *"Eve's Bayou:* Too Good to Be a Black Film?" *Cineaste* 23, no. 4 (1998): 26. For a more nuanced reading of the reasons for the film's success see Kara Keeling, *The Witch's Flight: The Cinematic, the Black Femme, and the Image of Common Sense* (Durham: Duke University Press, 2007), 149–51.

10. In the first few weeks of theatrical release the film made $13 million, after an initial investment of $4 million, making it a box-office success. The final domestic gross was nearly $15 million when it was pulled from theaters in March 1998. Lemmons's second film, *Cave Man's Valentine* (2001), also starring and co-produced by Jackson, suffered from a sophomore jinx, grossing a mere $687,081 domestically. *Talk to Me* (2007), a biopic about Washington D.C., radio personality Ralph "Petey" Green, was also a box office disappointment, only grossing $4.5 million domestically during its theatrical release.

11. When the Batiste children act out scenes from Shakespeare, it not only marks the family's class status but also foreshadows the film's disastrous ending when Cisely calls her brother and sister Tybalt and Mercutio, characters from *Romeo and Juliet*, another tale of star-crossed lovers.

12. Much like her role in the groundbreaking television comedy *Ally McBeal*, in which she played Renee Raddick, a sexually insatiable attorney and Ally's roommate, Carson's sexual availability is played for laughs. Renee is consistently frustrated by her lack of suitable lovers, and instead of being presented as Ally's equal she is consistently depicted as a "freak" whose sexual desires prohibit eligible partnership.

13. Quoted in Deborah Willis, *The Black Female Body: A Photographic History* (Philadelphia: Temple University Press, 2002), 89.

14. For Lemmons to cast Carroll against type annoyed some reviewers. After her initial shock, Carroll reportedly enjoyed performing without makeup and was relieved at not having to appear glamorous on film. Of course, the casting can also be attributed to Carroll's age. For an extensive discussion of Diahann Carroll's acting career and *Julia*, see Christine Acham, *Revolution Televised: Prime Time and the Struggle for Black Power* (Minneapolis: University Minnesota Press, 2004).

15. D. Soyini Madison, "Oedipus Rex at *Eve's Bayou;* or, The Little Black Girl Who Left Sigmund Freud in the Swamp," *Cultural Studies* 14, no. 2 (2000): 326.

16. Peterson theorizes that the black female body becomes "normalized" or perceived as "white" through two strategies, decorporealization and normalization. Carla

Peterson, Foreword, in *Recovering the Black Female Body*, edited by Michael Bennett and Vanessa D. Dickerson (New Brunswick: Rutgers University Press, 2001), xiii.

17. Although Aunt Mozelle presents another option of womanhood, Louis denounces his sister in front of the children and dismisses her "mystical" powers.

18. Sandra Grayson, *Symbolizing the Past: Reading "Sankofa," Daughters of the Dust, and Eve's Bayou as Histories* (Lanham: University Press of America, 2000), 55.

19. Julie Dash, Daughters of the Dust: *The Making of an African American Woman's Film* (New York: New Press, 1992), 32.

20. Angeletta KM Gourdine, "Fashioning the Body [as] Politic in Julie Dash's *Daughters of the Dust*," *African American Review* 38, no. 3 (2004): 505.

21. Viola is particularly disturbed by Bilal Muhammad's Muslim practices and makes a point of criticizing them around the children.

22. The colloquial expression *fixing the tit* suggests that Yellow Mary somehow physically mutilated her breasts in order to stop producing milk.

23. It is noteworthy that both Mozelle and Yellow Mary, the women in each film who have the most lovers, are childless, which undermines the myth of the promiscuous, fertile black woman.

24. Baker, "Not without My Daughters," 161.

Chapter 4: Narrating Sexuality in Contemporary African American Autobiography

1. A "52 percent increase in the number of black managers, professionals, technicians, and government officials" occurred during the 1980s. Richard Lugo, "Between Two Worlds," *Time*, March 23, 1989, 58.

2. Both quotations are from Charisse Jones and Kumea Shorter-Gooden, *Shifting: The Double Lives of Black Women in America* (New York: HarperCollins, 2003), 6–7.

3. Jonetta Rose Barras, "Literary Lockup," *Washington City Paper*, Oct. 28, 1994, 27; Henry Louis Gates Jr., Introduction, in *Bearing Witness: Selections from African American Autobiography in the Twentieth Century* (New York: Pantheon, 1991), 3–9; Ashraf H. A. Rushdy, *Neo-slave Narratives: Studies in the Social Logic of a Literary Form* (New York: Oxford University Press, 1999).

4. Robert B. Stepto, *Behind the Veil: A Study of Afro-American Narrative* (Urbana: University of Illinois Press, 1979), (a landmark book); William L. Andrews, *African American Autobiography* (Englewood Cliffs: Prentice-Hall, 1993); William L. Andrews, *To Tell a Free Story: The First Century of Afro-American Autobiography, 1760–1865* (Urbana: University of Illinois Press, 1986).

5. Lorene Cary, *Black Ice* (New York: Vintage, 1992), 6. Further citations to this work appear in parentheses.

6. Books such as Ellis Cose's *Rage of a Privileged Class* (New York: HarperCollins, 1993) and Gerald Early's anthology *Lure and Loathing: Essays on Race, Identity, and the Ambivalence of Assimilation* (New York: Allen Lane, 1993) describe "the soul-destroying slights at the heart of black middle-class discontent" and illustrates

the burden of persistent racism (5). The backlash against government-supported affirmative action programs, and the nation's mounting, increasingly conservative tone, frustrate many middle-class African Americans who assumed that with greater affluence and better education they would enjoy more acceptance. More recent autobiographies address issues of identity and advocate equality by illuminating the disappointments of black middle-class life.

7. Stephen Butterfield, *Black Autobiography in America* (Amherst: University of Massachusetts Press, 1974), 1.

8. Mary Burgher, "Images of Self and Race in the Autobiographies of Black Women," in *Sturdy Black Bridges: Visions of Black Women in Literature*, edited by Roseann P. Bell et al. (New York: Anchor Books, 1979), 107–22; Nellie Y. McKay, "The Narrative Self: Race, Politics, and Culture in Black American Women's Autobiography," in *Women, Autobiography, Theory; A Reader*, edited by Sidonie Smith and Julia Watson (Madison: University of Wisconsin Press, 1998), 96–107.

9. Nellie Y. McKay, "Nineteenth-Century Black Women's Spiritual Autobiographies: Religious Faith and Self-Empowerment," in *Interpreting Women's Lives: Feminist Theory and Personal Narratives,* edited by the Personal Narratives Group (Bloomington: Indiana University Press, 1989), 141.

10. bell hooks, "Writing Autobiography," in *Talking Back: Thinking Feminist, Thinking Black* (Boston: South End Press, 1989), 155.

11. Joanne M. Braxton, *Black Women Writing Autobiography: A Tradition within a Tradition* (Philadelphia: Temple University Press, 1989), 5

12. Nancy Mairs, *Voice Lessons: On Becoming a (Woman) Writer* (Boston: Beacon Press, 1994), 109.

13. Carolyn G. Heilbrun, "Non-Autobiographies of 'Privileged' Women: England and America," in *Life/Lines: Theorizing Women's Autobiography,* edited by Bella Brodzki and Celeste Schenck (Ithaca: Cornell University Press, 1988), 63.

14. Frances Smith Foster, "Adding Color and Contour to Early American Self-Portraitures: Autobiographical Writings of Afro-American Women," in *Conjuring: Black Women, Fiction, and Literary Tradition,* edited by Marjorie Pryse and Hortense Spillers (Bloomington: Indiana University Press, 1985), 25–38.

15. Burgher, "Images of Self and Race," 107.

16. Other contemporary autobiographies by black middle-class women, such as Gwendolyn Parker, *Trespassing: In the Halls of Privilege* (Boston: Houghton Mifflin, 1997) and Toi Derricotte, *The Black Notebooks: An Interior Journey* (New York: W. W. Norton, 1999), also address sexuality as an issue directed and controlled by class and racial identity.

17. See Lisa B. Thompson, "Sex Talk Black Women Represent Sexuality," Ph.D. diss., Stanford University, 2000), 1–27, for a delineation of the genealogy of black middle-class chastity and morality represented in African American literature.

18. Martin Carnoy, *Faded Dreams: The Politics and Economics of Race in American* (New York: Cambridge University Press, 1944), 14.

19. For discussion of legislation on African American social mobility see Martin Carnoy's examination of twentieth-century African American political and economic progress: *The Politics and Economics of Race in America* (New York: Cambridge University Press, 1994), 14. Carnoy states that a palpable difference exists in the quality of life among blacks because African Americans "who had attained middle-class status became more separated economically from the black working (and not working) poor" (13).

20. The belief that the middle class is a self-interested group that tries to emphasize their differences from most African Americans has been thoroughly argued by sociologists: E. Franklin Frazier, *The Black Bourgeoisie: The Rise of a New Middle Class in the United States* (New York: Free Press, 1957); Nathan Hare, *The Black Anglo-Saxons* (London: Collier Books, 1965). More recently, Bart Landry, *The New Black Middle Class* (Berkeley: University of California Press, 1987), and Mary Pattillo-McCoy, *Black Picket Fences: Privilege and Peril among the Black Middle Class* (Chicago: University Chicago Press, 1999), have disputed this claim by presenting the black middle class as more varied economically and socially.

21. Patricia L. Williams, *The Rooster's Egg: On the Persistence of Prejudice* (Cambridge: Harvard University Press, 1995), 149.

22. Dwight A. McBride, *Why I Hate Abercrombie and Fitch* (New York: New York University Press, 2004); Pattillo-McCoy, *Black Picket Fences;* Thomas M. Shapiro, *The Hidden Cost of Being African American* (New York: Oxford University Press, 2004); Melvin Oliver and Thomas M. Shapiro, *Black Wealth/White Wealth: A New Perspective on Racial Inequality* (New York: Routledge, 1997).

23. Shapiro, *The Hidden Cost,* 2. For a discussion of transformative assets, see Shapiro, *The Hidden Cost of Being African American.*

24. In her autobiography *Trespassing,* Gwendolyn Parker explains how she confronted an unwanted pregnancy in college with the help of her parents. Parker and her family handled the pregnancy quickly and privately to ensure her professional future. For a discussion of black women's reproductive rights see Dorothy Roberts, *Killing the Black Body: Race, Reproduction and the Meaning of Liberty* (New York: Pantheon Books, 1997). Although Roberts never specifically addresses middle-class black women, she analyzes how poor black women lack the power to control their reproductive fate.

25. Jill Nelson, *Volunteer Slavery: My Authentic Negro Experience* (Chicago: Noble Press, 1993). The wording appears on the back cover of the paperback edition.

26. Nelson, *Volunteer Slavery,* 23. Further citations to this work appear in parentheses.

27. The government study commonly known as the Moynihan Report after its principle author, Senator Daniel P. Moynihan, viewed the black family as troubled because "a very large percentage of Negro families are headed by females" (Moynihan, *The Negro Family: The Case for National Action* [Washington: U.S. Department of Labor, 1965], 9). The report further claimed that "at the center of the tangle of pathology is the weakness of the family structure. Once or twice removed, it will be found to be

the principal source of most of the aberrant, inadequate, or antisocial behavior that did not establish but now serves to perpetuate the cycle of poverty and deprivation" (30). For other views on the black family see Andrew Billingsley, *Climbing Jacob's Ladder: The Enduring Legacy of African-American Families* (New York: Simon and Schuster, 1992).

28. The mainstream media also put the issue at the forefront of black America's problems. Bill Moyers, for example, in *The Vanishing Family: A Crisis in Black America* (CBS News, 1986), echoed Moynihan's view that black males fail to participate in traditional family structure because of aberrant social values. *Newsweek* dedicated an entire March 23, 1987, issue, "Brothers: A Vivid Portrait of Black Men in America," to analyzing the plight of African American males. The November 1989 special issue of *Essence,* "Our Men: In Love, In Trouble—Let the Healing Begin," also examined the status of black men. For an extensive exploration of the "black male problem" see Pedro A. Noguera, "Reconsidering the 'Crisis' of the Black Male in America," *Social Justice* 24, no. 12 (1997): 147–66. Noguera questions the construction of a black male crisis in isolation from other members of the black community and suggests that it only exacerbates problems experienced by black males. See also Douglas C. Lyons, "The Other Side of the Male Crisis" *Ebony* 46, no. 10 (1991): 106–11, who states that despite the difficulties that some black men experience, others are "exercising unprecedented authority in some of society's most influential institutions" (107).

29. Since the 1990s, several articles in popular African American periodicals such as *Essence* have discussed the lack of black marriageable black males. The magazine often advises black women about "getting" and keeping a man. Charles N. Jamison Jr., "Where We Go Wrong Looking for Mr. Right," *Essence* (July 1991): 50–53, 112; Bebe Moore Campbell, "When He's Gotta Have It," *Essence* (Dec. 1990): 60–61, 127–38; Anita Randall, "Loving a Younger Man," *Essence* (April 1990): 58–60, 96–98. Although these articles follow the format of traditional women's magazines, the plummeting marriage rates make them all the more significant. See also Margaret M. Porter and Arline L. Bronzaft, "Do the Future Plans of Educated Black Women Include Black Mates? *Journal of Negro Education* 64, no. 2 (1995): 162–71; and Belinda M. Tucker and Claudia Mitchell-Kernan, "Psychological Well-being and Perceived Marital Opportunity among Single African American, Latina and White Women," *Journal of Comparative Family Studies* 29, no. 1 (1998): 57–73.

30. Robert Staples and Leanor Boulin Johnson, *Black Families at the Crossroads: Challenges and Prospects* (San Francisco: Jossey-Bass, 1993), 98.

31. The context in which black middle-class women experience marriage possibilities complicated the sexual and social landscape at the end of the twentieth century. Belinda Tucker and Claudia Mitchell-Kernan, eds., *The Decline in Marriage among African Americans: Causes, Consequences, and Policy Implications* (New York: Russell Sage Foundation, 1995). The study concludes that the shift in African American family formation pattern supports findings that "only 70 percent of black women born in the 1950s will marry," and "using more recent data . . . fewer than three of four black women overall can expect to marry, compared to nine of ten white women" (12). As a

consequence, the discourse constructs a crisis for heterosexual middle-class women because of the lack of available and satisfactory mates.

A glut of black self-help and relationship books addresses the black male crisis and the need for black middle-class women to contain their overly aggressive nature. In her review of black relationship books, Debra Dickerson reaffirms the importance of discussing the problems of mate selection in the African American community and cites statistics to underscore its seriousness: "In 1970, 68 percent of black families were headed by couples; it's 44 percent today. The black divorce rate tripled from 100 per 1,000 married persons to 300 per 1,000; only 35 percent of adult black women are married now, compared to 70 percent in 1960. Jesse Jackson made it clear to the nation that there are more young black men in jail than in all our colleges combined." Dickerson, "She's Gotta Have It: The Search for Black Men," *The New Republic,* May 6, 1996, 12–14, quotation on 12. Also see Robert G. Wood, "Marriage Rates and Marriageable Men: A Test of the Wilson Hypothesis," *Journal of Human Resources* 30, no. 1 (1995): 163–82, who supports ideas put forth by William Julius Wilson, who "proposed an explanation for the decline in marriage rates among blacks, particularly among poor, inner-city blacks, is due primarily to declining black male employment levels, resulting in a shrinking pool of acceptable marriage partners for black women" (163), and J. E. Blackwell, *The Black Community: Diversity and Unity* (New York: Harper and Row, 1991).

32. Lynne Segal, *Straight Sex: Rethinking the Politics of Pleasure* (Berkeley: University of California Press, 1994), 10.

33. Carole Vance, Introduction, in *Pleasure and Danger: Exploring Female Sexuality* (Boston: Routledge and Kegan Paul, 1984), 1.

34. John D'Emilio and Estelle B. Freedman, *Intimate Matters: A History of Sexuality in America.* (1988, repr. Chicago: Chicago University Press, 1997), 343.

35. Hazel V. Carby, "Policing the Black Woman's Body in an Urban Context," *Critical Inquiry* 18 (1992): 741.

36. Nelson complains that the discussion made her "feel like a victim of attempted rape" because colleagues condemn her for prior behavior (*Volunteer Slavery,* 111).

37. When a teenager and employed in a summer job, Nelson, like Cary, found herself ridiculed by other blacks. In Nelson's case, she did not know the nickname for Howard Johnson's and tried to "save face with a little elitism" (Ibid., 124).

38. hooks, "Writing Autobiography," 155, 157.

39. Burgher, "Images of Self and Race," 121.

Chapter 5: Sex, Travel, and the Single African American Girl: Andrea Lee's *Sarah Phillips*

1. Hazel Scott, "What Paris Means to Me," in *A Stranger in the Village: Two Centuries of African-American Travel Writing,* edited by Farah Griffin and Cheryl J. Fish (Boston: Beacon Press, 1998), 187.

2. Here I am thinking about Paule Marshall, *Praisesong for the Widow* (1983, repr. New York: Dutton, 1984); Toni Morrison, *The Bluest Eye* (1970, repr. New York: Pocket Books, 1972); Toni Morrison, *Song of Solomon* (New York: Knopf, 1977); Toni Morrison, *Tar Baby* (New York: Random House, 1981); Toni Morrison, *Paradise* (New York: A. A. Knopf, 1998); Toni Morrison, *Love* (New York: A. A. Knopf, 2003); Gloria Naylor, *The Women of Brewster Place* (New York: Viking Press, 1988); Gloria Naylor, *Linden Hills* (New York: Ticknor and Fields, 1985); and Gloria Naylor, *Mama Day* (New York: Vintage Books, 1989). See also E. Franklin Frazier, *The Black Bourgeoisie: The Rise of a New Middle Class in the United States* (New York: Free Press, 1957); and Nathan Hare, *The Black Anglo-Saxons* (London: Collier Books, 1965).

3. Barbara Christian, "Trajectories of Self-Definition: Placing Contemporary Afro-American Women's Fiction," in *Conjuring: Black Women, Fiction, and Literary Tradition,* edited by Hortense Spillers and Marjorie Pryse (Bloomington: Indiana University Press, 1985), 172.

4. See more recent novels such as Pearl Cleage, *What Looks Like Crazy on an Ordinary Day* (New York: Avon Books, 1997); Lorene Cary, *Pride* (New York: Anchor Books, 1998); Kristin Hunter Lattany, *Kinfolks* (New York: One World/Ballatine, 1997); Ntozake Shange, *Lilliane* (New York: Picador, 1995); Paule Marshall, *Daughters* (Atheneum, 1991); Caroliva Herton, *Thereafter Johnnie* (New York: Random House, 1991); Connie Briscoe, *Sisters and Lovers* (New York: HarperCollins, 1995); Connie Briscoe, *P. G. County* (New York: Doubleday, 2002); Benilde Little, *Acting Out* (New York: Free Press, 2003); Benilde Little, *Good Hair* (1996); Benilde Little, *The Itch* (New York: Simon and Schuster, 1998); Benilde Little, *Who Does She Think She Is?* (New York: Free Press, 2005); Dorothy West, *The Wedding* (New York: Doubleday, 1995); Diane McKinney-Whetstone, *Tempest Rising* (New York: William Morrow, 1998); Trisha R. Thomas, *Nappily Ever After* (New York: Random House, 2000); and Trisha R. Thomas, *Would I Lie to You? The Journey of Venus Johnston* (New York: Random House, 2005).

5. Sherley Anne Williams, "Roots of Privilege: New Black Fiction," *Ms.* (June 1985): 70.

6. This tendency is also discernable in African American drama; see chapter 2, "Staging Black Female Desire in Contemporary African American Autobiography."

7. Cheryl Wall, "Nella Larsen: Passing for What?" in *Women of the Harlem Renaissance* (Bloomington: Indiana University Press, 1995).

8. Alice Walker, *Meridian* (New York: Washington Square Press, 1976); Carlene Hatcher Polite, *The Flagellents* (New York: Farrar, Straus and Giroux, 1967); Ann Petry, *The Narrows* (1953, repr. Boston: Beacon Hill Press, 1988).

9. Mary Helen Washington makes a similar observation in *Invented Lives: Narratives of Black Women, 1860–1960* (New York: Anchor Press, 1987).

10. Morrison, *Song of Solomon,* 75.

11. Similarly, Morrison's protagonist in *Tar Baby,* Jadine, suspects that she is missing

something "essential" despite her success as a model and doctoral student. The novel attributes her rootlessness to an inability to cherish her black family members, her black lover, or the culture of the broader African diaspora. Morrison suggests that Jadine rejects her cultural and racial inheritance because of her affinity for Anglo- and Franco-European culture. By the novel's end she abandons the lover, returns to Paris, and reunites with her European boyfriend. Jadine's white lover represents her alienated sexuality and self-loathing. *Tar Baby* proposes that black middle-class women lack the essential elements for the race's survival. Throughout the narrative Jadine feels haunted by other, more authentic black women such as her lover's family members and the servants on the island, who comment that Jadine's "parts," the sexual pieces of her body, are bankrupt and faulty. She is an inauthentic and incomplete black woman.

12. Nedeed is quite similar to the patriarch in *Song of Solomon,* Macon Dead. Naylor suggests that Luther has an "unnatural" relationship with the corpses he receives in his mortuary, and the necrophilia confirms his role as the novel's villain. Morrison and Naylor indict both genders equally.

13. Naylor carries this theme over to her subsequent novel, *Mama Day.* The protagonist, Ophelia, returns to the Georgia Sea Island of her youth with her new husband, but her vanity and insecurity provoke a jealous neighbor to poison her. In order to survive, Ophelia must embrace her great aunt's folk wisdom; because she resists, her husband dies. Again, Naylor demonstrates that middle-class values are neither life-affirming nor community-sustaining. In all four novels Morrison and Naylor's heroines lack validating romantic relationships and sexual agency. Black middle-class women have few alternatives to a life of sadness, isolation, and sexual deviance.

14. Jill Nelson's *Sexual Healing* (New York: Agate, 2003), a novel about a brothel and spa that services upwardly mobile black women, fits both the African American romance and erotic fiction genres.

15. For a discussion in popular periodicals of the McMillan phenomenon, see Audrey Edwards, "Waiting to Inhale," *Essence* 23 (Oct. 1992): 77–78, 82, 118; Quincy Troupe, "A Conversation with Terry McMillan," *Emerge* 4 (Oct. 1992): 51–52, 56; and Karen Grisby Bates, "Possessing the Secrets of Success," *Emerge* 4 (Oct. 1992): 47–49. More complex representations of black middle-class sexuality have carried over onscreen with movies such as *Love Jones* (1997), *Hav Plenty* (1998), and *The Best Man* (1999), all of which have had varying degrees of box-office success. The screen adaptations of McMillan's *How Stella Got Her Groove Back* and *Waiting to Exhale* have been the most financially successful movies of the black romance genre. For a discussion of popular black film and representations of the black middle class see Valerie Smith, *Not Just Race, Not Just Gender: Black Feminist Readings* (New York: Routledge, 1998); and Elizabeth Alexander, "'We're Gonna Deconstruct Your Life!': The Making and Unmaking of the Black Bourgeois Patriarch in *Ricochet,*" in *Representing Black Men,* edited by Marcellus Blount and George P. Cunningham (New York: Routledge 1996), 157–71.

16. Thulani Davis, "Don't Worry, Be Buppie: Black Novelists Head for the Mainstream," in *War of the Words*, edited by Joy Press (New York: Three Rivers Press, 2001), 182. Other contemporary African American novels that depict the black middle class include Trey Ellis, *Platitudes* (New York: Vintage Books, 1988); Trey Ellis, *Home Repairs* (New York: Simon and Schuster, 1993); David Bradley, *The Chaneysville Incident* (New York: Avon, 1981); Stephen L. Carter, *Emperor of Ocean Park* (New York: Knopf, 2002); Stephen L. Carter, *New England White* (New York: Knopf, 2007); Diane McKinney-Whetstone, *Tempest Rising* (New York: William Morrow, 1998); Dawn Turner-Trice, *Only Twice I Wished for Heaven* (New York: Crown, 1996); Jake Lamar, *The Last Integrationist* (New York: Crown Publishers, 1996); Darryl Pinkney, *High Cotton* (New York: Farrar Straus and Giroux, 1992); Paul Beatty, *White Boy Shuffle* (New York: Houghton Mifflin, 1996); and Thulani Davis, *1959* (New York: Grove Press, 1992).

17. Washington, *Invented Lives*, 166.

18. Hazel V. Carby, *Reconstructing Womanhood: The Emergence of the Afro-American Novelist* (New York: Oxford University Press, 1987); Ann duCille, *The Coupling Convention: Sex, Text, and Tradition in Black Women's Fiction* (New York: Oxford University Press, 1993); Cheryl Wall, *Women of the Harlem Renaissance* (Bloomington: Indiana University Press, 1995).

19. du Cille, *The Coupling Convention*, 81, 87.

20. Carole Boyce Davies, *Black Women, Writing and Identity: Migrations of the Subject* (New York: Routledge, 1994), 134, 135.

21. Farah Jasmine Griffin and Cheryl J. Fish, eds., *A Stranger in the Village: Two Centuries of African-American Travel Writing* (Boston: Beacon Press, 1998), xiii.

22. Andrea Lee, *Lost Hearts in Italy* (New York: Random House, 2006), 8.

23. Lynne Segal, *Straight Sex: Rethinking the Politics of Pleasure* (Berkeley: University of California Press, 1994), 30.

24. Valerie Smith, Foreword, in Andrea Lee, *Sarah Phillips* (1984, repr. Boston: Northeastern University Press, 1993), xi.

25. Andrea Lee, *Sarah Phillips* (New York: Random House, 1984), 32–33. Further citations to this work appear in parentheses.

26. Sarah's prep school introduces her to whiteness more broadly, and she expresses the isolation she experiences there. Contradicting the assumptions of those who oppose affirmative action for academic reasons, Sarah explains, "Classes were easy for me, friends were hard" (54).

27. Paul Fussell, *The Norton Book of Travel* (New York: W. W. Norton, 1987), 13.

28. For an exploration of the migration of black writers to France see Tyler Stovall, *Paris Noir: African Americans in the City of Light* (New York: Houghton Mifflin, 1996); and Michel Fabre, *From Harlem to Paris: Black American Writers in France, 1840–1980* (Urbana: University of Illinois Press, 1991). See also the documentary *Africa to America to Paris: The Migration of Black Writers* (1997) by Jacques Goldstein and Blaise N'Djehoya. Faith Ringgold's exhibit *Dancing at the Louvre*, a collection of

painted quilts, features a fictional character, Willa Marie Simone, who finds herself posing nude for Henri Matisse and Pablo Picasso as well as meeting in cafes with prominent African American expatriates such as Lois Mailou Jones, Romare Bearden, Augusta Savage, and William H. Johnson. Ringgold's work particularly explores the complexity of the black female artist and expatriate in France and mirrors some of the concerns raised in *Sarah Phillips*. Collected essays on the exhibit appear in *Dancing at the Louvre: Faith Ringgold's French Collection and Other Story Quilts*, edited by Dan Cameron (Berkeley: University of California Press, 1998). Janet McDonald's autobiography *Project Girl* (Berkeley: University of California Press, 2000) and Shay Youngblood's novel *Black Girl in Paris* (New York: Riverhead Books, 2001) also center on young black women who venture to France in order to escape life in the United States.

29. James Baldwin, *Notes of a Native Son* (1949, repr. New York: Library of America, 1998), 106–7.

30. As Griffin and Fish note, "For the first time many expatriates encountered Africans from France's colonies and were introduced to decolonization struggles in these nations. As independence swept Africa, and when the formerly colonized began to immigrate to the country, mainly in the 1970s and 1980s, France's reputation for racial tolerance lessened among African Americans, especially as sections of the country made frightening turns to the extreme right" (*A Stranger in the Village*, xvi).

31. Mary Louise Pratt, *Imperial Eyes: Travel Writing and Transculturation* (New York: Routledge, 1992), 7.

32. Klaus de Albuquerque describes "the entry of young women into the sex tourism market dates to the early 1960s, when Scandinavian, British, and German women began to travel to the southern coasts of Europe" and its shift to "the Gambia, Kenya, or Ghana" ("In Search of the Big Bamboo," *Transition* 77 [1999]: 50).

33. Paulla Ebron, "Traffic in Men," in *Gendered Encounters: Challenging Cultural Boundaries and Social Hierarchies in Africa*, edited by Maria Grosz-Ngate and Omari Kokole (New York: Routledge, 1997), 240.

34. Terry McMillan, *How Stella Got Her Groove Back* (New York: Viking, 1996), 27.

35. In the Jamaican tourist industry, both African American women and native men negotiate their expectations. Klaus de Albuquerque contends that "African American women are known for their interest in long-term relationships with Jamaican men, and they represent a rent-a-dread's best chance to obtain a highly-coveted U.S. green card" ("In Search of the Big Bamboo," 51). Moreover, African American women are highly valued because it is presumed that they do not carry the same racial biases and "sexual hang-ups" as other women from the United States and Europe. In this way black female travelers become sexual agents with the power to negotiate the sexual landscape in their favor.

36. James Clifford, *Routes: Travel and Translation in the Late Twentieth Century* (Cambridge: Harvard University Press, 1997); Ali Behdad, *Belated Travelers: Oriental-*

ism in the Age of Colonial Dissolution (Durham: Duke University Press, 1994); Sara Mills, *Discourses of Difference: An Analysis of Women's Travel Writing and Colonialism* (New York: Routledge, 1991).

37. Aware of her pretension, Sarah confesses, "At that time, thank heavens, I hadn't seen or read *Jules and Jim,* so I could play the queen without self-consciousness, thinking—headily, guiltily, sentimentally—that I was doing something the world had never seen before" (7). Although she is not unique, Sarah is quite happy being different from what her parents expect and understand.

38. For useful discussions of Sara Baartman see T. Denean Sharpley-Whiting, *Black Venus: Sexualized Savages, Primal Fears, and Primitive Narratives in French* (Durham: Duke University Press, 1999); Anne Fausto-Sterling, "Gender, Race, and Nation: The Comparative Anatomy of 'Hottentot' Women in Europe, 1815–1817," in *Deviant Bodies: Critical Perspectives on Difference in Science and Popular Culture,* edited by Jennifer Terry and Jacqueline Urla (Bloomington: Indiana University Press, 1995), 19–48; Sander Gilman, *Difference and Pathology: Stereotypes of Sexuality, Race and Madness* (Ithaca: Cornell University Press, 1985); Janell Hobson, *Venus in the Dark: Blackness and Beauty in Popular Culture* (New York: Routledge, 2005); and the documentary *The Life and Times of Sara Baartman: The Hottentot Venus* (1999) directed by Zola Maseko. In addition, for discussions of Nella Larsen's middle-class heroines see Wall, *Women of the Harlem Renaissance* and duCille, *The Coupling Convention.*

39. For more on the myth of Galatea see Edith Hamilton, *Mythology: Timeless Tale of Gods and Heroes* (New York: Mentor, 1940).

40. See Don M. Enomoto, "Irreconcilable Differences: 'Creative Destruction' and the Fashioning of a Self in *Sarah Phillips,*" *MELUS* 24, no. 1 (1999): 209–34, for a discussion of Lee's treatment of "estrangement and alienation" in Sarah's development.

Epilogue

1. Anita Gates, "Brainy Women, Still Looking for Love," *New York Times,* June 20, 2006, E4; Linda Armstrong, "Single Women in the Spotlight," *Amsterdam News,* June 15–21, 2006, 22. For reviews of other productions of *Single Black Female* see F. Kathleen Foley, "'Female' Riffs of Feminist Rants," *Los Angeles Times,* April 9, 2004, E36; Erin Aubry Kaplan, review of *Single Black Female, LA Weekly,* April 2–8, 2004, 80; Robert Hurwitt, "'SBF,' Witty, Provocative, Seeks Audience," *San Francisco Examiner,* March 19, 1999, C5; Chad Jones, "A Different World: 'SBF: Single Black Female' Explores the Lives of Black Middle-Class Women," *Oakland Tribune,* March 13, 1999, 4; Sam Thielman, "Single Black Female," at Variety.com, http://review/VE1117937408.html?categoryid=33&cs=1 (June 12, 2008); Jerry Portwood, review of "Single Black Female" at Backstage.com, http://www.backstage.com/bso/news_reviews/nyc/review_display.jsp?vnu_content_id=1003816586 (June 13, 2008).

2. Lisa Thompson, "Single Black Female" (© 1998), unpublished manuscript, 73.

3. Jocelyn Elders et al., "Adolescent Sexuality and Public Policy: A Liberal Response," *Politics and the Life Sciences* 15 (March 1996): 281–323; Douglas Jehl, "One Gaffe too Many: Controversial to the End, Surgeon General Is Undone by Her Outspokenness," *New York Times,* Dec. 11, 1994, 4:2; Martin Fletcher, "Clinton Sacks His Health Chief in School Sex Furore," *Times of London,* Dec. 10, 1994, 1; Jeff Jacoby, "Look What's Missing from Lani Guinier's Book," *Boston Globe,* June 2, 1994, op-ed, 17; Maureen Dowd, "In 1994–Model Politics, Loyalty Is Often Optional Equipment," *New York Times,* March 20, 1994, 4:3; Peter Applebome, "Guinier Ideas, Once Seen as Odd, Now Get Serious Study," *New York Times,* April 3, 1994, 4:5; Patricia J. Williams, "Lani, We Hardly Knew Ye: How the Right Wing Created a Monster out of a Civil Rights Advocate and Bill Clinton Ran in Terror," *Village Voice,* June 15, 1993, 21.

4. Maureen Dowd, "Should Michelle Cover Up?" *New York Times,* March 8, 2009, WK10; Erin Aubry Kaplan, "First Lady Got Back," *Salon.com,* November 18, 2008, at http://www.salon.com/mwt/feature/2008/11/18/michelles_booty/ (November 30, 2008); Jack Cafferty, "My Crush on Michelle Obama," CNN.com at http://www.cnn.com/2009/POLITICS/03/03/cafferty.first.lady/ (March 21, 2009); Jeannine Stein, "Michelle Obama's Sleeveless Style," *Atlanta Journal Constitution,* April 3, 2009, at http://www.ajc.com/services/content/news/stories/2009/04/03/michelle_obama_sleeveless_dress.html (April 4, 2009).

5. Michele Wallace, "Variations of Negation and the Heresy of Black Feminist Creativity," in *Invisibility Blues: From Pop to Theory* (London: Verso, 1990), 236.

Index

affirmative action, 6, 14, 22, 103, 110, 164n6, 171n26
African American literature: power of absence theory, 70; sexuality and, 8; tragic heroine narratives, 44, 46, 65, 71, 119–20
African American theater: abolitionist dramas, 63–64; depiction of performance of middle-class black womanhood, 63; literary criticism and, 44–45, 156n7, 157n13; lynching plays, 44–45, 64, 154n61, 156n9; performance of intersectionality, 46–47; power of absence theory, 70; racial uplift paradigm in, 46, 156n9; real-life drama, interpreted, 50–51; revolutionary black theater movements, 46; tragic heroine narratives, 46, 71; use of for cultural interventions, 44–49; use of the erotic, 71; use of tragedy, 64; working-class women within, 46
African American Women in Defense of Ourselves, 31–32, 40–41, 153n45
agency: of black men, 167n28; contact zones and, 29, 134–35; culture of dissemblance, 4; sexual agency through class identity, 132–33; sexual freedom and, 131; social position and, 118; southern sites and, 16–17. *See also* sexual agency
Ain't Love Grand (Gibson), 62
alienated sexuality, 169n11
Ally McBeal (television show), 163n12
Alvarez, J. C., 28, 151n26

Andrews, William L., 98
Angelou, Maya, 48
antebellum period, 4, 9, 73, 81, 90, 145
anti-lynching dramas, 44–45, 64, 154n61, 156n9
Appropriating Blackness (Johnson), 142n8
asexuality, 3, 5, 63, 161n51
authenticity: autobiography and, 97, 101, 116–17; black middle-class and, 5, 17, 22; chastity and, 17, 24, 102, 145; class position and, 98–100, 101–2, 109–10, 112–13, 116–17; cultural mulattos, 5–6; interracial relationships and, 127–28; racial identification and, 169n11; racial loyalty and, 50, 61
autobiography: in African American traditions, 33, 97–102, 109, 116–17; of Anita Hill, 21, 42, 44, 97; authenticity and, 97, 101, 116–17; class identity, 17; of Clarance Thomas, 21, 148n5; of Gwendolyn Parker, 166n24; importance of autobiographical storytelling, 97–102, 106, 108–9, 110, 116–17; intersectionality and, 99; portrayal of authentic experiences, 97, 101, 116–17; sexual identity and, 17; slave narrative comparisons, 97, 99, 101; tendency to generalize, 99–100
Awkward, Michael, 58–59

Baartman, Sara, 132
Baker, Houston, 73, 77, 94
Baker, Josephine, 132

Baldwin, James, 129
Baraka, Amiri, 5, 45, 46
Best Man (1999), 74, 75–76
black arts movement, 45
Black Bourgeoisie (Frazier), 52
black church cultures, 55, 59–60, 160n35
black female bodies, 23, 58–59, 82–83, 125, 132–33, 163n16
black feminisms, 12, 30, 31–33, 55
Black Ice (Cary): acceptance as sexual beings, 98, 100–102, 104–9; autobiography overview, 17; class identity, 98–99, 100–101, 103–8; concealment of sexual experiences, 97–98, 100–102, 104–7; empathy with working-class, 103, 106–8; feelings of shame, 105, 106; first relationships, 105–7; importance of autobiographical storytelling, 97–102, 106, 108–9, 116–17; interracial relationships, 108; maternal training, 104; pregnancy, 105–7; racial authenticity, 98–100, 101–2; roles of privilege, 103, 105, 106–7, 108; sexual abuse/harassment, 105, 107–8; sexual codes, 104–5; transformative assets, 104, 105, 109
black intellectuals, 56
black lady, the: class position and, 25–26; gendered issues, 25–26; Lemmons on, 84–85; as public figure, 150n16; sexual experimentation, 67–68; usage of term, 6, 25–26, 144, 150n16
black masculinity, 52, 112, 160n37
black men: agency of, 167n28; black masculinity and, 52, 112, 160n37; black matriarchy and, 110; counterpublics of, 30; crisis narratives, 110–11, 167n28, 167n31; crisis narratives of, 167n28; emasculation of, 3, 6, 51; family structures and, 167n28; female promiscuity and, 58; marriageability of, 167n29; as public spectacle, 58; sexism and, 5; sexualities, 58, 130; sexual violence and, 5; violence and, 58
black middle-class: affirmative action babies, 14, 22; authenticity and, 5, 17, 22, 98–100, 101–2; blackness and, 5–6; definitions of, 5, 12–13, 14–15, 15–17; disappointments of, 164n6; growth of, 14–15; influence of the South on, 7, 16–18, 72–74, 77, 92, 93–94, 128–29; intimacy and, 120; minority status of, 15; normalization of, 7–8, 98–100, 103, 110, 116; racism and,

164n6; reliance on female sexuality, 135; representations of romance, 170nn13–15; residential segregation, 14–15; responses to affirmative action, 164n6; self-interests of, 5, 166n20; sexual dysfunction of, 5; whiteness and, 5, 119, 133, 171n26; women's issues and, 15
blackness, 5–6, 128, 133
Black Picket Fences (Pattillo-McCoy), 14–15
Black Women, Writing and Identity (Davies), 121–22
Blue Chip Black (Lacy), 15
body / embodiment, 82–83, 125
Boomerang (1992), 74
Boondocks, The, 1–2, 141n2
Branch, William, 45
Braxton, Joanne M., 99
Breaking All the Rules (2004), 74
Brooks, Daphne, 3, 44
Brothers (2001), 74
Brothers, The (Collins), 45
Brown, Henry "Box," 44
Brown, William Henry, 63
Brown, William Wells, 63
Brown Silk and Magenta Sunsets (Gibson), 62
Burgher, Mary, 101, 117
Bush, George Herbert Walker, 162n1
Bush, George W., 2
Butterfield, Stephen, 99

Carby, Hazel, 8, 112, 121, 143n18
Carnoy, Martin, 166n19
Carr, John W., 37
Carroll, Diahanne, 81–82, 163n14
Carson, Lisa Nicole, 79, 163n12
Carter, Stephen L., 14, 150n11
Cary, Lorene, 17, 118. See also *Black Ice* (Cary)
Case, Sue-Ellen, 156n7
Cave Man's Valentine (2001), 163n10
chastity, 17, 24, 71, 102, 145
Childress, Alice, 5, 45, 46, 63
Christian, Barbara, 12, 119
class expectations: community-sustaining relationships, 125; interracial relationships, 124–25; sexual explorations as defiance of, 131–32
class identity: chastity and, 71; class expectations, 130–32; impact on sexual develop-

ment, 98–99, 100–101, 103–8, 110–13; racial identification rejection, 169n11; sexual agency through, 132–33; sexual identity, 17; sexual stereotyping and, 145n50
class status: black womanhood and, 3; class mobility, 102; gender identity, 3; organizing around Hill/Thomas hearings and, 31–33; racial authenticity and, 98–100, 101–2, 109–10, 112–13, 116–17; racial identity and, 3; transformative assets, 104; victimization and, 60; working-class identity, 100, 105–7, 108
Cleage, Pearl, 46
Clean Sheets Can't Soil (Gibson), 62
club movements, 3, 103, 150n16
Cohen, Cathy, 7
Collins, Kathleen, 45
Collins, Patricia Hill, 8, 11
concealment strategies, 4, 97–98, 100–102, 104–7
contact zones, 29, 134–35
Cooper, Anna Julia, 6
Cooper, Helen, 2
coping strategies, 44, 48–49, 79. See also survival strategies
Cosby Show, The (television show), 22, 56, 74, 82, 147n68, 160n34, 160n36
Cose, Ellis, 15, 164n6
counterpublics, 29–33, 30, 41–42, 153n42
Coupling Convention (duCille), 121
Crenshaw, Kimberlé, 8, 61, 138, 152n36, 154n49
Cult of Domesticity, 3
Cult of True Womanhood, 3
cultural interventions, 44–45
cultural mulattos, 5–6
cultural policing, 144n24
culture of dissemblance, 4, 48, 57, 97

Daddy's Girls (2006), 74
Dancing at the Louvre (Ringgold), 171n28
Dash, Julie: on challenging notions of beauty, 89; sexual agency, 16–17; use of the South, 74, 77. See also *Daughter's of the Dust* (1991)
Daughter's of the Dust (1991), 89–94; family structures, 89; *Gnostic Gospels*, 93; limits of morality, 94; nonlinear African storytelling style, 77, 89; notions of beauty, 89; promiscuity within, 164n23; on romanticization of history, 93–94; sexual abuse/victimization, 91–92, 93; sexual agency within, 16–17; spiritual practices within, 77, 89–90, 90–91, 164n21; survival strategies, 89–90; use of the South, 74, 92, 93–94
Davies, Carol Boyce, 121–22
Davis, Thulani, 121
Dawson, Michael, 30, 153n37
de Albuquerque, Klaus, 172n32, 172n35
Decline in Marriage among African Americans (Tucker and Mitchell-Kernan), 167n31
Deliver Us from Eva (2003), 74
D'Emilio, John, 111–12
Designing Women (television episode), 152n30
Destiny's Daughters (Gibson), 62
De Veaux, Alexis, 45–46, 64
deviant sexuality, 13, 119–20, 170n12
Dickerson, Debra, 167n31
Dickerson, Ernie, 154n61
Dickerson, Glenda, 44, 167n31
Downie, Leonard, Jr., 141n1
Drama of King Shotaway (Brown), 63
Du Bois, W. E. B., 6, 30, 32, 45, 64, 91, 135
DuCille, Ann, 121
Dunye, Cheryl, 94
Dutchman, The (Baraka), 45
Dyson, Michael, 147n68

Ebron, Paulla, 129
Ellis, Trey, 5, 127, 171
emasculation, 3, 6, 51
eroticism, 59, 71, 94, 132, 162n60, 170n14
Escape; or, A Leap to Freedom (Brown), 63
Evers, Myrlie, 72–73
Eve's Bayou (1997), 78–89; coping strategies in, 79; critical reviews of, 78, 163n10; decorporealization (embodiment), 82–83; diversity of sexual identities within, 78, 82–85, 87–89; family structures within, 80–82, 86–88, 163n11; incest within, 87–88; limits of morality, 94; marriage in, 83–84, 86; negative stereotypes within, 78; normalization, 82–85; notions of beauty within, 79–80, 82–83; racial uplift paradigm, 82–83, 85–86; respectability, 78–79, 80–82, 86–88, 89; sexual agency within, 16–17; sexual development of characters,

79–81, 84–85, 87–88; spiritual practices within, 77, 80–81, 85, 164n17; tragic heroine narrative, 84–85; use of promiscuity within, 78–79, 80; use of the South, 74, 78–79, 81–82, 87, 88–89

family structures: black men and, 167n28; family formation, 104, 110, 167n31; female-headed households, 166n27; interracial relationships and, 127; marriage, 4, 83–84, 110, 127, 166n27, 167n31; maternal training, 54, 57, 104, 123–24; pathology of, 166n27; pregnancy, unwanted, 84, 105, 106, 107, 138, 166n24; sexual development and, 80–82; slavery trade and, 81; stability of, 4, 127; tensions between genders, 56
Fauset, Jessie, 4, 121, 122, 129, 143n17
feminism, 8, 11, 22, 102, 110
Ferguson, Roderick, 7
Fish, Cheryl J., 121, 122, 172n30
"For Colored Girls Who Have Considered Suicide When the Rainbow Is Enuf" (Shange), 69, 71
Foster, Frances Smith, 99, 101
Foucault, Michel, 145n36
Fraser, Nancy, 29–30, 31, 41, 153n42
Frazier, E. Franklin, 5, 52, 143n21, 166n20
Freedman, Estelle B., 111–12
Freeman, Roland, 40
Funnyhouse of a Negro (Kennedy), 45, 46, 64
Fusco, Coco, 48
Fussell, Paul, 128

Galatea (myth), 132
Gates, Henry Louis, 15, 156n7
gender identity: class status, 3; gender discontent, 155n64; gender roles, 81; male privilege and, 60; professional ambition and, 74–76; race and, 4–5; struggles of working class women and, 55; travel narratives and, 121–22
Gibson, P. J., 16, 43, 61–70, 135
Givhan, Robin, 144n33, 174n4
Gnostic Gospels, 93
gorilla stereotype, 52–54, 58
Gourdine, Angeletta KM, 91
Grayson, Sandra, 85–86
Great Goodness of Life: A Coon Show (Baraka), 46

Griffin, Farah Jasmine, 121, 122, 128–29, 172n30
Grimke, Angelina, 45
guilt, 103–4, 105, 106–7
Guinier, Lani, 139

Habermas, Jürgen, 28
Hammonds, Evelynn, 8, 12, 47
Hamri, Sanaa, 94
Hansberry, Lorraine, 64
Hare, Nathan, 5, 160n34
Harper, Francis, 150n16
Harris, Leslie, 94
Hart, Lynda, 158n20
Hav Plenty (1997), 74
Height, Dorothy, 72
Heilbrun, Carolyn, 100
Higginbotham, Evelyn Brooks, 3
Higgins, Tracy, 13
Hill, Anita: affirmative action and, 22; autobiography of, 21, 42, 44, 97; as black lady, 6–7, 15–16, 24, 25–26, 36–38, 53–54, 116; black women's responses to, 150n15; class status and, 26–28, 34, 137–38; conservative politics of, 22; desire for privacy, 26–27, 155n68; emotionality of, 27; feminism of, 22; as gorilla, 54; heterosexuality of, 38–40; impact on politics of sexuality, 22–23; interclass tensions invoked, 54; Leibovitz photo, 35; lesbianism and, 38–40; media representations of testimony, 151n24; national organizing around, 30–33; private sphere and, 34; professional ambition/status, 26–27, 28, 34, 151n26, 160n33; public performance of, 21–22, 39–41; public/private roles, 22–24, 26–27, 28–32, 34, 155n68; as race traitor, 27–28; racial authenticity of, 22; as racial victim, 25; reliability of, 16, 21–22, 24–25, 61; response to Thomas' memoir, 21–22, 148n1, 148n5; romantic life of, 35–37; sexual agency and, 58; on sexual harassment, 22, 40–41, 148nn5–6; southern roots of, 28; *vs.* working class representations, 26–28. See also *WOMBmanWARS* (Jackson)
Hine, Darlene Clark, 4
historical values, 3
homophobia, 68–69

hooks, bell, 8, 9, 13–14, 99, 116
Hopkins, Pauline, 46, 121, 150, 150n16
"How Being a Good Girl Can Be Bad" (Tolman and Higgins), 13
How Stella Got Her Groove Back (McMillan), 121, 130, 170n15
hypersexuality, 6, 48–49, 63, 71, 161n51, 163n12

I Know Why the Caged Bird Sings (Angelou), 48
In Living Color (television episode), 152n30
Insurrection (O'Hara), 64
Interesting Women (Lee), 122
interracial relationships: authenticity and, 127–28; racial fetishization in, 133; racial loyalty and, 127–28; racial objectification, 133; as rejection of cultural identity, 169n11; as rejection of racial identity, 169n11; as representation of alienated sexuality, 169n11; self-loathing through, 169n11; social expectations, 124–25
intersectionality, 8, 46–47, 99, 154n49
"Interstices: A Small Drama in Words" (Spillers), 9
Is Bill Cosby Right? (Dyson), 147n68

Jackson, Judith Alexa, 16, 43–44, 47–61, 50, 71, 159n26
Johnson, E. Patrick, 142n8
Johnson, Georgia Douglas, 46, 64
Johnson, Leanor Boulin, 111
Jones, Charisse, 97
Jones, Gayl, 5
Jong, Erica, 11, 146n53
Jules and Jim (1962), 131, 173n37
Julia (television show), 82, 163n14
Julien, Isaac, 144n24

Kaplan, Erin Aubry, 174n4
Kennedy, Adrienne, 45, 46, 64, 156n1
Killing the Black Body (Roberts), 166n24
King, Coretta Scott, 72–73, 162n1
King, Rodney, 53
Konvergence (Gibson), 62

Lacy, Karyn, 15
Landry, Bart, 14, 15, 146n62, 166n20
Larsen, Nella, 4, 121, 143n17

Lawrence, Charles R., III, 160n37
Lee, Andrea, 17, 118–19, 122–23. See also *Sarah Phillips* (Lee)
Lee, Spike, 94
Leibovitz, Annie, 35
Lemmons, Kasi: *Cave Man's Valentine* (2001), 163n10; sexual agency, 16–17; *Talk to Me* (2007), 163n10; use of the South, 74. See also *Eve's Bayou* (1997)
lesbianism, 12, 38, 68–69, 161n53, 162n56
Lewinsky, Monica, 22, 148n6
"liberated sex," 123
Lil' Bush (cartoon), 141n6
Linden Hills (Naylor), 119, 120, 170n12
Living with Racism (Feagin and Sikes), 15
Locke, Alain, 71
Long Time since Yesterday (Gibson), 61–70, 135; black lady, 66–68; critical reviews of, 62; defending sexuality, 43; diversity of sexual identities, 65–66; hypersexuality, 71; promiscuity, 65, 70; respectability, 66–68; self-realization within, 64; sexual agency, 43, 66–67; sexual conformity, 16; sexual identities in, 62, 63, 64–65; sexual stereotypes, 47; staging of actual sexual encounters, 70; suicide theme, 68–70; tragic heroine narratives, 44, 65
Lorde, Audre, 41
Lost Hearts in Italy (Lee), 122–23
Love Jones (1997), 74
Lubiano, Waheema, 6, 25–26
lynching: anti-lynching dramas, 44–45, 64, 154n61, 156n9; black bodies and, 23, 142n12, 149n10; as metaphor, 24, 25, 154n61; uses of in literature, 44–45, 64, 154n61
Lyons, Douglas C., 167n28

Mabry, Marcus, 7
Madison, D. Soyini, 82
Mairs, Nancy, 99
Malveaux, Julianne, 150n15
Mama Day (Naylor), 170n13
Mammy figures, 3
Manliness and Its Discontents (Summers), 15
marriage: black masculinity and, 110–11, 112, 167n29; class status and, 167n31; family structures, 4, 83–84, 110, 127, 166n27, 167n31; gender oppression, 12; interracial

180 · INDEX

relationships and, 127; monogamous relationships *vs.*, 13, 112, 113, 116, 123; performance of middle-class black womanhood and, 67–68; possibilities of, 110–12, 164n1, 167n29, 167n31; sexual repression, 12; survival of the black family, 127; unmarried women, 111
"Marriage Rates and Marriageable Men" (Wood), 167n31
Martin, Darnell, 94
Mask, Mia, 78
maternal training, 54, 57, 104, 123–24
McBride, Dwight, 104
McDowell, Deborah, 8, 145n39
McGruder, Aaron, 1–2
McKay, Nellie, 31, 99
McMillan, Terry, 120, 121, 130, 170n15
Mitchell, Michele, 15
Mitchell-Kernan, Claudia, 167n31
Modleski, Tania, 48, 158n20
monogamous relationships, 112, 113, 116, 123
morality, 4, 45, 71, 94, 113–14, 138–39, 143n18. *See also* respectability
Morrison, Toni, 5, 23, 53–54, 119–20, 144, 169n11, 170nn12–13
Moyers, Bill, 167n28
Moynihan, Daniel P., 110, 166n27
Moynihan Report (*The Negro Family*), 110, 166n27
My Grandfather's Son (Thomas), 21

Naylor, Gloria, 119, 120, 170nn12–13
Negro Family, The (Moynihan), 110, 166n27
Nelson, Alice Dunbar, 64
Nelson, Jill, 17, 97, 168nn36–37, 170n14. See also *Volunteer Slavery* (Nelson)
Nero, Charles, 4
Noguera, Pedro A., 167n28
Nottage, Lynn, 46, 156n1

Obama, Michelle, 1, 22, 174n4
O'Grady Lorraine, 81
O'Hara, Robert, 64
Ohio State Murders (Kennedy), 46
Oliver, Melvin, 14, 104, 146n62
Olney, James, 33
Onassis, Jacqueline, 72–73
"The Other Side of the Black Crisis" (Lyons), 167n28

Painter, Nell, 25, 160n33
Paris Blues (1961), 82
Parker, Gwendolyn, 165n16, 166n24
Parks, Rosa, 72
Parks, Suzan-Lori, 46–47, 68–69
Pattillo-McCoy, Mary, 14–15, 104, 147n65, 166n20
Pear, Robert, 146n60
performance of middle-class black womanhood: alienation from black community and, 50, 52, 54, 169n11; antebellum period, 4, 9, 73, 81, 90, 145; appearance/clothing, 7; asexuality and, 3, 5, 63, 161n51; decorporealization (embodiment), 82–83; diversity among middle-class females, 62–63; hypersexuality and, 63; influence of the South, 72–74; interclass tensions, 54–55; lesbians and, 63; literary depictions of, 4–6; marriage and, 67–68; maternal training for, 104, 123–24; in opposition to poor black women, 11; in the public sphere, 15–17; racism and, 53; self-involvement as, 121; as sexual beings, 2–3, 98, 100–102, 104–9, 110–13, 115–17; sexual stereotyping and, 145n50; working-class and, 14, 100, 105–7, 108. *See also* tragic heroine narratives
Peterson, Carla, 82, 163n16
Petry, Ann, 5
phallocentricism, 58–59
Pinkney, Alphonso, 14
Politics and Economics of Race in America (Carnoy), 166n19
post-civil rights narratives, 6, 123
Poussaint, Alvin F., 56, 147n68
power of absence, 70
Pratt, Mary, 129
pregnancy, unwanted, 84, 105, 106, 107, 138, 166n24
principle of reverse, 48–49
professional ambition/status: Anita Hill and, 26–27, 28, 34; depicted in romantic comedies, 74–76; gender identity and, 74–76; organizing around Hill/Thomas hearings and, 31–33; sexual development and, 104–5; stereotypes of, 54–55
promiscuity, 58, 65, 70, 78–79, 80, 129–30, 164n23
public/private roles, 22–24, 26–27, 28–32, 34, 155n68

public spheres, 4, 28–32, 30, 50–51, 153n37, 153n42

"The Race for Theory" (Christian), 12, 119
Race-ing Justice, Engendering Power (Morrison), 23, 53–54, 144n25, 152n36
Rachel (Grimke), 45
racial authenticity, 98–100, 101–2, 109–10, 112–13, 116–17
racial loyalty: authenticity and, 50, 61; interracial relationships, 127–28; silences and, 72–73; tensions between genders, 54, 55–56
racial uplift paradigm, 4–5, 6–8. 82–83, 85–86
Rage of a Privileged Class (Cose), 15, 164n6
Rahman, Aishah, 46
Raisin in the Sun (Hansberry), 64
"Reconsidering the Crisis of the Black Male in America" Noguera, 167n28
Remaking Respectability (Wolcott), 15
representation of sexuality: definitions of, 12–13
reproductive rights, 166n24
respectability: black womanhood and, 3; impact on sexual development, 97–98, 100–102, 104–6, 108–9; limits of, 67–68; politics of, 3, 7–8
Rice, Condoleezza, 1–2, 6–7, 22, 72, 141n6, 142n7, 144n29, 144n33, 145n49, 159n22, 162n1
Rich, Frank, 148n1
Richards, Sandra, 45, 70, 156n7
Righteous Propogation (Mitchell), 15
Ringgold, Faith, 171n28
Roberts, Dorothy, 166n24
romance genre: black middle-class representations of, 170nn13–15; depicted in films, 74–78; romantic comedies, 74–76
Rose, Tricia, 9–10
Ross, Stephen, 17
Russian Journal (Lee), 122

Sarah Phillips (Lee), 17, 118, 121–35; affirmative action, 171n26; class identification, 123–25, 130–31, 135; class position, 123–25; cultural/racial inheritance, 123–25; fetishization of whiteness, 127, 133; in France, 131–34; interracial relationships, 124–25, 127–28, 131–32; overview, 17, 118; racial objectification, 132–34; romantic relationships, 121–22; self-loathing in, 127, 131; self-understanding in, 135; sexual agency within, 131; sexual explorations in, 121–22; sexual freedom in, 121–22, 123; as travel narrative, 121–22; whiteness in, 171n26
Scott, Hazel, 118, 122
Segal, Lynn, 13, 110, 111, 123
self-loathing, 127, 131, 164n6, 169n11, 189n11
self-realization/self-knowledge, 64, 127–28
sex tourism, 17, 128–32, 172n32, 172n35
sexual abuse, 3, 50–55, 60–61, 91–92, 93, 105, 107–8, 160n37
sexual agency: Anita Hill and, 58; class identity and, 60, 132–33; in *Daughter's of the Dust* (1991), 16–17; in *Eve's Bayou* (1997), 16–17; influence of Southern heritage on, 73–74; innocence *vs.*, 58–59; in *Long Time since Yesterday* (Gibson), 43, 66–67; male privilege, 60; in *Sarah Phillips* (Lee), 131; sex tourism and, 172n35; victimization and, 58–59; in *WOMBmanWARS* (Jackson), 43–44, 57, 58–59
sexual desire: black lesbians and, 12; class position and, 4–5; consequences of, 121; expressions of, 120–21; physical appearance, 127; in popular fiction, 11–12, 146n53; racial loyalty and, 6; social position and, 4–5
sexual development: community expectations, 100–101; dominant cultural norms, 100–101; family structures and, 80–82; impact of class identity on, 98–99, 100–101, 103–8, 110–13; inappropriate sexual discourse, 100–101; maternal training for, 104; professional ambition and, 104–5; respectability and, 97–98, 100–102, 104–6, 108–9; social status and, 97–98, 104–6, 108–9, 111–12; tragic heroine narrative, 100–101; transformative assets, 104
sexual deviance, 119–120, 170n12
sexual experiences: concealment of, 97–98, 100–102, 104–7, 111–13, 116–17; travel narratives and, 122–23
sexual exploitation, 3; the South and, 73–74
sexual exploration: agency within, 131; geographic boundaries and, 128–32; nonprocreative sexual experiences, 67–68; sex tourism and, 128–32; travel narratives and, 121–23

Sexual Healing (Nelson), 170n14
sexual preferences, 161n53
sexual scandals, 16, 44, 138–39, 148n6, 152n30
Shameful in Your Eyes (Gibson), 62
Shange, Ntozake, 46, 69, 71, 119
Shapiro, Thomas M., 14, 104, 146n62
She's Gotta Have It (Lee), 94
Shifting (Jones and Shorter-Gooden), 97
shifting strategies, 97–98, 104–5, 106–7, 108–9, 110, 112–13
Shorter-Gooden, Kumea, 97
Sikes, Melvin P., 15
silences, 97–98, 101, 103, 105
Single Black Female (Thompson), 137–38
Sister, Sister (1992), 82
60 Minutes interview (2007), 21–22
slave narratives, 4, 97, 99, 101
Smith, Anna Deavere, 46, 50–51, 159n26
Smith, Valerie, 123, 135
Snitow, Ann, 11–12
social status: bisexuality and, 14; heterosexuality and, 14; impact on sexual development, 97–98, 104–6, 108–9, 111–12; quality of life and, 164n6, 166n19; social mobility, 164n6, 166n19
Something New (2006), 74
Song of Solomon (Morrison), 120, 170n12
Soul Food (1997), 74, 76
South, the, 7, 16–18, 72–74, 77, 92, 93–94, 128–29
Speaking Truth to Power (Hill), 16, 33–34, 97
Spence, Eulalie, 46
Spillers, Hortense, 8–9, 53, 71, 161n51
spiritual practices, 74, 77, 89–90, 90–91, 164n17, 164n21. *See also* black church cultures
Staples, Robert, 111
Stepto, Robert B., 98
stereotypes: acting against, 24; appropriation of, 13–14; of black masculinities, 52–53; black matriarch, 54–55; black men as predator, 58; of black middle-class womanhood, 52–55; culture of dissemblance and, 4; gorilla stereotype, 52–54, 58; homophobic, 68–69
Stolen Women and Longing to Tell (Wyatt and Rose), 9–10, 145nn49–50
Strange Justice (1999), 154n61

Stranger in the Village (Griffin and Fish), 122, 172n30
strategies of concealment, 48
Summers, Martin, 15
survival strategies, 3, 4, 89–90, 97, 127
Symbolizing the Past (Grayson), 85–86

Talk to Me (2007), 163n10
Tapestry (De Veaux), 45–46, 64
Tar Baby (Morrison), 169n11
Terrell, Mary Church, 150n16
Thomas, Clarence: autobiography of, 21, 148n5; memoir, 21–22, 148n1; mother's voice invoked in *WOMBmanWARS*, 54; racial loyalty and, 54; as racial victim, 25; reflections on senate hearings, 21–22, 148n1; *60 Minutes* interview (2007), 21–22
Thomas-Hill hearings, 154n54; confirmation vote, 152n32; critical writings on, 149n8; criticism of media coverage, 60–61; emergence of gender discontent, 155n64; interclass tensions, 54–55; invocation of Southern heritage in, 73; referenced in television programs, 152n30; reflections from Thomas, 21–22, 148n1; *Strange Justice* (1999), 154n61; in *WOMBmanWARS* (Jackson), 60–61
Tod, the Boy, Tod (Wilks), 45, 64
Tolman, Deborah, 13
"Traffic in Men" (Ebron), 129
tragic heroine narratives: literary depictions of, 44, 46, 65, 71, 119–20, 170n13; promiscuity *vs.*, 70; sexual development and, 69, 119–20; suicide and, 47. *See also Long Time since Yesterday* (Gibson)
tragic mulatto figures, 5, 119, 143n17
transformative assets, 104, 105, 109
travel narratives: of black writers in France, 122, 128–29, 130, 131–34, 171n28; class identification, 128–29; escape and, 128; exile and, 121–23; racial identity and, 121–22, 128–29; self-understanding through, 127–28; southern migration and, 128–29
Trespassing (Parker), 165n16, 166n24
Truffaut, Francois, 131, 173n37
Tucker, Belinda, 167n31
Turning South Again (Baker), 73
Two Can Play That Game (2001), 74

"Two Nations of Black America" (1998), 15
Tyson, Mike, 50, 55, 160n37
Tyson-Washington stories, 50–55, 60–61, 160n37

Unveilings (Gibson), 62

Vagina Monologues (Ensler), 162n60
Vance, Carole, 111
Vanishing Family (1896), 167n28
Voice Lessons (Mairs), 99
Volunteer Slavery (Nelson): acceptance as sexual beings, 98, 110–13, 115–17; autobiographical overview, 109; class identity, 109, 111, 112–13, 115; class privilege, 115; concealment of sexual experiences, 97–98, 111–12, 113–14, 116–17; importance of autobiographical storytelling, 97–102, 110, 116–17; intimacy beyond sex, 114–16; middle-class morality, 113–14; monogamous relationships, 112, 113, 116; National Association of Black Journalists meeting, 113–14; racial authenticity, 109–10, 112–13, 116–17; racial identity, 112–13; reproductive freedoms, 111; sexual agency, 112, 113, 114; sexual exploration, 111, 112, 113; unmarried status, 111, 112–13, 115

Wall, Cheryl, 121
Wallace, Michelle, 139, 174n5
Washington, Desiree, 50, 54, 58–59, 161n40
Washington, Mary Helen, 121
Wells, Ida B., 150n16
West, Dorothy, 4, 143n17
"What Paris Means to Me" (Scott), 118
White, Deborah Gray, 3, 30–31, 32
White, E. Frances, 8
whiteness, 5, 119, 133, 171n26

Why Did I Get Married? (2007), 74
Wiegand, Shirley, 38–39
Wilks, Talvin, 45, 64
Williams, Patricia L., 103–4, 174n3
Williams, Sherley Anne, 119
Wilson, William Julius, 167n31
Wine in the Wilderness (Childress), 46
Winfrey, Oprah, 72
Wolcott, Victoria, 15
WOMBmanWARS (Jackson), 49–61; black church cultures, 55, 59–60; as challenge to stereotypes, 71; critical reviews of, 49; defending sexuality, 43–44; as documentary drama, 50–51; family structures, 57–58, 71; gender tensions, 55–57; Gorilla character, 52–54, 58; impact on community, 71; interclass tensions, 50, 54–55; maternal training invoked, 54, 57; racial authenticity, 50; racial loyalty, 50, 61; reliability of black women, 57, 61; sexual agency, 43–44, 57, 58–59; sexual harassment, 58; sexual stereotypes, 47–48; strategies of concealment, 48; Thomas-Hill hearings in, 44, 50, 53, 54, 60–61; Tyson-Washington stories, 50, 58–59, 60–61, 54–55; use of media representations, 49–50, 60–61; victimization and, 60
Wood, Robert G., 167n31
working-class identity: in African American theater, 46; interclass tensions, 54–55; performance of middle-class black womanhood and, 14, 100, 105–7, 108; sexual agency and, 60; sexual stereotyping and, 145n50; suicide and, 69; victimization and, 60
"Writing the Absent Potential" (Richards), 70
Wyatt, Gayle, 9–10, 145nn49–50

THE NEW BLACK STUDIES SERIES

Beyond Bondage: Free Women of Color in the Americas   *Edited by David Barry Gaspar and Darlene Clark Hine*
The Early Black History Movement, Carter G. Woodson, and Lorenzo Johnston Greene   *Pero Gaglo Dagbovie*
"Baad Bitches" and Sassy Supermamas: Black Power Action Films   *Stephane Dunn*
Black Maverick: T. R. M. Howard's Fight for Civil Rights and Economic Power   *David T. Beito and Linda Royster Beito*
Beyond the Black Lady: Sexuality and the New African American Middle Class   *Lisa B. Thompson*

LISA B. THOMPSON is an associate professor in the department of African and African Diaspora Studies at the University of Texas at Austin and the author of the play *Single Black Female*.

The University of Illinois Press
is a founding member of the
Association of American University Presses.

University of Illinois Press
1325 South Oak Street
Champaign, IL 61820-6903
www.press.uillinois.edu